How to Plan Your
Dream Vacation
Using the
Web

Elizabeth Dempsey

 CORIOLIS GROUP BOOKS

an International Thomson Publishing company I(T)P®

Albany, NY ▪ Belmont, CA ▪ Bonn ▪ Boston ▪ Cincinnati ▪ Detroit ▪ Johannesburg ▪ London ▪ Madrid
Melbourne ▪ Mexico City ▪ New York ▪ Paris ▪ Singapore ▪ Tokyo ▪ Toronto ▪ Washington

PUBLISHER	**KEITH WEISKAMP**
PROJECT EDITOR	**TONI ZUCCARINI**
COPYEDITOR	**CAROLINE PARKS**
COVER ARTIST	**GARY SMITH/PERFORMANCE DESIGN**
COVER DESIGN	**ANTHONY STOCK**
INTERIOR DESIGN	**MICHELLE STROUP**
LAYOUT PRODUCTION	**ROB MAUHAR**
PROOFREADER	**MICHELLE STROUP**
INDEXER	**LUANNE O'LOUGHLIN**

The Coriolis Group, Inc.
An International Thomson Publishing Company
14455 N. Hayden Road, Suite 220
Scottsdale, Arizona 85260
602/483-0192
FAX 602/483-0193
http://www.coriolis.com

Printed in the United States of America
ISBN 1-57610-130-4
10 9 8 7 6 5 4 3 2 1

How to Plan Your
Dream Vacation
Using the
Web

To Phil, my beloved travel companion.

Acknowledgments

The hard work, dedication, knowledge, and travel sense of some remarkable people made this book possible. I offer grateful acknowledgment to the following:

To my fiancé, Phil Kurczewski, for his steadfast love, support, and assurance, which encouraged me throughout the process of writing this book.

To Keith Weiskamp, for the book's concept and for giving me the opportunity to put it into words.

To Toni Zuccarini, for her diligence, smart revisions, and expert assistance. I couldn't have done it without her.

To Caroline Parks, for her keen editing eye and for cleaning up my writing and catching the "little things" that could have fallen through the cracks.

To everyone in the Production department of Coriolis Group Books who transformed my manuscript into this book.

To Shannon Karl, for her guidance and backing that got this book off the ground.

To Anne Dempsey-Kotowski, for helping me research the book's content with such enthusiasm.

To Jay Cohen, my travel correspondent in Asia, for the many excellent travel suggestions.

To my friends who passed useful information my way, especially Jody Smith, Liz Meagher, and Lucy Root, who were always on the lookout for great travel Web sites. And to Susan Lubeck for letting me borrow her laptop computer for six months.

To my parents for giving me my first opportunity to see the world.

And lastly, to the many travelers I spoke with who filled me in on their travel plans, experiences, and habits, which gave me great insight for the pages of this book.

Contents

CHAPTER 5 PLANES, TRAINS, AND RENTAL CARS: GETTING WHERE YOU WANT TO BE 131

CHAPTER 6 RESERVATIONS ASIDE: FINDING ACCOMMODATIONS 173

CHAPTER 9   TROTTING THE GLOBE: TRAVEL TO FOREIGN LANDS   285

CHAPTER 10   EXPLORING THE WILD LIFE: ADVENTURE TRIPS   323

Introduction

Even if you've never been on the Internet, *How to Plan Your Dream Vacation Using the Web* can teach you how to use the World Wide Web to save time and money while planning your vacation.

With *How to Plan Your Dream Vacation Using the Web*, you'll learn how to use the World Wide Web to plan and book your own vacations, and you'll never need to buy another travel guide again. As your own online travel agent, you'll shave *hundreds of dollars* off vacation expenses. No matter where you plan to go or how tight your budget is, the abundant travel resources on the World Wide Web can help you plan your trip of a lifetime.

In this book, you'll learn how to save money on your vacation through special offers that aren't advertised anywhere except on the Web. You'll discover promotional discounts, last-minute deals, online auctions, and discount mailing lists on everything from airline flights to hotel rooms, rental cars to cruises. You can also access low rates through the Web sites of discount brokers, Web sites offering information on travel passes, and sites that provide recommendations on where to save while exploring all corners of the globe.

Using the Web, you'll find the most current prices, so you can plan your budget accordingly. Comparison shopping is easy—visit a few Web sites listed in this book to discover the best deals and make your reservations online—in a fraction of the time it would take you otherwise.

How to Plan Your Dream Vacation Using the Web shows you where to access flight schedules, reserve theater tickets, discover great hotels, and rent a car online, so everything will be taken care of when you reach your destination. You'll discover where to find up-to-the-minute currency exchange rates, take online language lessons, and learn about the culture and etiquette of other countries before traveling abroad. You can even receive realtime weather forecasts for your destination before you pack, read travel advisories from the State Department on health conditions, and browse online travel magazines and guidebooks to get the experts' views about what's hot and what's not—without paying subscription fees. On the following pages, you'll discover how to do all this and more—and you don't need to be an Internet virtuoso to do so.

I've spent hundreds of hours sorting through online travel resources so you don't have to—and I've listed the best of them in this book. In addition, I offer useful tips to help you save money while traveling. *How to Plan Your Dream Vacation Using the Web* puts you in control of your travel plans, and your travel costs, so you can plan the vacation of your dreams.

The Only Travel Book You'll Ever Need

CHAPTER 1 TOPICS

- SAVE TIME AND MONEY WHEN PLANNING YOUR TRIP BY USING THE WEB

- ACCESSING VAST ONLINE TRAVEL RESOURCES

- GREAT ADVICE IS A CHAT AWAY

- THE ENTERTAINING WAY TO MAKE TRAVEL ARRANGEMENTS

Chalk it up to the American way. The longing to travel, find adventure, experience other cultures, and eat fattening foreign foods is shared by people across the United States. Author John Steinbeck summarized this common ambition in *Travels with Charley*, a narrative about Steinbeck's journey across the country with his dog in a makeshift RV: "I saw this look and heard this yearning in every state I visited. Nearly every American hungers to move."

Every once in a while, we just need to pack up and get away from it all. Nothing feels better than being on vacation. The word itself evokes a sense of relaxation and well-being. The problem with a vacation, though, is planning it. In doing so, we often add to the stress that prompted the need for a break in the first place.

Remember that anxious, frantic feeling you experienced before you left on your last trip—a perception that you needed a vacation just from planning the vacation? You spent hours skimming brochures to find a decent place to stay, and even more time on hold with hotel concierges, airline assistants, and foreign restaurateurs who spoke little English. You packed your suitcase with hefty guides and travel books that contained a pound or two of excess information.

Even when you had a travel agent plan your trip for you, you paid for it in hidden increased travel fees. (Ever wonder how travel agents make their money?) And more often than not, while on your trip, you considered how you would have done things a little differently had you planned it yourself.

Today there is a better way. Organizing your trip using the World Wide Web makes vacation planning convenient, inexpensive, and actually a whole lot of fun.

The World Wide Web, or just Web, as it's commonly referred to, is part of the Internet. The Web is made up of graphical documents called pages or sites that contain text, art, and links to other Web pages. These Web pages are created by universities, companies, organizations, and just regular people like you and me, and are instantly accessible by other Internet users.

One of the great things about the Web is that it's made up of thousands of Web pages loaded with information, graphics, and photos from the travel industry. Hotels, resorts, airlines, national parks, restaurants, tourist attractions, travel tours, budget travel clubs, travel magazines, travel television shows, and many other travel organizations (phew!) have gotten online to provide you with information and convenient service.

When you use the Web to plan your vacation, you are your own travel agent. Once you know how to plan and book your own trip, locate tourist information, and check out the best travel Web sites, you'll never go back to those old, cumbersome guidebooks. If you have a computer, a modem, and an Internet account, the world is at your fingertips. You have all the necessary tools right in front of you to get the best deals, find the most accommodating resorts, and plan your itinerary.

So surf the Web before you go surfing off the north shore of Oahu. Cruise the information superhighway before you cruise the Las Vegas strip. Sign on with Netscape before signing in at that four-star hotel. See a pattern here? The Web was practically made for travelers.

In this chapter we'll explore how the Web makes vacation planning easier, more convenient, more fun, and just plain better than the old-fashioned way. Why should *you* use the Web to plan your dream vacation? Read on.

Time Is On Your Side

The Web lets you plan and book your vacation from the comfort of your home computer chair, at your convenience, and in a small amount of time. With a few clicks of your mouse, you're ready to see the world.

Time Keeps On Tickin'

Let's face it, sitting on hold with Muzak; waiting for brochures from the mail carrier (they don't call it snail mail for nothing); driving to bookstores, libraries, and travel agencies for information; and then actually booking your vacation (more Muzac for your listening pleasure) is a complete waste of your time.

Why bother when you can do all that and more in one session at your computer? The Web saves you time in the long run through its unique services.

For instance, you can actually book your plane flight without ever picking up a telephone. Plenty of Web sites, such as Southwest Airlines (**www.iflyswa.com**), offer flight schedules and ticketless travel. At Southwest's Web site, shown in Figure 1.1, you enter the location of where you would like to fly to and from, and your travel dates. Southwest then gives you the flight schedule specific to your information, including departure and arrival times, flight numbers, and

Figure 1.1 Book your flight from Southwest Airline's Web site.

the days of the week the flights are offered. The fares listed also include those for children, youths, seniors, and round-trip tickets.

Once you've chosen your flight, clicking your mouse on an icon will secure your reservation. You'll then receive your flight confirmation via email—with no Muzac ringing in your ears, and far more quickly than if you had called the airline to book the ticket.

It's Up To You

On the Web, you navigate and choose information that *you* think is vital; you never have useless information crammed down your throat. No more listening to travel agents trying to sell you vacation packages you're not interested in, or automated-voice systems leading you through a tangle of useless garble. With the Web, you're in control.

Remember, how much time you spend on the Web is up to you. There is lots of information out there, and, if you so choose, you can spend hours online. Or you can plan a whole vacation in one short sitting.

Let's Talk Convenience

Using the Web, you never have to leave your house—or your home office. After a long day of work, errands, or chores, it's just plain comforting to know you can get things done from home. The Internet makes life a whole lot easier, and more relaxed, when you can get your tasks done without the run-around.

The Web also offers the convenience of making your travel arrangements on your own time. The Internet is open 24 hours a day. It doesn't close at midnight, on Sundays, on holidays...ever. Why not make your plans when you want to?

It's So Easy

Most travel-industry Web sites have your satisfaction in mind. The truth is, the sponsors of those sites want your business and they want to keep you coming back to their site. Most travel Web sites, whether commercial or non-profit, cater to you and have your ease-of-use in mind. Therefore, many of them are easy to navigate, fun to read, have colorful icons to click on, and are a breeze to operate. One visit to **www.hilton.com**, a few clicks here, a few key strokes there, and you're booked at the Hilton in Charlotte, North Carolina (see Figure 1.2).

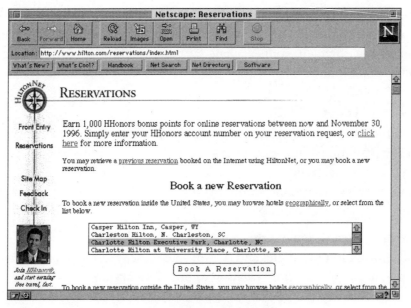

Figure 1.2 Reserve your room on Hilton's Web site.

Convenience is the key. Vacations are for getting rid of stress, not creating more of it.

Travel Byte

Remember, saving time depends on your cruising speed along the information superhighway. Things can move pretty slowly on the Web if you have a slow connection. Speed things up by investing in a high-speed modem. It will save you time and money in online and long-distance charges. For more information on modem speeds, check out Chapter 2.

Conserve Your Cash

The Web saves you money by eliminating service costs and a middle man, and by directing you to great bargains, temporary fares, and discounts that you never knew existed.

Don't Mess With Mr. In-Between

Travel agent services may seem free, but they're not. Service costs are hidden in the prices of your tickets and travel packages. According to *USA Today*, using the Internet for travel arrangements eliminates "a middle man that accounts for 10 percent or more of ticket prices." The Web rids you of the need for a travel agent, so you pay less for your trip.

Other price hikes can be found in package-tour rates. A tour that includes plane flights, ground transportation, meals, accommodations, and daily guided outings can often cost a lot more than if you had arranged each step of the trip separately. You can end up paying for the convenience of not arranging everything yourself.

Last-Minute Miracles

The Web offers discounts you can't get anywhere else, especially great temporary and last-minute deals. Many companies, such as airlines and hotels, offer last-minute discounts to book all their seats and rooms. Loads of last-minute information like this is available to you on the Web. Airline companies, such as American Airlines (**www.americanair.com**), offer extremely low rates to

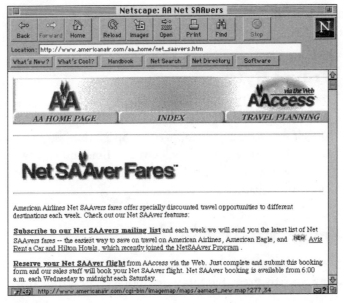

Figure 1.3   Net SAAver fares from American Airlines.

last-minute flyers, as shown in Figure 1.3. Many companies also offer introductory prices for new services, and discounts that aren't advertised anywhere else.

Monthly travel publications can't fill you in on these great deals because of the lengthy lead times they require to produce and distribute such publications. But by checking into a few Web sites, you can get updates on these promotional and temporary discounts each week, or even daily. Join email lists like Royal Caribbean Cruise Line's E-list (**www.rccl.com**), shown in Figure 1.4, and receive regular updates on promotions and special offers.

You can also find coupons on the Net, as well as discounts for online customers. The Net offers a surplus of deals on everything from hotel accommodations to theme park entrance fees.

A Few Dollars Here, A Few Dollars There

Vacation books, travel magazines, language guides, budget planners, and maps are all "little extras" that can substantially raise the price of your trip—quickly. Why not get all these extras for free?

The Web has some information from popular travel books such as *Let's Go, Fodor's,* and *The Lonely Planet* (see Figure 1.5). Check out articles from online

Figure 1.4 Royal Caribbean Cruise Line's Web page.

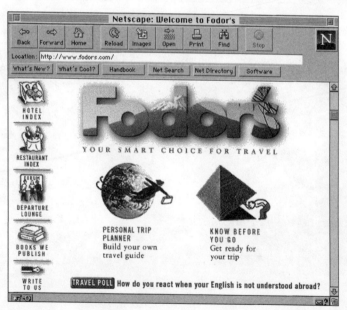

Figure 1.5 Find comprehensive information from Fodor's travel books.

magazines like *Condé Nast Traveler* and *Travel & Leisure* on everything from roughing it in Tibet to flamenco guitarists in Arizona. You can even print out maps locating attractions to visit in Paris (**www.parisnet.com**), shown in Figure 1.6. Read them, print them out, and stick them in your suitcase. It's virtually free from the Web.

Amazing Information At Your Fingertips

The Web has thousands of sites on vacation planning, and more sites make their debut every day. Read up on geography, history, regional food, different cultures, travel tips, destinations, fares, and anything else you can think of, right from your one-stop-shop, the Web.

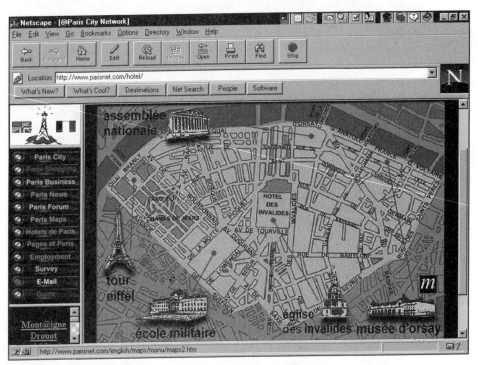

Figure 1.6 *An online map to monuments in Paris.*

Travel Sites Galore

The Web's thousands of travel sites are distinct and diverse, so you're bound to find just what you're looking for. From Web pages of large cruise lines to your neighbor's home page about San Diego (see Figure 1.7), the Web has something for everyone. There's more than enough information to satisfy your every travel need.

We're Talking Volumes

Travel agents, however well-informed, are simply not encyclopedias. Could your travel agent give you detailed information about the menu of a restaurant in Milan? Could he give you etiquette lessons for bargaining at an Israeli bazaar? There's no possible way you can get this much information on planning a trip anywhere else. The Web isn't just one encyclopedia, either—it's thousands of encyclopedias rolled into one vast network of information.

Not only is the number of sites impressive, but so is the quantity of information on those sites. Many are jammed with useful and interesting information. Companies and organizations like using the Web as a vehicle to reach you

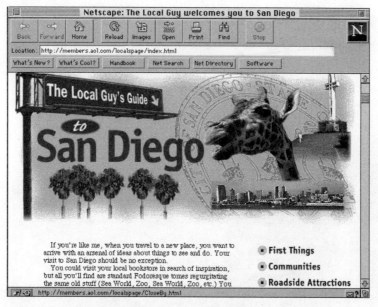

Figure 1.7 The Local Guy's Guide to San Diego Web page.

because there is so much room to work with. Brochures, with their costly production prices and restricted size, limit the amount of information that can be provided. Web sites can be filled with lots of information, because there are few size limitations.

For this reason you'll find extended versions of printed articles on some Web sites. In the July/August issue of *National Geographic Traveler*, I read a terrific article about whitewater rafting down Idaho's Selway River. In August, when I stopped by National Geographic Traveler Online (**www.nationalgeographic.com/traveler**), the publication's Internet counterpart (see Figure 1.8), I was thrilled to find an expanded version of the same article, complete with photos, animation, audio bird calls, wildlife-watching tips, and a contest to win my own river expedition.

Take It With You

Don't bother lugging thick travel books with you in your carry-on bag—there's no need to tote around all those excess pages that don't pertain to you or your trip. Simply print the information you think you'll need right off your computer. Before you leave, look up the daily hours of the Metropolitan Museum of Modern Art in New York (**www.moma.org**), shown in Figure 1.9, and

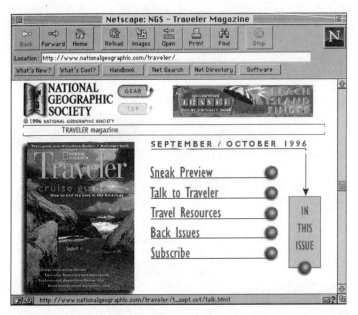

Figure 1.8 Read articles from National Geographic Traveler online.

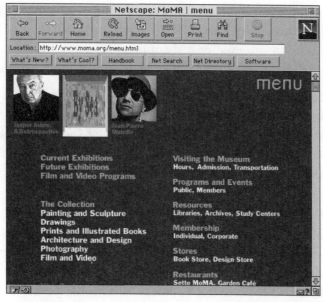

Figure 1.9 The Web page of The Metropolitan Museum of Modern Art.

avoid carrying an extra 30 pages on the museum's history and past exhibitions. Save room in your luggage for souvenirs—take only what you need with you.

The Travel Industry Has Caught On

Most companies have gotten hip to the information age. They've realized, or are realizing, that a Web site is practically free advertising. You may have noticed how many print ads, as well as television commercials, now post their company's Web address. The Web helps companies reduce the costs of customer support, telephone lines, and data entry. With the Web, companies and customers both win.

Just The Facts

The Web gives you up-to-the-minute information you can't find anywhere else. It even offers real-time facts and figures.

No Hang Time

Traditional travel books simply can't give you the up-to-date information you need to plan the ultimate vacation. By the time a reviewer visits individual hotels, guest houses, and restaurants, and publishes a critique and other information, the analysis may be out of date. But by using the Web, food critics and travel writers can write reviews, post them on their Web sites, and get the facts to you all in one day. The Web can give you the latest travel information available.

As you know, the world is fast-paced and constantly changing. What may have been true three months ago is not necessarily true today. How can you avoid getting stuck in road construction in Seattle, or showing up to the Louvre on the one day of the week it's closed? With the Web, you can find up-to-the-last-minute details you simply cannot get anywhere else.

Immediate Information

Many sites are updated daily, giving you the very latest news on the travel industry. You can also have daily emails sent to you so that you are always informed. Because they come via email, there is no junk mail to throw away, just the latest tips, fares, and updates. What could be more convenient than having great travel news delivered to you?

Travel Byte

Make sure that you want the information you sign up to receive. As email becomes a more common way to communicate, junk email is becoming more of a problem. Be choosy about what you sign up for, and be sure to reply to any companies that have sent you unsolicited email and tell them to take you off their list.

The Web also allows you to get real-time details. That means you receive information as it's happening. Guidebooks can't predict a hurricane in Miami, but computers can (see Figure 1.10).

Read details on weather conditions, currency exchange rates, traffic reports, and more. Stay informed.

The Interactive Net

Traditional travel books allow only one-way communication. With the Web, news travels both ways and you are involved. A book may not answer your specific questions, but interactive Web sites can.

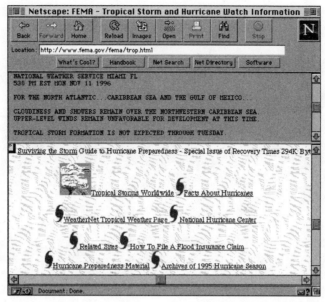

Figure 1.10   Check for tropical storms on the Federal Emergency Management Agency's Web site.

Part Of The Action

The Internet allows you to interact with others through your computer, and lets you take an active role in making your plans. Posting questions to the resort you had in mind can help make your decision easier. Asking questions such as, "Do you offer vegetarian meals?" and "Do you allow pets?" will provide you with the answers you need to make the right choices.

While the answers to your questions may not be instantaneous, at least you don't have to sit on hold, or get transferred from one clerk to another. You can turn off your computer, do your laundry, wash your car, and then log on later to read the reply. It is now quite common for companies to have online customer support.

Why Bother With Pushy Salespeople?

Reserve your hotel rooms, plane flights, and rental cars without ever talking to a sales agent. You can choose only the information you *want* to know. If you "frankly don't give a damn" about plantation homes of Atlanta, but would like to visit the Coca-Cola Museum that's based there, you can browse only that

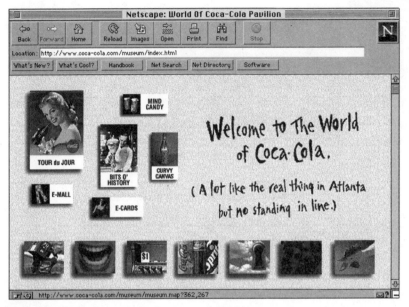

Figure 1.11 The Coca-Cola Company's Web page.

information on the Web, as you can see in Figure 1.11, and receive detailed facts on the museum's hours and fees, and even learn how many Coca-Cola soft drinks are slurped up every second of every day.

The Web enables you to custom pick your information. With many travel guidebooks, it's spoon-fed to you, and you only get the information offered in the guide. If you want more information on the Coca-Cola Museum, you have to find and sift through another book. With the Web, simply run a search or click on a related or linked site and retrieve all the information you want.

Get Expert Advice

The Web gives you access to thousands of experts on everything from gourmet dining to hiking the jungles of Peru. Get information from those in the know. They're waiting to hear from you.

Get In The Know

One of the greatest things about the Internet is that you have access to specialists in the travel industry. Have you ever read an article on a destination and wanted to ask the writer a few questions you felt were left unanswered? Ever see a travel television show and want to ask the host what she *really* thought about the places she visited?

Many Web sites, such as those of Texas Monthly (**www.texasmonthly.com**) and Travel Update (**www.travelupdate.com**), shown in Figure 1.12, give you the opportunity to ask those questions. From their Web sites, you can post questions to the authors about their travel experience, or to the television host about accommodations.

Learn From Travelers All Over The World

Meet travelers like yourself to share information, recommendations, and advice. Learn from the experience of others.

Chit Chat

In addition, many travel sites have chat sessions. Chat sessions let you read others' opinions and take part in topical discussions over the Internet. You can post your own questions and get some answers, and also read the questions

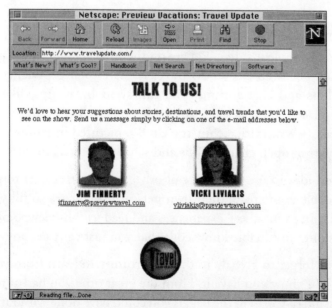

Figure 1.12 Post questions to the television hosts of Travel Update.

and answers of others. These chat sessions are often scheduled at designated times, and some occur at regular times each month or week. Remember the Web version of the Selway River rafting article I found on National Geographic Traveler online? In addition to all the other things I mentioned, they also offered chat sessions with the article's author and whitewater rafting outfitters.

Travel Byte

What makes chat sessions unique is that they're one of the only places on the Web where people will tell you where *not* to go. You'll almost always get an honest opinion.

You can also receive tips, post questions, and participate in chat sessions with world-famous photographers, leading scouts and guides, presidents of travel companies, and more. And the best thing is that you can get their advice and tips *free*.

Just by visiting sites, you can hear from travel professionals. Amtrak employees are experts concerning their trains. Knowledgeable city administrators provide information to The Chicago Office of Special Events Web site. Learn from people who know their stuff.

Meet Fellow Trekkers

Millions of people just like you are on the Internet, and more are hooking up every day. The Web lets fellow travelers share their experiences with you. In travel clubs and chat forums, you can swap travel tips, likes and dislikes, favorite places, and packing tips with others all over the world. Sites like TravelTalk (**www.trvltips.com/traveltalk**), pictured in Figure 1.13, invite you to take part in open chat sessions and scheduled travel discussions.

It's a good idea to use the advice of other travel enthusiasts to plan your trip. Some people even create their own personal Web sites to fill you in on their travels. Learn from others' experiences and read various viewpoints. Experienced travelers offer invaluable knowledge that you just can't get anywhere else.

And don't forget to give them the opportunity to learn from you. Offer your input—you know you have it. From the great time you had at the Pink Palace on the island of Corfu to the haggis you could have done without in Edinburgh,

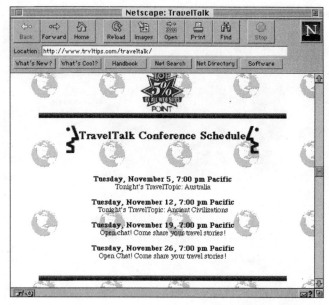

Figure 1.13 Chat with other travelers at the TravelTalk Web page.

Scotland, the Net allows you to share your impressions as well as receive insight from others.

Cool Things Books Can't Do

Most travel Web sites are entertaining and fun to explore. They can be colorful, creative, and amusing, and actually make preparing for your vacation enjoyable.

Cyber Fun

The Web offers so many cool features that no other medium can; the best of them being the virtual tour, or cyber tour. Web tours vary from site to site, but many of them contain video clips, audio narration, and interactive maps of possible getaway spots.

Yes, you can actually watch video clips of your potential destination—everything from landscapes to activities—on your computer. Local people, accommodations, and whatever else you can think of can be found in these clips. You may also find films of tourist attractions, museums, galleries, and ski slopes. At the Web site of Outward Bound (**www.outwardbound.org**), an organization that focuses on adventure travel for learning and self-discovery, you can watch a video clip

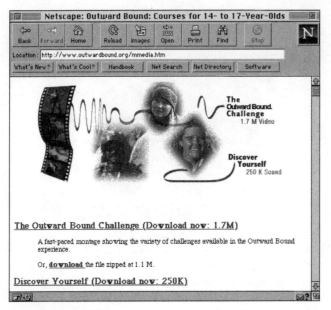

Figure 1.14 Watch video clips from Outward Bound's Web site.

of people taking part in the different endeavors offered (see Figure 1.14). These clips give you a sneak peek at wherever you're planning to go and whatever you're planning to do, and you can watch them right in your browser.

You can hear lots of great tunes, narration, and sound clips from Web sites, too. Listen to bird calls and bear growls, recordings from famous people like Ansel Adams, and music. I visited the Web site of French Polynesia (**www.fix.net/~wdavis/fp_home.html**) and listened to a recording of the local music of the islands. You may also listen to live broadcasts over the Internet, and hear archived segments of travel radio programs.

Interactive maps enable you to locate tourist attractions and other points of interest from a map on your computer screen. Find detailed information about a region, city, suburb, or neighborhood. Some mapping programs even allow you to enter a street address, and it will mark it for you right on your online map.

Many sites also feature animation, extensive photo galleries, and blinking or rotating icons that lead you to the information you're looking for. You can find visually appealing and stimulating graphics, such as 3D art and virtual reality, and live Internet cameras, like the ones found at the Disney Web site (**www.disney.com**), shown in Figure 1.15. Internet cameras take a snapshot of a certain spot every few minutes, and transmit it over the Web.

Figure 1.15 A live camera snapshot of Disney World.

See For Yourself

The following chapters illustrate how the vast resources of the World Wide Web can be used to plan every detail of a vacation, from choosing a destination to booking the flight home. You'll find Web addresses to hundreds of travel-related Web sites and learn how to use them to enhance your vacation and reduce costs.

You'll learn how to purchase your airline tickets, receive incredibly low rates on everything from hotel rooms to cruises, and reserve your rental car online. By visiting the numerous Web sites listed, you can gather information on daily hours and ticket prices of museums, art galleries, and top tourist attractions in your destination, and learn about local happenings, such as cultural festivals, sporting events, upcoming theater productions, and concerts. You'll also discover how to obtain your passport, take online language lessons, purchase your traveler's checks, and check current exchange rates.

The Web makes planning a vacation just as fun as being on one. Keep reading to discover all the exciting travel sites that await you.

CHAPTER 2

Internet 101

CHAPTER 2 TOPICS

- NAVIGATING YOUR WAY
  THROUGH CYBERSPACE

- EMAIL, MAILING LISTS,
  AND NEWSGROUPS

- GETTING CONNECTED

Y ou now have a good idea how the World Wide Web can make your travel plans complete. However, you still may not quite understand exactly what the Internet is or how the Web works. This chapter will give you all the Internet basics you'll need to plan your dream vacation. While avoiding technical details and computer-guru jargon, Internet 101 will get you up to speed on what all this information superhighway stuff is about. You'll read what the Internet and World Wide Web are, learn how to navigate your way around cyberspace, and find out how to get connected.

What Is The Internet?

The Internet is a revolution in progress, an entirely new means of human interaction that has forever changed the way people communicate worldwide. Radically transforming how the world shares and distributes information, the Internet has altered the way people work, play, and conduct their daily lives. Just think—by hooking up to the Internet, not only are you planning your vacation, you're making history!

The Mother Of All Networks

The nucleus of the Internet is a number of linked supercomputer networks owned and operated by universities, government agencies, research institutions, Baby Bell telephone companies, and long-distance services. Other computer networks are linked to this principal system, and other networks are linked to them. That's why, as you may have heard, the Internet is referred to as "a network of computer networks." All these interlinked computers follow a common set of communication rules, called *protocols*, that allow them to communicate with one another all over the world.

The Internet is not located in any particular place and is not operated or controlled by any specific organization. Any person, no matter what age or nationality, can read and post information on the Internet. In addition, in the United States, the Net is uncensored, so you have the freedom to do everything from speaking your piece to booking your own airline flights.

Anyone can access the Internet, and you don't have to be a computer genius to do it. Many libraries, universities, and community groups offer free Internet services.

The World Wide Web

The World Wide Web, or Web, is the most user-friendly of all areas on the Internet and is made up of millions of Web sites. A Web site is a linked group of related digital documents, called *pages*, that contain text and graphics. The home page of a Web site is usually the first page a visitor sees. Similar to the cover of a publication, home pages typically contain the site's name, company logos, an index, and other information on what you can find among the digital pages. The Travelocity home page shown in Figure 2.1 is a good example of an informative Web site.

The Lowdown

Sites on the World Wide Web are created using Hypertext Markup Language (HTML). HTML commands, which determine the organization and appearance of text and images on a Web page, are read by Web browsers, free software programs you can get on disk to install on your computer. Commands used to create Web pages are written in plain text.

For instance, if you wanted to create your own Web page named "My Trip to Taipei," you would tell the browser to insert that title using this command:

```
<TITLE>My Trip To Taipei</TITLE>
```

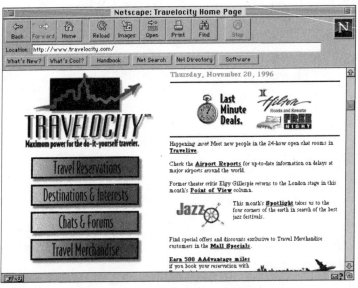

Figure 2.1 The home page of the Travelocity Web site.

To enhance a certain word in the text of your page, you would use similar commands. The command in the line

```
Taipei is an <B>amazing</B> city
```

would make the word "amazing" appear in bold text. The different command in

```
Taipei is an <U>amazing</U> city
```

would tell the browser to underline the designated word.

By reading these HTML commands, the Web browser displays the Web site on your screen. The finished product may contain text, photos, 3D graphics, video, sound, and more.

Because the HTML commands are only understood by Web browsers, you cannot visit Web sites without a browser. Netscape Navigator and Microsoft's Internet Explorer are very popular. Web browsers are also available free through online services like America Online.

The technology called hypertext enables documents to be linked. You use hypertext technology when you click on an underlined or highlighted word in a document to view a related document. For example, you may visit the Web site of CNN's Travel Center and find a link to a site about Berlin, as shown in Figure 2.2. If you click on the highlighted text you'll be transported to a Web page in Germany.

Hypertext documents are often linked so seamlessly that you may not even notice you were transported to a different Web site than the one you started with. One danger of following hypertext links is that you can lose sight of your original destination or become sidetracked. That's not necessarily a detriment; however, if you're working on a deadline, or the cost of online time is important to you, it may be something to watch out for.

URLs

Each Web site has a Universal Resource Locator, or URL. URLs are Web addresses. Specifying a URL tells the computer where to go on the Web and gives the precise location of the document you want. For example, the URL for American Express Travel is **www.americanexpress.com/travel**.

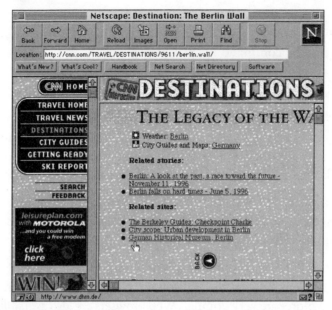

Figure 2.2 Hypertext links are a great time-saving and indexing feature of the Web.

You may notice that many Web addresses contain "http://" when they appear in the location box of your browser. For instance, the URL of the Berlitz Web site appears as **http://www.berlitz.com**. However, you don't need to enter the http:// part of the address when you're typing it into your location box; you need only type in "www.berlitz.com" when you want to visit the site.

Travel Byte

Always write a URL exactly as you read it. Many Web browsers are punctuation- and case-sensitive when reading Web addresses. If you find a Web site address listed in a magazine, mentioned on a television program, or written anywhere else, make sure you type the address in the exact same way, strange capitalization, punctuation, and all. Then you'll be sure to arrive at the site you had in mind.

During your cybertravels, you may come across an unfriendly "404 Not Found" error message when pursuing a link to a Web page. Sometimes Web sites will move to a new URL, change names, or stop being maintained by their creators. When this happens, the old URL no longer exists on the server and is little more than an address to Web nothingness. This message may also appear when a URL is not entered correctly, so always double check those addresses and include all those "dots" and "coms."

Web Browsers

If you would like to check out Web sites, you must have a Web browser. There are many browsers available: Mosaic, IBM's Web Explorer, and Microsoft's Internet Explorer to name a few, but the most popular browser right now is Netscape Navigator, shown in Figure 2.3. You may receive Netscape Navigator software when you sign on with an Internet Service Provider (more on ISPs later in this chapter). If not, call Netscape Communications at 414-528-2555. If you already have a browser, but want to use Netscape Navigator instead, visit **www.netscape.com** to download the latest version.

NETSCAPE DETAILS

Log on to the Web with Netscape and the first thing you'll see is Netscape's opening page. This page is your lift-off site. Above the page is a toolbar with a

Figure 2.3 Netscape Navigator's Web browser.

series of buttons. These buttons make surfing the Web quick and easy. Here's a list of what each button does:

- *Back*—Returns you to the last Web site you visited.
- *Forward*—Returns you to the Web site you just backed up from.
- *Home*—Delivers you to Netscape's home page (or whatever page you've designated as the home page).
- *Reload*—Reloads the Web page you're visiting. Click this button when you experience an incomplete transfer of graphics or text.
- *Images*—Allows you to turn the graphics on your Web page on and off. If you choose not to see them (for instance, if you have a slow modem and pages take a long time to load), click the button. If you then choose to see them, click it again and they'll appear.
- *Open*—Allows you to type in a Web site address. (You can also do this directly in the Netsite or Location box.)
- *Print*—Lets you print Web pages.
- *Find*—Enables you to conduct a keyword search of the current Web page.
- *Stop*—Halts the loading of a Web page.

Directly below these buttons, you'll find Netscape's URL in the Netsite or Location text box. Click on the box to highlight Netscape's home page URL. To go to another page, simply delete this address, type in the new URL, and press Enter. You can also head off to another site by clicking on the "Open" button, and enter the address there.

Other features Netscape offers are a daily listing of "cool" sites to visit, access to newsgroups and mailing lists, and easy loading of software enhancements to Web sites.

CHECKING OUT THE SITUATION

Every so often you'll find that accessing a Web site takes an unusually long period of time. When this happens, you may be curious to know what's holding things up. Netscape lets you find out by providing status messages across the bottom of its browser window. These messages keep you informed on each stage of your data transfer. The four stages of a data transfer using Netscape appear in this sequence:

- *Looking up Host*—Netscape is translating the domain name of the URL into the host computer's IP (Internet Protocol) address. (You only need to know the URL.)

- *Contacting Host*—Netscape is waiting for the host computer to accept the request. If the host computer is busy, you may be stuck in limbo for a spell.

- *Host Contacted Waiting for Reply*—The host computer has accepted Netscape's request.

- *Transferring Data*—Netscape is receiving data from the host computer and is delivering it to your computer screen. You may experience a lag at this point also. If your data transfer is interrupted, try again by using Netscape's reload button.

PLUG-INS

As I mentioned earlier, many Web sites offer video clips, virtual reality graphics, audio narration, and lots of other cool features. For some sites, simply clicking on an icon enables you to immediately enjoy a feature without fuss. For others, you need to download and install software that will let you access the feature. These free software "plug-ins," as they are referred to in Netscape, must be downloaded and installed onto the hard drive of your computer.

Netscape automatically lets you know when you need a plug-in, what plug-in to install, and offers you the chance to download it at that time. Be sure to follow the instructions you're given by Netscape. Once you have saved the plug-in, you may begin installation. When you're finished, you'll probably need to relaunch your browser and reload the Web page that required the plug-in. Figure 2.4 shows you the Netscape plug-in warning.

Plug-ins, like Omniview's image viewer in Figure 2.5, often enhance Web site graphics. While downloading and installing plug-ins seems (and sometimes is)

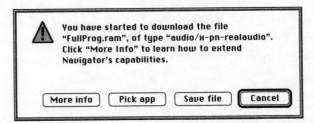

Figure 2.4 Netscape lets you know when you need a plug-in.

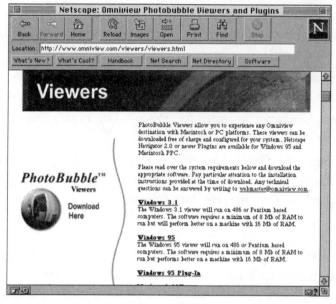

Figure 2.5   A plug-in from Omniview that allows you to see 360 degrees of an image.

a lengthy process, it is worth the extra effort. Once installed, plug-ins will work with any Web site you visit. For example, if RealAudio narration is offered on two different Web sites, you only need to install the plug-in once. It is then available for all your Web surfing. Plug-ins consume lots of disk space and memory, so be selective when choosing them. Plug-ins are offered for download at numerous Web sites. Two top picks are Macromedia's Shockwave for real-time interactive multimedia (**www.macromedia.com**), and Progressive Networks' RealAudio Player for sound (**www.realaudio.com**).

Travel Byte

When you install a plug-in, make sure to jot down the name of the file and where it is located in your computer directory. This way, if you try a plug-in and feel it does not deserve your disk space or memory, you can easily uninstall it.

BOOKMARKS

Another cool feature of browsers like Netscape are bookmarks (or Favorites in Internet Explorer). Bookmarks give you easy access to your favorite Web pages, and you don't have to retype the URL each time you visit the site.

For example, visit a Web site you really enjoy, maybe Microsoft's Expedia Travel Center (**expedia.msn.com**). If you decide you'd like to return, simply pull down the Bookmarks menu and choose Add Bookmark. When you pull down the Bookmarks menu again, you'll see the name of the Expedia site there. When you want to visit the Expedia Web site again, return to "Bookmarks" and find their name. Another click, and you're there.

After you've surfed and bookmarked your way through cyberspace, you may find your bookmark list has grown to epic proportions. To get rid of bookmarks you don't want anymore, go to the Bookmarks menu and choose Go To Bookmarks. Then simply select the bookmark you want to get rid of and press the Delete button. You should follow a similar process for Favorites in Internet Explorer.

Search Engines

The number of Web sites that exist is staggering, and finding your way around can be a real challenge. Search engines, programs that allow you to look up information stored in immense databases, make navigating the Web a great deal easier. You can find links to numerous search engines, such as Yahoo!, WebCrawler, Lycos, InfoSeek, Excite, and HotBot, by either clicking on the Net Search button beneath the Netsite box or by using the Directory menu. There are many search engines out there, and each engine yields different search results. Test them out and decide which one works best for your particular search.

Search engines can help you locate Web sites regarding general subjects such as "travel," to a particular item such as "Smithsonian Museum in Washington, D.C." To use a search engine, enter the words that describe the information you're looking for into the search area on the engine's home page.

These words, appropriately called "keywords," are the keys to accessing the information you need from the Web. If you would like to find information on travel in Holland, enter the keywords "travel" and "Holland." The program will then present a list of Web addresses that will take you to sites about Holland.

Unfortunately, keyword searches are not always this easy. Sometimes your searches will turn up sites that have nothing to do with what you're interested in. When this happens, you need to narrow your search by using more specific keywords. Instead of travel, you may enter "cycling" to receive fewer and more appropriate addresses of related sites.

On the other hand, some keyword searches may return only a smattering of listed Web links. This can happen when your search is too specific (like searching for "villas in northern Italy that rent to Americans").

Submitting keywords to a search engine is a trial-and-error process. Continue offering keywords until you find a combination that unleashes the information you're looking for.

Travel Byte

A few tips on conducting a search:

- Make sure your keywords are spelled correctly.
- Use keywords that suggest the subject you're interested in.
- Use alternate words to make a search complete: "airplanes," "airlines," and "flying" all pull up different Web site listings.
- Try variations on words: submit "airline" as well as "air-lines" and "fly" as well as "flying."

Remember to try alternate routes if at first you don't succeed. I ran a search for Bora Bora and did not find what I was looking for—but I was led to a few sites on French Polynesia, where there was plenty of information on Bora Bora and her sister islands.

YAHOO!

Yahoo! (www.yahoo.com) is a great search engine for finding all sorts of travel information. It lists sites according to subject titles and sorts them into appropriate subject categories so you can find what you're looking for quite easily. Figure 2.6 shows the results of a Yahoo! search.

To search for Web sites with Yahoo!, type its URL into Netscape's Netsite or location box, or find Yahoo! by clicking Netscape's Net Search button. After arriving at Yahoo!, enter the subject in which you're interested in the text box

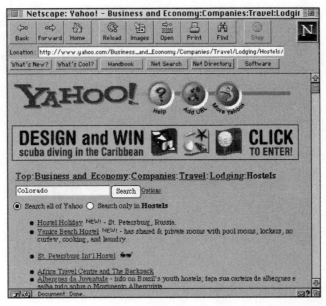

Figure 2.6 A Yahoo! search for sites about youth hostels in Colorado.

at the top of the screen and click on the Search button. When receiving your results, you may see a number in parentheses after a category listing. This number indicates how many sites exist under this category. For example, I conducted a search using the words "Colorado" and "skiing." The search pulled up 68 links to Web sites on skiing in Colorado; sites on equipment rental, resorts, ski clubs, tour operators, the Ski Hall of Fame, and everything in between were included. Don't worry if you see hundreds of sites under your item's heading—sites under your subject will probably be separated into more categories. Just keep clicking on your related categories to narrow your search down.

WEBCRAWLER

Another popular search engine is WebCrawler (**www.webcrawler.com**). This search engine is operated by America Online, and conducts your search by document title and content. WebCrawler, like other search engines, divides categories into departments to make your searches a little easier. In addition, WebCrawler may offer site summaries of particular sites, so you know the site's content ahead of time. Figure 2.7 shows the different categories WebCrawler gives you to help narrow your search. However, you can also search the standard way, by entering keywords in the text box and clicking Search.

Figure 2.7 Search in WebCrawler's individual departments.

HOTBOT AND EXCITE

Both HotBot (**www.hotbot.com**) and Excite (**www.excite.com**) can help you find plenty of links to travel-related Web sites. In addition, HotBot lets you customize your keyword search by date, location, and media type, and provides either detailed or brief Web site summaries—the choice is up to you. The Excite search engine provides Web site reviews. Search results are sorted by their relevance to your keywords: the better the match, the higher the percentage of relevance.

Electronic Mail

Electronic Mail, or email as it is most commonly referred to, allows you to exchange computer-generated messages with co-workers, siblings, friends, and others all over the world. Anyone who has email access can send and receive messages to and from anyone else with email access.

With email, there's no postage to pay for, you don't need to wait for the postman each morning, and it costs a whole lot less than calling long distance (it only costs you the few seconds of online time it takes to send the message).

In addition, messages sent and received are easy to organize and store for future reference. Another great thing about sending email is that etiquette is less formal than when sending a letter, even in the business world. Instead of drafting a formal statement on letterhead with proper headings and such, simply forward someone a friendly email message. However, keep in mind that although email travels at the speed of light, you must still take time to compose and spell-check your letter or note. Business email messages with spelling errors can convey a sloppy or unprofessional image.

Travel Byte

Make sure your Internet Service Provider equips you with an email address when you register for service. Online services like America Online and CompuServe also give you an email address where you can receive email.

How To Reach You

An email address is similar to your phone number or street address in that it's a way for you to be contacted personally on the Net. Each part of a person's email address contains instructions about where and to whom the message should be delivered.

The first half of an email address identifies the user's name. For example, my email address is **dempsey@ais.net**. Dempsey is my user name as well as my last name—so it's easy for people to remember. Unlike a Web URL address, an email address contains an @ sign. The @ sign means "at" and indicates that the rest of the address is the domain name. This is the same name that my Internet Service Provider (ISP) uses. If you also have an Internet account through an ISP, you'll probably be assigned its domain name. The same holds true for online services. America Online users have "aol.com" in their Internet addresses. CompuServe subscribers have "compuserve.com" in theirs. "Net," which means network organization, is also part of the domain name in my Internet address. Other domain names may include "gov" for a government agency, "com" for a company, and "org" for a non-profit organization.

Email messages like the one in Figure 2.8 are a quick, informal, and inexpensive way for Net users to communicate privately with each other.

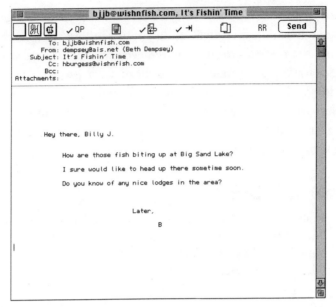

Figure 2.8 A message via email.

A Sig Of Your Own

Personalize your email messages and newsgroup postings by including a signature, or sig, at the end of your messages. A sig provides information to others on how to contact you. You may want to include your name, email address, physical address, phone number, or fax number, if you have one. Keep your sig concise—the netiquette standard is no more than four lines. No one wants to read a lengthy sig at the end of every message. Also avoid adding useless information like smileys, graphics, quotations, and advertisements.

Right Back At Ya

After sending an email message, you may find it has been returned to you. This happens because the message was sent to an inaccurate or invalid email address. Just as when a letter sent via U.S. mail is "returned to sender," email messages may be sent back "Returned Mail:User Unknown." When this happens, check the email address to make sure the one you entered was correct.

Travel Byte

Type your messages before you connect to the Net. Most email programs allow you to compose messages offline, and then send them when you go back online. This way, you won't use up, or pay for, unnecessary time on the Internet.

Mailing Lists

A mailing list is composed of a group of subscribers who share a common interest. When one subscriber sends an electronic message to the mailing list's main email address, that message is sent to all the subscribers on the list.

When you become a subscriber to a mailing list, you receive regular email messages from the list's sponsor. If you have a message you'd like to share with the group, send it to the main email address. The sponsor then decides whether or not to include your message in the next mailing. Mailing lists do not allow you to post messages to individual subscribers.

How To Subscribe

To subscribe to a mailing list, you may need to send an email message to the sponsor, letting them know you'd like to be added to the list. When doing this, you must follow some specific steps to ensure that you have been added. Most lists are automated by a listserver, a computer program that maintains mailing lists. For the listserver to understand your command, you must be very specific.

To subscribe to a mailing list, send an email to the site's email address, such as **travel-advisories-request@stolaf.edu**. In the message body, type:

Subscribe (the name of mailing list) (your first name) (your last name).

I would enter:

Subscribe Travel Advisories Elizabeth Dempsey.

Other mailing lists, like that of US Air, require you to subscribe from the company's Web site. To do this, simply click the button on their site that reads "add to mailing list" and type in your email address.

No matter which way you subscribe, a confirmation email message should be sent to you. The message informs you that you are indeed a subscriber and will receive regular mailings. Keep this message. It will probably tell you how to submit messages to the sponsor for distribution. In addition, it will let you know how to terminate your subscription if you choose to do so.

FINDING TRAVEL MAILING LISTS

There are lots of mailing lists on travel. Here are a few good ones:

U.S. State Department Travel Advisories
Warns travelers of hazardous conditions worldwide.

To subscribe: Email **travel-advisories-request@stolaf.edu**

US Air's E-Saver Mailing List
Informs subscribers of weekly discounts on airfare.

To subscribe: Visit the Web site **www.usair.com**

Cruise News
Reports on special offers, provides industry news and contests.

To subscribe: Email **cruisers@ns.nc.ndl.net**

Green Travel
For environmentally conscious travelers.

To subscribe: Email **majordomo@igc.org**

TravAble
Information for disabled travelers.

To subscribe: Email **listserv@sjuvm.stjohns.edu**

Eurotrip Newsletter
Recommendations and tips for European travel.

To subscribe: Visit the Web site **www.eurotrip.com**

WHERE TO FIND MORE LISTS

To find more mailing lists, visit these Web sites, or hunt for more using search engines like Yahoo!

Publicly Accessible Mailing Lists (PAML)
www.neosoft.com/internet/paml/

Indiana University Mailing List Archive
scwww.ucs.indiana.edu/mlarchive/

List of Email Lists on the Internet
catalog.com/vivian/interest-group-search.html

Tile.Net/Lists
www.tile.net/tile/listserv/

Liszt Searchable Directory of Email Discussion Groups
www.liszt.com

Newsgroups

If you want to receive a variety of viewpoints on a particular subject, you can read messages from others on the Internet through Usenet newsgroups. Unlike mailing lists, newsgroups allow numerous people to post messages and articles for others to read. You, too, can post messages to groups of people on the Internet. From a list, choose a particular article or a topic you're interested in, and take a look. Most Web browsers include a built-in news reader, which allows you to view and post messages.

When you first visit a newsgroup, read the Frequently Asked Questions, or FAQs, and then check out some of the articles. These articles consist of strings of discussions, called "threads." But before you jump in and post a message, read a few of the different discussions. There are quite a few unwritten rules to follow when joining a newsgroup. Heed the following rules before you post messages of your own.

Take All Members Of The Group Into Consideration

Newsgroups are international. Avoid mentioning references to the popular culture of your country, such as television shows, movies, and other things many members may not be aware of.

When replying to someone's newsgroup message, consider mailing the person directly instead of posting to the newsgroup. You need to decide whether or not your response is of value to everyone in the group. If you feel your message would really only benefit that one person, be considerate and send them a personal message via email.

Keep It Short

State your messages and responses clearly, and make them as concise as possible. The limit for posting a response is usually half a screen. In addition, keep to the newsgroup's subject topic. Don't post irrelevant information.

Refer To Previous Postings

Always refer to the article you're replying to so that others can follow the discussion thread. Also make sure to be descriptive in your subject header and refer to what you will be discussing.

Newsgroups To Use

There are plenty of newsgroups on travel, and new messages may be read daily. Here are a few to get you going.

Travel-Related Newsgroups

alt.travel—General travel discussions

rec.travel—More general travel discussions

alt.travel.road-trip—Road trips

rec.travel.cruises—Cruises

rec.travel.marketplace—Even more general travel discussions

rec.travel.resorts.all-inclusive—All-inclusive resorts

rec.travel.air—Air flight

rec.travel.miscellaneous—You got it; more general travel discussions

rec.travel.bed+breakfast—Bed and breakfasts

Travel Newsgroups For Specific Regions

Here are a few regional newsgroups you may also want to look into. If you are looking for discussions of major cities, visit the regional newsgroup that the city is located in. For instance, you can find information on traveling to Seattle in **rec.travel.usa**.

alt.travel.canada—Travel in Canada

fj.rec.travel.world—World travel

rec.travel.africa—Travel in Africa

rec.travel.asia—Travel in Asia

rec.travel.australia+nz—Travel in Australia and New Zealand

rec.travel.carribbean—Travel in the Caribbean

rec.travel.europe—Travel in Europe

rec.travel.japan—Travel in Japan

rec.travel.latin-america—Travel in Latin America

rec.travel.usa—Travel in the United States

rec.travel.usa-canada—Travel in the United States and Canada

Online Lingo

Communicating your emotion in writing can be a challenge. Written text lacks the inflection of the human voice, so what may be written purely in jest may be read literally or vice-versa. Thankfully, Net users have come up with online smileys, or emoticons, to let their true feelings be known. Smileys are used in informal online chat sessions and in email messages to make sure the reader on the other end interprets the message as intended.

Text characters on your keyboard create the facial expressions of smileys. A happy smiley is made using a colon for eyes, a hyphen for a nose, and a right parenthesis for a mouth. :-)

Here's a list of common smileys and their meanings:

:-) signifies happiness

:-(signifies sadness

:-/ signifies skepticism

; -) signifies you're joking (notice the wink)

:-0 signifies surprise

:-X signifies that you'll keep the message top-secret

:-& signifies that you're tongue-tied

Abbreviations are also frequently used on the Net. They save your fingers the extra keystrokes when writing email messages and cut down on lag time during online chats. Use them to comment on messages, too. Some abbreviations are used more than others in different forums. Abbreviations you may come across include:

- BRB—I'll be right back
- BTW—By the way
- FYI—For your information
- GMTA—Great minds think alike
- IMO—In my opinion
- LOL—Laughing out loud
- PMFBI—Pardon me for butting in
- TIA—Thanks in advance

Travel Byte

QUIET PLEASE! Never type your messages in all capital letters, unless you want to make a scene. Using all caps is considered shouting on the Net, and is not considered polite "netiquette."

Getting Connected

There are four main elements you'll need to get connected to the Net: a computer, a modem, a phone line, and an Internet account.

Some computers, called the *Internet backbone*, are directly connected to the heart of the Internet. As stated earlier, these few hundred computers are owned by government agencies, universities, research organizations, and companies in the telephone industry. To access the Internet, your computer needs to be linked to a computer that's connected to the Internet backbone. Direct access to the Internet backbone can cost hundreds to thousands of dollars a month, and that's a little too steep for most of us. The majority of users get Internet access through an Internet Service Provider. An ISP pays this expensive fee and subleases its bandwidth to users for a monthly fee.

What It Will Cost You

Internet access through an ISP connection costs about $20 to $30 a month for up to 150 hours of use. Many areas have lots of ISPs to choose from, and prices vary with the amount of competition. In other areas, there may be one or only a few ISPs to choose from. In that case, you may have little choice as to how much you will pay. As more and more people get on the Internet, more ISPs are cropping up. And that trend is likely to continue as the Internet and its number of users grow.

Finding An ISP

You can find a list of ISPs in the Yellow Pages under "Internet" or "computer." Also check with local computer stores, or look for advertisements in local computer publications.

You should research the ISP's reputation, technical support availability, and price. In addition, look for an ISP that provides you with a SLIP/PPP account. This type of account is best for Web surfers and for people who are just getting acquainted with the Net because it enables use of the World Wide Web, works well with high-speed modems, and is user-friendly.

Online Services

Online services, like America Online and CompuServe, can also connect you to the Internet. The difference between ISPs and online services is that online services provide their own information in addition to Internet access. These features are structured in an organized manner into categories and departments. Information on online services is overseen by their parent companies, and the posted material of vendors, organizations, and publications is controlled. In addition, subscribers may be charged fees to access certain departments.

Online services like America Online (shown in Figure 2.9) provide Internet access as well as services of their own, which can be of great value depending on your needs.

Online services used to differ from ISPs in that they typically charged by the hour. At the time this book was written, America Online had just changed from hourly rates to charging a flat monthly fee, similar to ISPs.

Figure 2.9 *Logging onto America Online.*

Other online services still charge by the hour, which works very well for many people. When billed this way, you are allotted a certain number of hours every month and charged an even rate for that number of hours. If you exceed that number, you are charged overtime. If you plan to spend lots of time checking out all the great travel resources on the Internet, you may want to go for a flat fee.

Friendly Neighborhood FreeNets

A FreeNet is a community organization that provides free access to the Internet. The computing systems of FreeNets may be based at local colleges, libraries, or community centers. Some FreeNets even offer users dial-up access from their homes. In addition, they often provide other community services and offer a variety of information on local goings-on from their Web site.

While some FreeNets do not supply full Internet access because of virus and security issues, others provide users with email, Usenet news, chat forums, and other useful services. The degree of Internet access depends on the individual FreeNet; some FreeNet lines are often busy due to neighborhood Web surfer overload, while others have regularly accessible lines.

To find out if there is a FreeNet in your neck of the woods, email the National Public Telecommuting Network at **info@nptn.org**.

First Things First: A Computer

If you don't own a computer, use one at a library, a university, or a community FreeNet. Any computer will suffice when surfing the Internet, but if you are purchasing one, there are two very important factors to consider: memory and speed. Running large programs, like Web browsers, can take up a huge chunk of memory, and if you have only a little bit of memory on your computer, things can run pretty darn slow, or not at all.

Buy a fast computer that has lots of memory, or RAM. To move at an acceptable speed using Netscape and other browsers, it's a good idea to have at least a 486 computer with 33 megahertz for speed, and 8 megabytes (MB) of RAM. While 8 MB of RAM gives you reasonable performance, anything higher will really get you moving. RAM is upgradable, so you can easily increase the amount of RAM on your computer by having additional memory chips added.

Check out publications such as *Consumer Reports* and *PC Magazine* to read about the best computers and what they cost, and to determine your own computer needs.

Getting To Know Your Modem

A modem is your key to the information superhighway. Modems allow computers to communicate with each other over standard telephone lines, which allows you to chat with people worldwide via the Net.

A modem works by changing digital data from your computer into an analog signal that can travel along ordinary telephone lines. The modem receiving the call then changes the analog signal back into digital data that your computer can understand. This alteration of digital data into analog data and back again is called modulation/demodulation, hence the name "modem," and is what allows two computers to communicate with each other.

There are basically three models of modems to chose from: external, internal, and PC. PC Cards, made for laptop computers, are the smallest of all modems and look very much like credit cards. PC Cards do everything the other modems do, and are great for when you're on the road.

Speed

A modem sends data to other modems in electronic pieces, called "bits." The speed at which a modem sends this data is measured in kilobits per second, written as Kbps on your modem's packaging. High-speed modems decrease the time it takes to download and upload graphics and text on the World Wide Web, and quickly transport you anywhere on the Internet.

High-speed modems available today are 28.8 Kbps (fast), 33.6 Kbps (faster), and 56 Kbps (the fastest of them all). A high-speed modem will cost more than those with lower speeds, but it is worth the investment. A fast connection saves you lots of time downloading graphics (which can be excruciatingly slow with a poky modem), and saves you money through lowered hourly service charges or long-distance fees. It's a good idea to buy the fastest modem you can afford.

A WORD ABOUT 56 KBPS MODEMS

Fifty-six Kbps modems work a little differently than standard 28.8 and 33.6 Kbps modems because they only cruise along the Internet at 56 Kbps in one direction. By taking advantage of today's digital phone networks, these modems bypass the analog-to-digital conversion when going from the server to your computer.

When you connect to a Web site, you'll cruise to that site at either 28.8 or 33.6 Kbps, but when receiving the graphics, text, sound, video, or anything else from that site, you'll receive it at 56 Kbps. That's twice as fast as 28.8 Kbps modems. While you can't connect with other home users at 56 Kbps, you can receive large graphic files from the Web in seconds—a great idea if you're planning to spend lots of time on the Internet. The speed and reliability of today's top modems, such as U.S. Robotic's line (Figure 2.10), make Net surfing a no-wait proposition.

A Last Word On Speed

The time it takes to transfer data to and from computers connected by the Internet, and to load graphics onto your computer screen, can either be painstakingly slow or quite swift. There are a number of things you can do to accelerate your Internet connection and get up to speed:

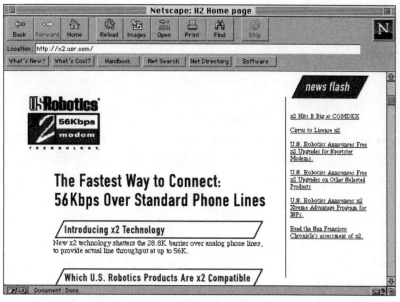

Figure 2.10   The home page of U.S. Robotics, a leading modem manufacturer.

- Buy a high-speed modem. In the long run, it's worth the extra dollars to buy the fastest modem available. Today, 56 Kbps is the fastest speed obtainable over standard telephone lines.

- Make sure your ISP has direct Internet access. If it's connected to the backbone, you'll move faster.

- Avoid high-traffic times. Just as on real highways, the Internet has traffic jams and crunches at certain times of the day, which may force you to move at a snail's pace. Avoid late afternoon and evenings whenever possible.

- Don't load images. If you only need the text of a Web site, and don't need to view any fancy graphics or pictures, choose the option on your browser that allows you to bypass images (on Netscape this is under the Options menu). That way you won't spend unnecessary time waiting for unwanted visuals to load.

- Buy a fast computer that has lots of memory, called RAM. Your computer should have 8 MB of RAM or more for good performance.

Laptop Companions

Having a laptop computer and modem with you on your vacation is convenient for finding the up-to-the-minute information you need from the Internet. If you want to access a bus schedule or check alternate routes when London Tube stops are temporarily closed, the information is right at your fingertips. Keeping an electronic journal on file and staying connected to friends back home via email are also good reasons for taking your notebook on the road. Laptop computers are smaller and lighter than ever, which make carrying them with you easy on your back.

On the other hand, using a laptop computer and modem on your vacation can be a major pain in the neck. First of all, you will need local ISP and online service numbers for wherever you will be, unless you don't mind paying monstrous long-distance charges. Secondly, if your hotel does not have RJ-11 phone jacks to plug your modem into, you won't be able to access the Internet at all. There are technical ways to bypass this problem, which involve taking apart your hotel telephone, but I'm not going to go into that. (What fun would dissecting phones be on your vacation?)

If you plan to spend your travel time outside of the United States, you are in for more challenges. The further you travel from the U.S., the more difficult it will be to get connected to the Internet. International phone systems make hooking up your American modem an adventure. You'll also need to obtain international ISP numbers—that is, if your ISP offers international access.

In addition, electrical appliances of most foreign countries operate on 220 volt alternating currents. The United States operates on 110 volts. This difference may cause headaches when plugging in your computer.

If you feel adventurous, and are willing to give taking your laptop a try, follow these steps before you leave on your trip:

- Email or call your hotel to make sure your hotel room has a standard RJ-11 phone jack for plugging in your modem.
- Check the Web site or call the customer service number of your ISP or online service to get the local access numbers of locations you'll be visiting.
- Take the customer service numbers of your ISP or online service with you in case difficulties arise.

- If you will be traveling abroad, check your computer's users guide or call customer service to see if you computer can adapt to 220 volt alternating currents, and buy an electrical adapter.

- Purchase a sturdy combination lock to lock up your laptop when it is not in use.

Other Options

Check with the hotels you'll be staying at to see if personal computer access is available to you. Many hotels have business centers that offer free computer and modem use to their guests. In addition, cyber cafes, coffee houses that offer online access to customers, are popping up in major cities worldwide. Check out Chapter 4 to see if there is a cyber cafe at your destination.

Learn More About The Web On The Web

With the Internet's growing popularity, many magazines about the World Wide Web have sprung to life. Publications like *ComputerLife*, *NetGuide*, and *Yahoo! Internet Life* offer readers useful information on Web sites, new software and software upgrades, commonly encountered problems, and industry news. But you don't need a subscription to the actual magazine to access the articles, features, and product reviews they provide—visit their Web sites to get it all for free! These online, or electronic, magazines, as seen in Figure 2.11, reflect the appearance and content of the real publications. You can get loads of information at the following Web sites to help you find your way around cyberspace and to keep you in-tune with hot topics.

ComputerLife
www.zdnet.com/complife

This online magazine offers advice for surfing the Web; monthly columns on Web activities, such as online dating; and reviews of up-and-coming Web sites. You'll also access daily tips and "downloads of the day." Visitors may communicate with each other via the message exchange.

NetGuide
www.netguide.com

NetGuide features live events and tools to help you surf the Web. You'll find links to numerous Web sites on business, entertainment, news, politics, health, sports, and more. Use the "snap guides" to connect to Web sites that teach you how to cook, cope with stress, invest your money, and look up your family history.

Yahoo! Internet Life
www.zdnet.com/yil

"Your guide to the best on the Web" is this site's motto. Visit *Yahoo! Internet Life* to read features and articles about what's hot on the Net. Also check out Web sites of the day, read site reviews, and attend "Surf School" to receive surfing tips and to post your questions to the "Surf Guru."

Online Vacation Planning

After spending some quality time surfing online waters, you'll be ready to plan the vacation you've been dreaming of. Chapter 3 will show you how Web sites featuring locations all over the world can help you choose the perfect getaway spot.

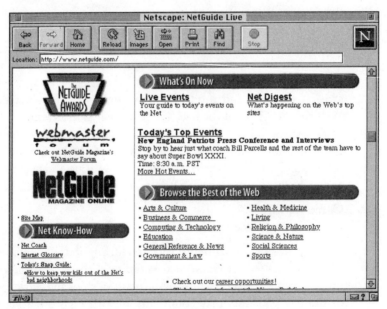

Figure 2.11 Learn more about the Web from online magazines.

CHAPTER 7

Whetting Your Wanderlust: Choosing A Destination

CHAPTER 3 TOPICS

- TRAVELING THE WORLD WITHOUT LEAVING HOME

- READ THE BEST OF POPULAR TRAVEL BOOKS AND MAGAZINES ONLINE

- PAY A VIRTUAL VISIT TO YOUR DESTINATION BEFORE BOOKING YOUR FLIGHT

- USING THE WEB TO CHOOSE YOUR DREAM DESTINATION

With so many intriguing out-of-the-way places to explore, distant lands to investigate, and cultures to experience, it's hard not to drop everything and take off into the horizon. Unfortunately, you may not be able to afford the time or money it takes to trek around the whole planet, but that doesn't mean you can't still harmonize with lots of far away places.

The Virtual Tourist

Using the World Wide Web, you can investigate the wide world around you right from your computer. Visit virtual destinations you may some day want to check out in person, or stop by Web sites of places you know you'll never see live, like the Chihuahuan desert (**www.desertusa.com/index.html**), or Antarctica (**www.terraquest.com/antarctica**), shown in Figure 3.1. Thousands of Web sites about regions around the globe are ready and waiting for your perusal. By visiting Web sites on various countries, states, and cities, you can get a true feel for a nation, a locale, or a community, and learn about the many wonders of the world.

In this chapter, you'll learn how the Web can help you decide what your perfect vacation may be. Web sites of travel magazines, guide books, television

Figure 3.1   Make a virtual visit to Antarctica with the TerraQuest expedition.

programs, as well as those of cities, states, and countries, are listed here. Use them to gather ideas about places you'd like to visit.

New Ways To See The World

The Web enables you to interact with environments like never before. You can observe live camera images of Mt. Fuji (**www.city.fujiyoshida.yamanashi.jp/ english/root.html**), behold the Grand Canyon by a 3D map, as shown in Figure 3.2 (**www.kaibab.org**), read a daily newspaper from Athens, Greece (**www.athnews.dolnet.gr:8080**), and listen to concerts from the House of Blues in New Orleans (**www.liveconcerts.com**)—all by way of the Internet.

So take your brain on a remarkable journey. It's a great way to discover all sorts of potential destinations. Traveling the world by the Web is enlightening, and it costs a whole lot less cash than tramping the globe on foot.

Travel Byte

Pay attention to the source of a Web site's content. Information provided by a commercial airline, or a city's tourism bureau, may be less impartial than the advice of travelers who've flown with the airline, or who have visited the city themselves.

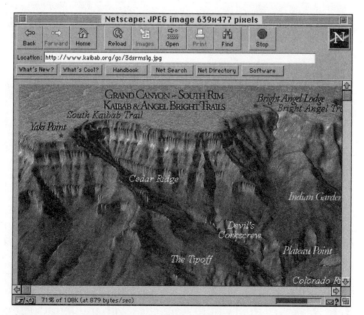

Figure 3.2 A 3D map of the Grand Canyon.

Online Travel Magazines

Through articles written by professional journalists, as well as recreational travelers, online magazines (also known as 'zines), such as Where Magazines International (**www.wheremags.com**), shown in Figure 3.3, offer diverse perspectives on world destinations. Read these accounts to familiarize yourself with exotic far away and some not-so-far-away getaway spots. The impressions gained can give you ideas about where you'd like to go.

The following travel 'zines are great resources.

Condé Nast Traveler
travel.epicurious.com/travel/g_cnt/home.html

Submit your top vacation priorities and Condé Nast Traveler's "concierge" will suggest a destination tailored to your preferences. The online publication provides editors' picks for great getaway spots and hotels, as well as suggestions and personal accounts of world travel on everything from elephant safaris to Paris nightlife.

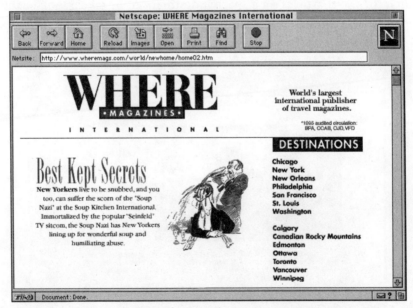

Figure 3.3 The home page of Where Magazines International.

The Connected Traveler
www.travelmedia.com/connected/

This Web-exclusive publication of "worldly words, sound, and light" shown in Figure 3.4 delivers articles and tidbits from travels across the globe. The editor provides personal picks on hotel accommodations and theater productions, and includes "best soup" in the dining category. Departments include "The Art of Travel" photo galleries, "Stories," and "Environment and Culture."

Destinations
www.travelersguide.com/destinations/destcovr.htm

Recommendations for off-the-beaten-path excursions, as well as not-so-unusual vacations, can be found at this site. Two feature articles accompany every issue. Check the editorial calendar to see what topics are on the way, or look over past issues and read previous features. Traveler contributions are encouraged.

Epicurious Travel
travel.epicurious.com

Search for travel articles on a specific destination, or take a look at the "most popular destinations" information provided by Fodor's. The Food section

Figure 3.4 An interesting read from the pages of The Connected Traveler Web site.

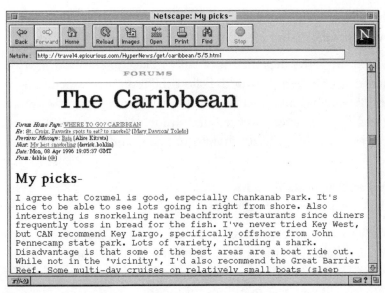

Figure 3.5   Input from a recreational tourist at Epicurious Travel.

provides "delectable dispatches from well-fed wanderers," including input from gourmet travel editors. Chat forums, like the one shown in Figure 3.5, allow you to share your impressions with other travelers, and a gallery of cool maps is also provided.

Fine Travel Magazine
204.188.48.61/finetrav/contents.htm

This site's collection of travel articles covers destinations, like Clint Eastwood's home town, and vacation activities, such as chartering yachts. Regular features cover camping, cruises, skiing, sight seeing, and adventure trips. Read suggestions of what to see and do, and take a look at travel writer bios. This site offers abundant links to other World Wide Web sites.

National Geographic Traveler
www.nationalgeographic.com/traveler

This online publication offers bi-monthly features that include photos and articles on a variety of national and international destinations. You can post notes on the travel message boards, including scenic drives and national park expeditions. Check out the winning pictures from the yearly photography competition, too.

Sally's Place
www.bpe.com

Pop into the travel department of Sally's Place to read articles from a pair of writers that have seen the world. Follow them on their expeditions to Morocco, Istanbul, Vienna, and other locations, and down the world's great rivers, such as the Nile, Danube, Yangtse, and Rhine. Also read recommendations on places to visit, things to do, hotels, markets, and more from Sally as well as other travel journalists.

Travel at the Speed of Light
vanbc.wimsey.com/~ayoung/travel.shtml

Visitors to this 'zine can read personal accounts "written by travelers from Alberta to Zaire." Peruse articles on eco-tours to adventurous trips, with titles such as "Fear & Lodging," "Oozing into Uzbekistan," and "33 Days of Hell on Wheels." If you have questions for the travel writers, contact them through the email links provided.

TravelAssist
travelassist.com/mag/mag_home.html

Read a wide assortment of travel articles from the magazine's current and past issues. Readers can look up archived articles by destination, and features on cruising, food, airlines, and B & Bs (Bed and Breakfasts) are also included. Articles incorporate links to Web sites about related topics. In the "Ask the Agents" section, your questions are answered by volunteer travel agents, vendors, and tour operators. There's lots of travel links at this site, too.

Travel File
www.travelfile.com

Check out the destination of the month, which offers tourist information, recommended activities, and other "Destination Details." Search for a particular U.S. location from archived Web content and read the latest news on eco-tours, golf packages, dog sledding expeditions, and more. View the calendar of events and check out current ski conditions. You can also get connected to Web sites of tourism offices.

Travelmag
www.travelmag.co.uk/travelmag/

"Independent travel on the Internet" is this online magazine's tagline. Stop by this site to connect to Web pages of worldwide destinations. Visitors can check out feature articles on everything from caving in South Africa to kayaking in New Zealand. Articles on crime and health issues abroad are also included, as well as quirky "news of the world."

TravelPage
www.travelpage.com

TravelPage features "information that will help you decide where to go and how to get there." Read destination recommendations, as well as favorite cruises, airlines, and hotels across the globe. Links to Web pages on hundreds of specific locations are also provided, and the search engine feature makes finding links to a particular destination a snap. Participate in the reader travel poll to contribute your two cents to the site.

Travel & Leisure
pathfinder.com/@@RtpJOQUAlHo7xkq3/travel/TL, or go to www.pathfinder.com, then click on "Travel & Leisure."

Travel articles provide extensive information, including pricing specifics and contact information, on numerous vacation getaways. Click on an interactive map in the "Great Cities of Europe" section, and take a virtual tour of Lisbon, Prague, Brussels, Berlin, and other frequented destinations. You'll find 360 degree panoramic views, video clips of top attractions, walking maps, and more. Also check out the "Best Deals," "Strategies," and "Eat, Sleep & Drink" departments.

Vapor Trails
www.vaportrails.com

Departments at this site cover eco-tourism, cheap trips, and world cuisine. Information for senior travelers is also provided. The site suggests vacation activities, on everything from deep sea diving to snowshoe hikes, and articles on personal expeditions abound. Join the free mailing list to receive updates on current travel deals and discounts.

Travel Byte

Web sites of newspapers such as *USA Today* (**www.usatoday.com/life/ travel/ltfront.htm**) and the *Chicago Tribune* (**www.chicago.tribune .com/travel**) offer regularly updated travel articles and photos from their print travel sections.

Digital Travel Books

Many printed travel publications offer the same or similar content on their Web sites. Regional and city summaries detail things to see and do, and describe a destination's atmosphere and flavor. Browse the Web's online travel books to gain insight from various travel writers.

The Berkeley Guides
www.tripod.com/bin/travel/browser/

This site is packed (I mean *packed*) with information of global proportions. Peruse the guide for details about travel in Central America, Europe, Mexico, and the Pacific Northwest. Click on the country of your choice to receive an introduction, then delve deeper into specific regions and cities. You'll find out about "getting around" and what to do "after dark," among other useful topics. View maps and read specifics about where to eat and sleep, and what to explore, according to your budget. Create your own personal planner to save topics of interest.

Fodor's
www.fodors.com

The first stop on your visit to this site should be to the "Personal Trip Planner." You will be led through a series of checklists. Choose a destination and click on your travel preferences. When you're done you'll receive detailed recommendations on where to stay, places to dine, and sights to see, according to your particular travel profile. Read "what's hot" in major cites, with great photos included, as well as Fodor's top picks on activities and attractions all over the world. Also, listen to Fodor's radio program online.

Frommer's
www.mcp.com/frommers

Updated daily, this site (Figure 3.6) offers unique views on travel, advice on getting discounts, and industry travel news. The "Outspoken Encyclopedia of

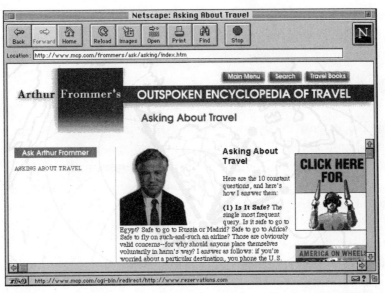

Figure 3.6   Common travel questions are answered at Frommer's Web site.

Travel" presents advice on off-beat trips and alternative methods of traveling the globe, including "new ways to visit old destinations" and "new modes for travel." The "Vacations for Real People" news magazine found on the site provides a daily editorial and the "Ask Arthur Frommer" section answers common travel inquiries. In addition, message boards with titles such as "Been There? Done That?" give you the chance to communicate with other travel hounds.

Gault Millau Travel Guides/Gayot's Guides
www.gayot.com/index.html

Find information through featured items, such as places to dine on Valentines Day. The site lists editors' choice picks of hotels or restaurants from one of their books, with reviews and facts on each listing. Check out Gayot's restaurant database—you can search a city for the top restaurants according to your tastes. Restaurant updates will even be emailed to you if you choose. Links to other Web sites, such as the Travel Channel, are also included.

Let's Go
www.letsgo.com

The Let's Go Web site offers insight into the experiences of many of the book's travel writers. "Tales from the Road" offers personal accounts about locations from Italy to India. The "Expose" section provides writer bios and details of their adventures, including "the wackiest traveler met." Read travel articles by writing competition winners, too.

Lonely Planet
www.lonelyplanet.com

From the extensive information on worldwide destinations, to the photo galleries from Lonely Planet travel photographers, this is a great resource for travelers. Zoom in on detailed maps, and gather destination-specific information on culture, activities, history, economy, and environment. Watch slide shows of landscapes and common scenes of each destination, and check out "Facts at a Glance" for quick reference. You can also read articles from professional travel writers as they trek the planet, as well as reports from the average traveler on recommendations, scams, and useful tips. Don't have a particular destination in mind? Then take a "Mystery Tour" to visit random corners of the globe.

Moon Travel Handbooks
www.moon.com

The whole text of the *Road Trip USA Handbook* can be found at the Moon Travel Web site. You can read detailed itineraries on several trips across America, including "Route 66: The Mother Road" and "U.S. 93: Montana to Mexico." Information from the *Survival Guides* can also be found, covering U.S. cities such as Seattle, Memphis, New Orleans, and New York. Visitors can read city-specific information on finding their way around town, seeing the sights, and learning where to eat. Also read interesting travel articles from the current and previous issues of the *Travel Matters* newsletter.

The Rough Guides
www.hotwired.com/rough

Navigate your way through this site to discover a wide variety of information on world destinations. You'll read city descriptions, with lengthy summaries on neighborhoods, attractions, and anything else a city has to offer visitors. You can get clued in to day trips outside the city proper as well. Check out recommendations in the "eat" and "sleep" sections, and visit the "threads" to hear what other travelers have to say about each destination.

TimeOut
www.timeout.co.uk

The City Guides (see Figure 3.7) offer extensive information on major cities all over the world, including Madrid, Amsterdam, Paris, London, Tokyo, New York, and San Francisco. Everything from cafes to bath houses are included, in addition to details about accommodations, museums, sightseeing, and music. This site even lists movie theaters, what's playing, and show times. Free registration is required to access the features and events listings. Also check out the Guides to Eating and Drinking in Paris, and in London.

Cyberprograms

Web sites of travel television programs also provide information on a variety of destinations. In conjunction with their TV counterparts, these Web sites regularly feature vacation recommendations. The online features are archived so you can easily look up a destination that was featured three months ago.

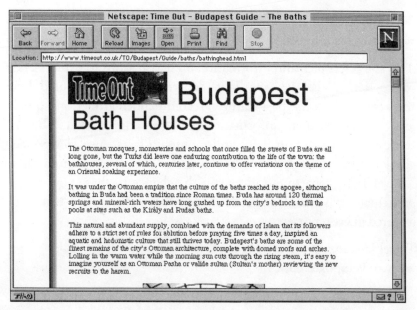

Figure 3.7 Learn about different cultures on the pages of TimeOut.

CNN Travel Guide
cnn.com/TRAVEL/index.html

Through linked pages and photos, this travel guide takes you on virtual journeys with titles such as "Inside the Big Easy" and "Cruising Twain's Mississippi." The world-wide city guides will link you to related Web sites, and provide zoomable city and forecast maps. Check out the ski update for "mail from the trail" and current snow and weather conditions.

Europe Through the Back Door
www.ricksteves.com

This site is chock full of great travel tips and also provides further details on a "country-by-country basis." Suggested itineraries, with a history lesson and descriptions of each stop along the way are included. Recommendations for daily activities, transportation, accommodations and places to eat are also mentioned, as well as a brief language lesson. Check out the featured "back door" destination and past issues of the free newsletter, and don't miss the included scripts from the television program.

The Travel Channel
www.travelchannel.com

This site offers plentiful information on destinations to explore and vacations to experience. Visit the "Spotlight" department, with a featured destination of the week, and browse past features, recommended attractions, quick language lessons, and pertinent information about the destination. The ski vacation section provides terrain maps and mountain facts. Also view video clips and check out the photo gallery, which includes 360-degree panoramic views. The "Travel Talk" department gives you the chance to share your travel tips and participate in scheduled discussions on hot topics. Also read articles from featured guest reporters.

Travel Update
www.travelupdate.com

Similar to the television program, this site guides you to numerous Web sites on travel. Read informative articles, and find Web links to a vast array of locations. You'll also find links to vacation activities, such as elephant tours, safaris, rail excursions, and whale-watching trips. The site is regularly updated with content from each week's show, and you can also look into previously aired episodes to peruse past features and find links to even more Web sites.

Finding Your Way To A Destination

There are thousands upon thousands of Web resources regarding regions, countries, states, and cities all over the world. No maps of the World Wide Web exist to guide you through these multitudinous sites, but there are helpful roadside assistants that can give you a few pointers along the way.

References

Visit Web sites that link you to all the corners of the world: the sites that make it their business to connect you to World Wide Web locales. Sites like Eurolink (**syselog.com/eurolink**) connect you to pages of nations in Europe. eGO Travel (**www.ego.net**) links you to virtual states, from Arizona to Wyoming. USA CityLink (**www.usacitylink.com**), shown in Figure 3.8, connects you to city sites across the globe. Check into these types of Web sites to get yourself linked to digital destinations.

Figure 3.8 Sites like USA CityLink can lead you to city-specific Web sites.

Search Engines

Stop by your friendly neighborhood search engine. Search engines like WebCrawler, Excite, Lycos and Yahoo!, which is shown in Figure 3.9, have their own travel departments. You'll find copious lists of virtual locations— just click on links or conduct searches for specific locales. You may want to narrow your search down by choosing options such as "search only travel" instead of "search all of Yahoo." Otherwise you may wind up with more sites than you'll know what to do with.

Looking For Links

When browsing a Web site, look for links to other pages about that destination. One Web page may link you to a new page, and that page may connect you to more Web pages, and so on and so on. For example, a Web site about Italy, such as the one in Figure 3.10, may link you to Web pages on Italian cooking, Italian opera, hotels in Florence, or other sites on "touring the boot." One terrific site can lead you on an infinite journey of interlinked and related sites. In addition, don't forget to search for links when you visit the online travel books, magazines, and other great resources listed in this book.

Figure 3.9 A search for Washington D.C. in Yahoo!

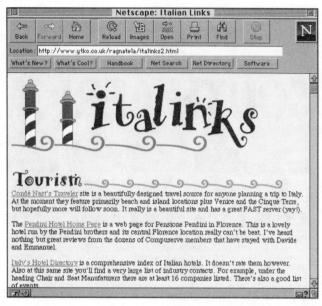

Figure 3.10   The Italinks Web page connects you to other sites about Italy.

Virtual Countries

Traveling to foreign countries by way of the Web may allow you to catch up on your world history, get introduced to interesting and diverse people, discover unfamiliar lands, view colorful images of exotic places, and virtually taste test regional cuisine. In addition, you can read about distinct regions, cultural happenings, and historical landmarks, and view images of the local architecture.

Web pages for travel in foreign countries, such as the South African home page shown in Figure 3.11, may be created by national tourist organizations and tourism bureaus, or just regular folks who live in that country. Some are created by Americans who have resided, traveled, or studied abroad.

When you visit Web sites of foreign countries, you may come across foreign languages, too. Some sites' text may be written entirely in Italian, Spanish, or Dutch. Many sites are multilingual, giving you a number of languages to choose from. The Web pages of the Montreal Museum of Fine Arts (**www.mmfa.qc.ca**) give you the option of viewing the site in English or French. However, don't worry about not understanding foreign travel pages. There are hundreds of sites on the Web that are all about foreign lands but have English text.

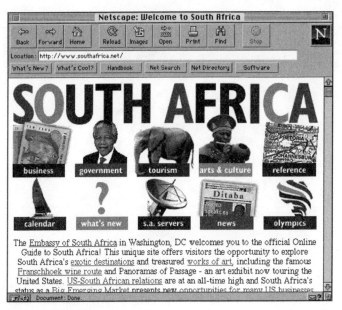

Figure 3.11 A South African home page.

Digital States

You don't have to look to foreign lands to find fascinating places. In the United States, there's a wide range of diverse regions to visit, and there are a vast number of Web sites to explore. Web pages from tourist associations and travel bureaus can fill you in on happenings throughout all 50 states. These sites may describe state-wide attractions, scenic thoroughfares, or even state fairs and music festivals. I read all about the Traverse City Cherry Festival from a Michigan Web page, made a visit that summer, and still have the cherry pits to prove it. You can also learn about state parks, the state's history, and people of the region. Many of these sites have local flavor and are packed with photos of points of interest.

Travel Byte

A great starting point for finding Web sites about a particular state is that state government's homepage. Enter a URL that follows this easy pattern

www.state.(state's postal abbreviation).us

to visit these sites and get linked to other Web sites about that state. For instance, to visit the state of Oregon, type "www.state.or.us/" as your URL, and get transported to "Oregon Online."

Cybercities

Many state Web sites link you directly to the Web pages of the cities in that state. City sites can direct you to the best local restaurants, give you tips on where to shop, and direct you to hole-in-the-wall theaters. They can also take you into local neighborhoods, such as New York's Little Italy and San Francisco's Japantown, shown in Figure 3.12. You'll locate the coziest pubs, hottest dance clubs, and trendiest coffee shops in town.

Here are a few good resources for finding Web sites about cities around the world.

World City Guide
www.world-travel-net.co.uk/cities

Select from a list of world cities and get connected to a vast number of related Web sites, including those of tourist organizations and travel bureaus. Links to destination-specific information on politics, culture, geography, history, economy, as well as food and drink and sports and leisure, can be found on this site.

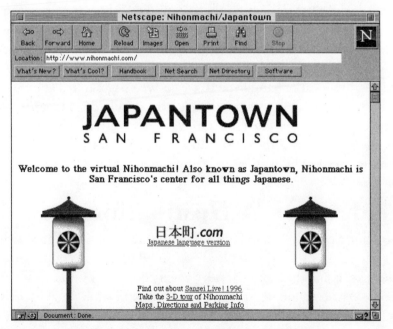

Figure 3.12 A Web page about San Francisco's Japantown.

Metroscope
www.metroscope.com

Metroscope provides hundreds of links to city Web sites. Neatly categorized into departments, these Web site links cover topics on art, culture, and media. You'll also get connected to city guide sites, and sites covering night clubs, theme parks, and popular attractions.

 City Guide USA
cityguide.lycos.com/index.html

This site covers a wide assortment of U.S. cities, with regular features highlighting a particular city. Links to Web sites fall under topics such as city attractions, places to eat, and local sports. Visitors should also check into the "local flavor," "vital stats," and "hot spots" departments. In addition, the location-specific site links are accompanied by a descriptive city summary.

Written From The Road

Some of the most fascinating reading on the Web comes from people who've already traveled to where you want to go. You may come across these personal travelogues, such as the one shown in Figure 3.13, while journeying the depths of the Web. These sites are usually created by individuals who have trekked to a location, and lived to create Web pages to tell about it. They may recount the path of a journey, give you details on encounters with local people, or include outlined itineraries and descriptions of scenery and wildlife. Travelogues are great for getting an intimate feel for a destination, and many of them overflow with entertaining and useful information.

Deciding On A Destination

Deciding where you want to go is an important decision. You may have only a few sacred days off from work a year, so be sure to make the most of them. There are many things to consider when choosing a vacation spot that many people overlook, or never even consider until after they've arrived at the chosen location. The beach may sound great as you're staring out your window at falling snow and gusting winds, but seven straight days of lying idle may get old quickly if you're an active person.

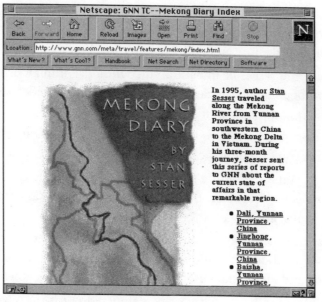

In 1995, author Stan Sesser traveled along the Mekong River from Yunnan Province in southwestern China to the Mekong Delta in Vietnam. During his three-month journey, Sesser sent this series of reports to GNN about the current state of affairs in that remarkable region.

- Dali, Yunnan Province, China
- Jinghong, Yunnan Province, China
- Baisha, Yunnan Province,

Figure 3.13   Mekong Diary, a Web travelogue.

It's a good idea to really consider what you want from a vacation before making any decisions. Prioritizing what's important to you can make the difference between just-a-vacation and a *dream* vacation.

Here are a few things to consider:

- What vacations have you enjoyed in the past and why? Looking back to great experiences can give you ideas for future trips. Visit Web sites of places you've visited to refresh your memory.

- How much money do you have to spend? Use the Web to research costs of airline tickets, hotels, and entertainment.

- How long will your trip be? Will you accomplish what you want to in that amount of time? Check out all there is to see and do using Web sites about a particular city or region.

- Do you want to learn a thing or two along the way? Or is play your main objective? Web sites about museums and art galleries, in addition to those of beaches and theme parks, can help you decide what type of vacation is right for you.

- What do you like to do for fun? Would you like to include these activities in your trip? Look up Web sites on topics of interest, including horseback riding, snorkeling, and golf.

- Would you rather be in natural surroundings, or in an urban setting? Web pages about national parks, as well as those of major cities, may inspire you.

- What time of year do you plan to travel? Is this the best time of year to visit the destination you had in mind? Many destination-specific sites inform you of typical weather conditions and seasonal activities.

- Would you rather visit a popular destination, or one that is unfrequented by travelers? Sites about popular attractions, as well as off-the-beaten-path excursions, abound on the Web.

- What are your goals? Do you want to get in shape? Relax? Enjoy the outdoors? Web sites about spas and other healthy vacations, as well as sites about hiking and biking trails around the country, can give you some good ideas.

- Would you rather rough it or be pampered? Visit the Web sites of camp-grounds, or those of spas and resorts, to help you choose.

Travel Byte

Take a minute or two to visualize yourself on your dream vacation. Where do you picture yourself? What do you see yourself doing? Follow your imagination—it can lead you on the trip of a lifetime.

Other Considerations

Another matter to think about is who you will be traveling with. Is this a family trip? If so, you'll want to consider what everyone, including the kids, have in mind for the getaway. Even if you're traveling with just one, two, or a few other people, you should find out what your travel partners have in mind. Arguing about the day's itinerary can be a real drag when you're supposed to be enjoying yourself. Make sure you have a consensus before you go.

Also, be sure to consider the special needs of travelers in your group. Allergies, special diets, motion sickness, illnesses, and physical impairments are all important factors to bear in mind when choosing a location. If there's a chance someone in your party will need medical attention, make sure there's a hospital or care unit nearby. (More about health care on the road in Chapter 4.)

Even if you have a region, country, state, or certain climate in mind, choosing exactly where to visit can often be a tough call. The Web can give you an overview of many different locations, with sights and sounds to boot.

Knowing What To Look For

When cruising the Web, make sure to take a close look at what each location has to offer. Is the location chock full of historical landmarks and monuments to visit? Are there sporting activities to watch and take part in? Are there museums that kids would find exciting? Plunging into the World Wide Web can help you decide what location is the best for you.

Here's a list of things you may want to look into when checking out potential destinations on the Web.

- *Orientation*—Many sites have automated tours, or virtual tours of the location. These can give you a real feel for a locale through photos, film clips, and extensive information.

- *How much things cost*—Get an overall sense of how costly the trip may be by finding out approximate prices of entertainment, cultural events, and restaurants.

- *Surrounding areas*—Check out the different neighborhoods of a city and look for offshoot excursions and attractions.

- *Potential activities*—Search for sights to visit. Check out calendars of events, and explore everything from jazz clubs to art galleries to hiking trails.

- *The local spirit*—What are you looking for to flavor your trip? Investigate new cultures and lifestyles.

After all is said and done and cybersearched, you may end up with a plan that diverges from your original itinerary. Don't worry, your research has probably helped you make a wiser, more thought-out decision.

Sites To See

There are thousands of location-based sites on the Web, and some are better than others. The following list is not comprehensive; I've just chosen a few I think are worth a look.

With each listing, I've included:

- The real-world locale
- The name of the Web site
- The URL that takes you there
- A brief description of the material offered on the site, including its cool features

Keep in mind that the Internet changes every day, so information on a Web site may also change at any time.

U.S. Cities

Boston, Massachusetts
The Boston Web
bweb.com/bostonweb

Zoom-in maps, photo tours, and a daily calendar of events makes this site on Bean Town a real trip. There are plenty of suggested places to go and things to do, all categorized by neighborhood—you'll find everything from late night restaurants to theater performances.

Chicago, Illinois
Chicago Mosaic
www.ci.chi.il.us

Hang on to your hat during this virtual tour of the Windy City. Discover sights to see and museums, aquariums, and galleries to visit by using an interactive map. Find out about cultural festivals and neighborhood events, and use the search engine to find exactly what you're looking for.

Miami, Florida
Miami Perfectly Seasoned
www.miamiandbeaches.com

You can practically feel the tropical breezes as you peruse the attractions and beaches of Miami at this site. Visit neighborhoods like Coral Gables, Coconut Grove, and pastel-colored South Beach, and find out what's happening with a calendar of events. While you're there, take the Miami trivia quiz and find out what you don't know about one of America's favorite vacation destinations.

NASHVILLE, TENNESSEE
Music City USA
Nashville.musiccityusa.com

Catch up on the latest news and happenings in Music City. Find attractions, shopping, and nightly entertainment from Bluegrass to Pop, and of course, straight Country. Also, read Nashville trivia facts, and find out what's the latest at the Grand Ole Opry.

NEW ORLEANS, LOUISIANA
New Orleans Online
www.neworleansonline.com

This Web site provides loads of suggestions for things to see and do while in N'awlins. Take a virtual streetcar tour of the city's attractions, and look up local restaurants according to your Creole/Cajun cravings. And the coolest feature of all: listen to jazz while you surf!

NEW YORK, NEW YORK
The NYC Insider
www.TheInsider.com/nyc/

Check out the Big Apple with this site's detailed and useful information. Lots of information is provided on popular attractions like the Statue of Liberty and the David Letterman show, in addition to the city's "hidden treasures." There are also suggestions on ways to save some money, and a daily survival guide.

SAN FRANCISCO, CALIFORNIA
San Francisco Online
www.sanfranciscoonline.com

This regularly updated site keeps you informed about the city's hotels, restaurants, and shopping in Union Square. Visit San Francisco's best tourist attractions, and stop by the city's neighborhoods, from Haight-Ashbury to Fisherman's Wharf.

SANTA FE, NEW MEXICO
Santa Fe
www.nets.com/santafe

No need to go all the way to Santa Fe: Simply visit this site, shown in Figure 3.15, to learn about the city's attractions, history, and the culture of

Hispanic and Native Americans in New Mexico. Also read about current happenings, climate, geography, hotels, and restaurants.

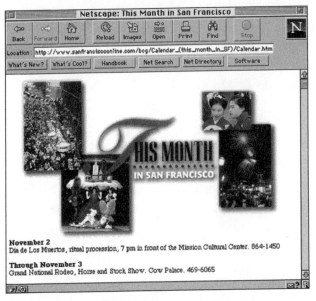

Figure 3.14   Leave your heart in virtual San Francisco.

Figure 3.15   A Web page from The Santa Fe Convention and Visitors Bureau.

VAIL, COLORADO
VailNet
www.vail.net/index.html

Snow, snow, and more snow—this site provides information on skiing, snowboarding, Nordic skiing, snowshoeing, snowmobiling, and more (see Figure 3.16). Find information on ski schools, rental equipment, and lodging, too. Don't forget to come in from the snow to eat—you'll find information on everything from sleigh-ride dinners to recipes from local chefs.

International Cities

HONG KONG
Hong Kong Wonder Net
www.hkta.org

This entertaining site is brimming with information, from news of the week to the many festivals and events taking place each month (see Figure 3.17). You're greeted with an audio welcome, and can watch a video clip on sights to see while in Hong Kong. Take advantage of the interactive tour guide, where you receive a customized list of suggested attractions to visit.

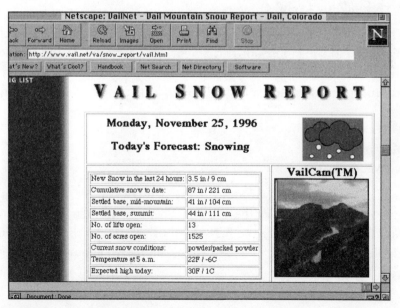

Figure 3.16 Check the daily snowfall in Vail, Colorado.

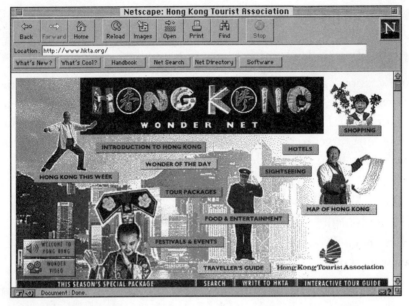

Figure 3.17 Cool graphics of the Hong Kong Wonder Net Web page.

LONDON, ENGLAND

LondonNet

www.londonnet.co.uk

This site has everything you'd want in London except the fish and chips! Visit Big Ben and the Houses of Parliament, chat for a bit in the London forum, and view a pictorial guide of the city's famous landmarks. Also find a list of current runs in the theater district, and the "gig guide" on upcoming concerts.

MOSCOW, RUSSIA

Moscow Guide

www.moscow-guide.ru

You'll receive a warm welcome at the Moscow Guide, where you can find out what's happening at the Bolshoi Theater and take a virtual tour of the Kremlin, as shown in Figure 3.18. Visit other areas of the capital city, including Red Square and "the Golden Ring," and learn about Russian folk art and traditions.

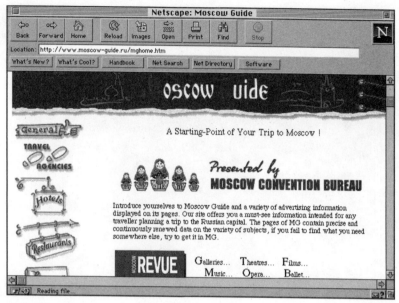

Figure 3.18 Tour the Kremlin with the Moscow Guide.

PARIS, FRANCE
The Paris Pages
www.paris.org

With so much history and background information on the City of Lights, this site is *tres magnifique*! Read details about individual cafes; view interactive maps on monuments, museums, and the Metro (Figure 3.19); and view images of Parisian life. It's up to you whether to read the text in French or English.

SYDNEY, AUSTRALIA
Sydney Interactive Visitor's Guide
webwin.com/tourism

Take a virtual trip down under when you visit this site on Sydney. Find lots of great photos and information on attractions to see, including the koalas. Investigate the city's neighborhoods, take tours of museums, and check out the beaches without the risk of sunburn.

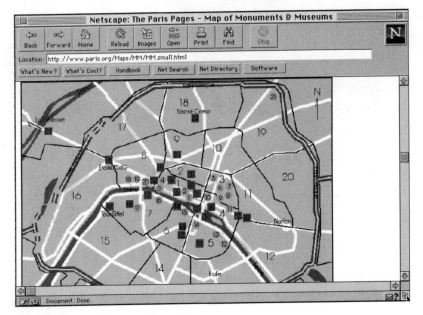

Figure 3.19 The Paris Pages Web site.

U.S. States

ALASKA
Alaska
akcache.com/alaska

Visit "America's last great frontier" region by region. Travelers can learn about outdoor activities and find approximate fees for everything from salmon dinners to canoe rentals. Catch weekly forecasts of auroral activity and be sure to read the information on how to keep bears away from your camp!

ARIZONA
The Arizona Guide
www.arizonaguide.com

Learn about the Grand Canyon State, territory by territory. Read about the cities, from Phoenix to Tucson to Mesa. Look up happenings with a calendar of events and conduct keyword searches of the site. And of course, there's plenty of info on the Grand Canyon itself.

HAWAII
Hokeo Hawai'i
www.visit.hawaii.org

Put on your lei and stay awhile! Learn about Hawaii's majestic islands via interactive map. Overflowing with information, this site will teach you about Hawaii's past and present. Discover out-of-the-way places to explore and natural wonders to behold. A calendar of events is also provided.

MAINE
Destination Maine
www.destinationmaine.com

Discover what Maine has to offer by conducting searches according to activity, region, or season. Read updated, informative articles on suggested outings, scenery to view, and attractions to visit.

MONTANA
Montana Big Sky Country
travel.mt.gov

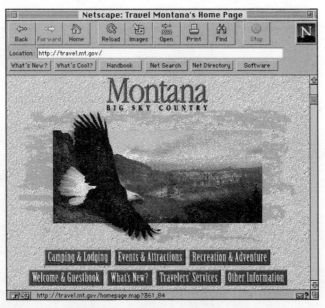

Figure 3.20 The virtual outdoors of Montana.

The natural surroundings of Montana await you at this site, with plentiful information on wildlife and state and national parks, including Yellowstone. There's lots of information on outdoor recreation, too, provided according to the season.

TEXAS
TravelTex
www.traveltex.com

Take in the down-home flavor of this Texas Web site (see Figure 3.21). Watch slide shows of travel tours, learn about terrain, and receive updates on events in the Lone Star state. Plan your trip with an interactive itinerary, collect screen savers, and send virtual postcards to your friends.

Countries

ARGENTINA
Argentina: The Land of Six Continents
turismo.gov.ar

From The Great Waters Rain Forest to the Patagonian Atlantic, this site is chock full of information, with nice maps and colorful photos. Read about

Figure 3.21   A Texas-style Web page.

nature reserves, out-of-the-way excursions, and the city of Buenos Aires. A daily itinerary is also offered.

BARBADOS
Barbados Tourism Encyclopedia
www.barbados.org

Plan your itinerary with an interactive sightseeing map and a calendar of events. Read "fun facts" and take a look at the photo gallery of fauna, local people, natural attractions, and scenic outlooks of this tropical destination.

CANADA
Gold, Grizzlies and Then Some
parallel.ca/yukon

Take the Klondike quiz and learn about Canada's untamed Yukon. View "a modern day trail map," learn about the Klondike gold rush, send virtual postcards, and play with cool Canadian puzzles.

COSTA RICA
Costa Rica
www.cool.co.cr

View this site's beautiful images of Costa Rica, and find information on diving and surfing in not one, but two, oceans at this tropical destination. Also read plenty of background information on the country itself and on recommended attractions. You'll also find a helpful searchable database of hotels at this site.

ECUADOR AND THE GALÁPAGOS ISLANDS
Virtual Galápagos
www.terraquest.com/galapagos/

Visit blue-footed boobies and other wondrous creatures on your virtual tour of the islands (Figure 3.22). Follow adventurers on their journey with maps, photos, and daily updates. This site also covers the islands' history, Darwin's visit, the theory of evolution, and eco-tourism.

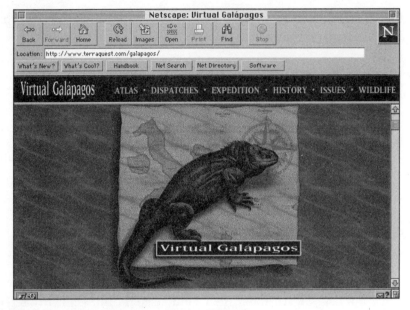

Figure 3.22   Venture to the Virtual Galápagos.

EGYPT
Egypt's Information Highway
www.idsc.gov.eg/tourism

Read about relics to see in Egypt, from the Sphinx to the pharaohs' tombs. Check out the 3D graphics, and step into the "Cairo Café," where you can play with puzzles and translate your name into hieroglyphics.

INDIA
Welcome to India
www.tourindia.com

Read information on the land "where temple elephants exist amicably with the microchip." Learn about people, music, traditional dances, and curries—even check out the history of the sari. The site also includes details about the states and regions: everything from hiking the Himalayas to shopping in New Delhi.

IRELAND
Access Ireland
www.visunet.ie/welcome.html

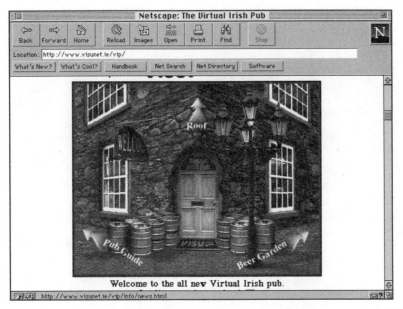

Figure 3.23   Stop by Ireland's virtual pub.

Your first stop: the Virtual Irish Pub, shown in Figure 3.23, where you can chat with other wearers of the green about politics, history, sports, music, and other topics. Take a virtual tour of the countryside, and find extensive background on Ireland's rich cultural heritage and great novelists and poets.

ITALY
In Italy Online
www.initaly.com

Visit hill towns, castles, and out-of-the-way treasures. This site (Figure 3.24) offers recipes, and suggests drives through the countryside. Learn about the country by region—the site features a different region each month. Also post questions to the message board.

KENYA
KenyaWeb
www.kenyaweb.com

This site presents an extensive chronicle of Kenya's history, and provides regional information on one of the most popular destinations in Africa. Learn

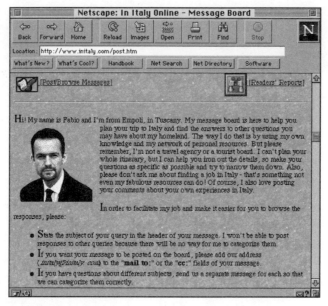

Figure 3.24 Post messages on the In Italy message board.

about the native animals and use the interactive map to find facts about wildlife parks and reserves.

KOREA
Korea National Tourism Organization
www.knto.or.kr

Visit this Web page for lots of information on the people, culture, and festivals of Korea. Learn about religion and temples, stop by museums and attractions, visit Seoul, and learn about "everything kimchi" in the food department.

NORWAY
Norway Online Information Service
www.norway.org

Learn about Norway's past and present, from the Vikings to current political issues. Read articles on local food, contemporary arts, and architecture. Also visit Oslo, Norway's capital, and discover "fun facts from a to z."

Figure 3.25   The Web page of New Asia Singapore.

SINGAPORE

New Asia Singapore

www.travel.com.sg/sog/

This Web site of the "Lion City" is full of information on attractions, including neighborhoods, temples, landmarks, and gardens (Figure 3.25). You'll also find appetizing descriptions of the exotic cuisine, facts on Singapore's cultural past as well as its present, and a video clip about the island.

SPAIN

Discover Spain

www.spaintour.com

Read about everything Spanish, from the thriving cities of Madrid and Barcelona to seaside villages. Learn about tapas, historic buildings, and special events.

TAHITI

Tahiti Explorer

www.tahiti-explorer.com

The cool blue tropical waters of Tahiti welcome you to this site. Watch videos of activities to do and sights to see. Find information on the sister islands of

Bora Bora, Moorea, Maupiti, and others. Also read about Tahiti's flora, local music, and dances.

The Next Step

Once you have decided where to spend your vacation, you need to begin preparing for your trip. Now is the time to stock up on particulars to help plan your itinerary. The Web sites listed in Chapter 4 can make that step easier, and can help you shop for luggage, improve you photography skills, and provide information on any immunizations you may need.

Practical Preparations: Details Before You Hit The Road

CHAPTER 4 TOPICS

- PLANNING YOUR ITINERARY

- SHOPPING FOR TRAVEL ESSENTIALS ON THE WEB

- PACKING TIPS

- STAYING HEALTHY ON THE ROAD

- PHOTO 101 ON THE WEB

Stuffing suitcases, digging beach towels from the closet, running to the mall for last-minute necessities, and locking the house up tight are rituals you may perform before leaving on vacation. While sitting down at your PC may not have been part of your routine in the past, you may want to consider adding it to your list in the future.

By spending just a short session at your computer and on the World Wide Web, you can gather lots of information to better equip you on your journey. For instance, by visiting weather Web sites, like those of the Weather Channel (**www.weather.com**) and Intellicast (**www.intellicast.com**), you'll find real-time weather conditions at your destination. Seeing satellite images and reading forecasts about incoming cold fronts can alert you to pack the appropriate clothing for a chilly week ahead. Instead of packing shorts and sandals, you'll probably want to pack sweaters and electric socks. That may not have been the ideal conditions you had in mind for your trip, but at least you'll be dressed properly.

Knowing the weather and what to pack for your trip is one of the keys to a glitch-free vacation (Figure 4.1).

Figure 4.1   Check the weather in Prague before you pack for your trip.

The Web can also provide you with invaluable information on trip preparation itself, including packing tips. And why not learn from the health experts about avoiding Montezuma's revenge, and receive pointers from professional travel photographers on capturing memories to last a lifetime?

Your Vacation Blueprints

The idea is simple: Smart travelers plan ahead. By reducing the stress that unavoidably comes with traveling, planners make the most of vacation time and keep track of what they set out to accomplish. Checking out the scene beforehand allows you to preview the sights and decide which seem most interesting to you. Then, when you arrive at your destination, you will use your time to the fullest. For instance, you can avoid wasting an afternoon at a museum that does not pique your curiosity by reading up on a city's museums before you visit. By perusing the Web, you may decide that the Museo del Prado is more your style than the Centro de Arte Reina Sofia. Know before you go to get the most out of your trip.

Planning ahead also allows you to reduce time wasted on transportation. By researching where attractions are located, you can plan to stop by sights in the same area at one time, so you spend as few hours as possible commuting. Wouldn't you rather spend that extra time relaxing on a beach or exploring one of the world's famous art galleries than crammed into expensive cabs or crowded buses?

In addition, mapping out a course of action before departure can prevent glitches along the way. Figure out where you will be and when, and make your hotel reservations ahead of time. This greatly reduces the chance of not getting a room, or a *decent* room, for the night.

Making The Itinerary

Preparing for a trip does not mean plotting out every hour of each day and snuffing all spontaneity from a journey (leaving room for some impulsiveness is a must). Instead, it's about devising a course of action to use as a general guide.

Begin plotting an itinerary by researching your destination as much as possible. There are numerous Web sites that can divulge the details you need for planning your trip. Sites filled with travel information, such as Expedia, shown

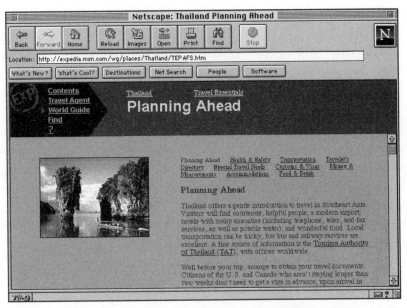

Figure 4.2 Get the particulars to plan your itinerary at Expedia.

in Figure 4.2, and Travelocity can give you particulars on everything from theater productions during your stay to outdoor activities offered in an area. Discover corner cafes to visit, galleries to browse, off-the-beaten-path excursions to take, and everything in between.

Travelocity
www.travelocity.com

Visit the "Destinations and Interests" section to learn about sights to see, restaurants, and upcoming events at your destination. You can also view maps, photos, and "video tours" of countries all over the world. Scheduled chat sessions let you get the scoop on your destination from travel columnists or others in the business.

Expedia
www.expedia.com

Expedia's "world guides" offer information on over 250 destinations in Asia, the Caribbean, Europe, the Middle East, Hawaii, North America, and the South Pacific. You'll find quick facts on the country you plan to visit and learn about the geography, history, culture, and people of the region. Also review "travel essentials" about food, accommodations, safety, transportation, and money matters. Experienced travelers offer destination-specific recommendations in the chat forums.

AT&T Worldwide
www.att.com/traveler/pip/pip.html#form

Create your itinerary using this site, as shown in Figure 4.3. You provide your top trip priorities, select the city you plan to visit, and then peruse suggestions on things to do and see. You'll read city summaries and recommendations for shopping, outdoor activities, where to eat, museums, and after-dark activities. Once you've chosen what you'd like to do on your trip, you can view your itinerary, print it out, and take it with you.

Travel Byte

Before you depart on your vacation, leave a copy of your itinerary with a friend or family member. That way people at home will know where to contact you in case of emergency.

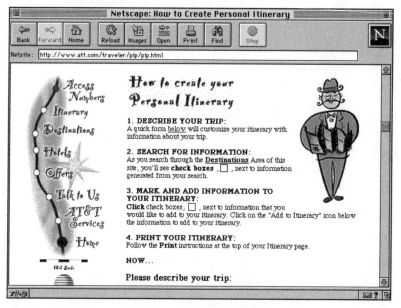

Figure 4.3   Plan your travel itinerary on the Web.

Doing Your Homework

Look to online magazines such as Travel & Leisure (Figure 4.4) and online travel books, like *Fodor's*, listed in Chapter 3. With online travel publications you can read reviews and travel articles by writers who have already been to your destination. Web sites listed in Chapter 7 can also provide you with numerous ideas of what to see and do on your excursion. By checking into these sites, you can get the full scoop on what your vacation spot has to offer, and you can plan your days' itinerary before you depart.

When visiting Web sites, jot down whatever catches your fancy, or easier yet, print out the articles, reviews, and suggested sights to see. After you've collected plenty of information, narrow the subject matter down according to what is most important to you—separating the must-sees from the maybes. You can then work the activities into a daily schedule, keeping in mind the amount of vacation time you have. Create an outline of where you would like to spend each day and what you plan to do while you're there.

Remember to allow ample time to soak up the atmosphere and culture of wherever you plan to visit. By rushing from one monument to the next in Washington D.C., you may miss out on experiencing the hub-bub of Dupont

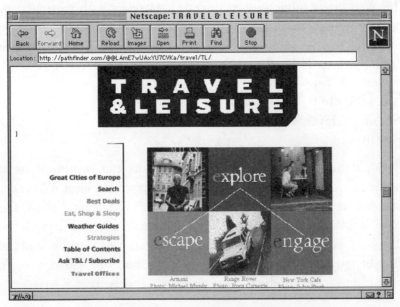

Figure 4.4   Read reviews from online magazines like Travel & Leisure.

Circle, the beauty of the Georgetown University campus, and the ethnic diversity of the Adams-Morgan neighborhood. Give yourself time to take it easy.

Plan to visit what seems interesting to *you*. If the thought of exploring Napoleon's tomb gives you a thrill, and a climb up the Eiffel Tower seems uninspiring—bypass the tower. You don't need to visit an attraction just because "everybody else does it." When traveling in a group of people with different views on the sights to see in Paris, or anywhere else, plan a day to separate from one another to do your own thing. The group can meet up later that night for dinner and lively conversation about the day's activities.

Travel Byte

Consider purchasing an open-jaw ticket for your trip. These tickets allow you to fly into one city and leave for home from another.

When designing your vacation blueprints, consider your special needs. Disabled travelers may have limited mobility, or may need a travel companion who can offer assistance. Seniors may be interested in vacationing with others in their age group. Women may be especially concerned about safety.

The Web offers numerous resources for travelers with particular needs and concerns. Online magazines, organization home pages, and sites for networking with other travelers are available to you. The following sites offer information for disabled, senior, and women travelers.

FOR DISABLED TRAVELERS
Disability Travel Services Online
www.dts.org

Through this organization's Web site, visitors can communicate with one another about traveling with a disability, as shown in Figure 4.5. Travelers may subscribe to mailing lists for networking with others, and the DTS bulletin board is full of posted inquiries and comments. Electronic guidebooks offer city-specific information on transportation, accommodations, and the accessibility of museums, sports centers, hospitals, and medical clinics. You'll also find links to travel products, tour operators, and assistance services.

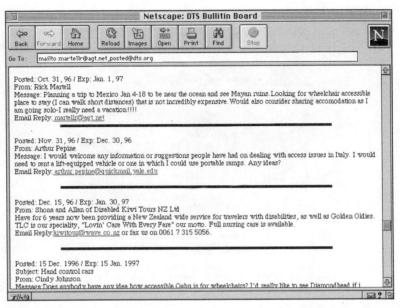

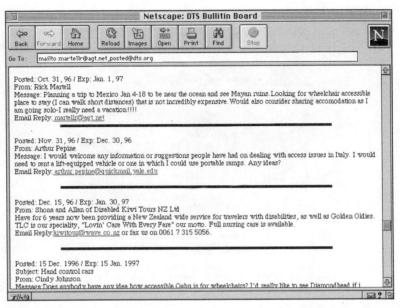

Figure 4.5 Read comments, recommendations, and advice from other disabled travelers.

Global Access
www.geocities.com/Paris/1502

This "network for disabled travelers" features articles written about visits to distant lands (Figure 4.6). You'll read about experiences on safaris, airline flights, and resorts from disabled travelers' perspectives. Check out the travel tips for those with special needs and read letters from other visitors to the site.

Disability Net Holiday/Travel News
www.globalnet.co.uk/~pmatthews/DisabilityNet/Holidays/HolidaysNews.html

News that may be of interest to travelers with disabilities is posted on this site. Read updates on newly opened wheelchair accessible hotels, guest houses, and inns. Find out about park trails that offer audio cassette guides and Braille signs, and cruise ships and safaris that offer easy access.

Access-Able Travel Source
www.acess-able.com

This site informs readers of new tours, travel discounts, and promotions like free magazine offers. In addition to offering information about organizations

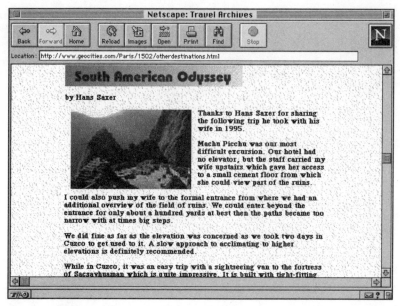

Figure 4.6 Articles written by disabled travelers are offered at the Global Access Web site.

for disabled travelers, the site provides summaries of related magazines, books, and newsletters, including contact and pricing information. The site also features tours and offers lots of links for disabled travelers.

FOR SENIOR TRAVELERS
Elderhostel
www.elderhostel.org

Elderhostel offers short-term educational programs for seniors in countries around the world. The home page provides information on the organization, courses offered, accommodations, pricing, and available scholarships. Search the seasonal online catalogs to review course descriptions and find a program that suits your interests. You can register for programs right from the Web site.

Grand Times
www.grandtimes.com

Grand Times is "exclusively for active retirees." The online magazine offers departments on cooking and relationships as well as travel. Look to the latter to read articles about discount accommodations, traveling by RV, and taking trips with the grandkids or family pets.

Today's Seniors
NovaTech.ON.CA/seniors/mrtstrav.html

This online magazine offers travel articles written for seniors by seniors, as shown in Figure 4.7. Numerous articles are offered, including many from past issues. Read about ski trips, mountain treks, cruises, riding the rails, and excursions at sea. You'll find articles about international travel, birding tours, and impressions of castles, cathedrals, and parks as well.

For Women Travelers
Maiden Voyages
www.maiden-voyages.com

The online version of *Maiden Voyages* magazine offers women travelers opportunities for networking and sharing comments, tips, and experiences. Read features in "The Journal," and other articles by guest writers. You'll find information on tours and accommodations run by and geared toward women. Also participate in the site's survey to let them know about your travel preferences and habits.

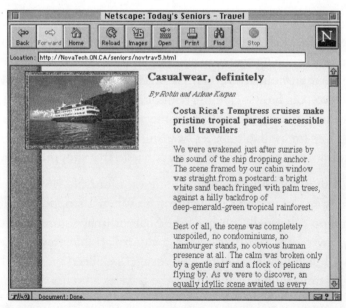

Figure 4.7   Read travel articles written by active seniors in online magazines.

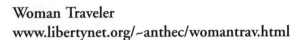

Woman Traveler
www.libertynet.org/~anthec/womantrav.html

This organization arranges independent international trips for small groups of women. Read about their travel style and philosophy, and how they are unlike most travel tours. Fill out the travel questionnaire to help the group decide where to go next—and if you're a woman, you are invited to join. The motto of the site is "happiness is a well-stamped passport."

Travel Byte

In parts of Asia, women dress more modestly than in the West. To help prevent some forms of sexual harassment, women should wear clothing that covers their legs and arms.

Shopping Made Easy

One of the ways to get you and your trip in order is by doing some shopping—online shopping, that is. From buying those electric socks to purchasing a travel iron, you can buy great merchandise right from the Web at cybermalls and cyberstores.

At cybermalls, you can stop by online versions of many popular stores found in your local shopping center, in addition to thousands of other shops all over the planet. There are numerous cybermalls to choose from that are open all day and all night. So you can browse clothing boutiques, wilderness outfitters, kitchen-supply outlets, and grocery markets anytime you choose. But instead of circling parking lots for available spaces, waiting in long check-out lines, and dealing with uninformed sales people, you get hassle-free shopping done in no time.

Need to shop for some items for your vacation? No problem. Shop at such Web sites as DreamShop in Figure 4.8. When I stopped by Time Warner's DreamShop cybermall, I visited The Sharper Image store, where, while looking at travel bags, I discovered a great collapsible travel bike, perfect for packing. I then headed over to The Voyager's Collection, where I found a very cool dual-time-zone wristwatch for the traveler who has everything.

Another option is to bypass the mall and visit your favorite stores and catalogs right at their Web sites. Find luggage and other travel goods at the Web pages of JCPenney (**www.jcpenney.com**) and Spiegel (**www.spiegel.com**). At

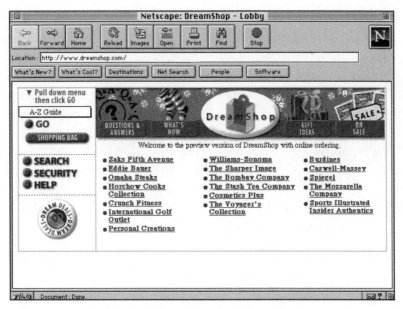

Figure 4.8 Time Warner's DreamShop cybermall.

cyberstores, you can view merchandise photos, read detailed product descriptions, and find up-to-date, specific information that otherwise may not have been available to you.

Travel Byte

Order free travel brochures off the World Wide Web by visiting the World Wide Brochure site (**www.wwb.com**). You'll find email links to thousands of travel companies that will send you free brochures on what they offer. Conduct key word searches to order free road maps, cruise guides, tourism directories, adventure vacation magazines, and travel brochures according to your interests.

But Is Online Shopping Safe?

Many people are reluctant to shop online because they feel uneasy about disclosing credit card numbers over the Internet. While concern is understandable, giving such information on the Net is worth no more anxiety than giving a credit card number to a mail-order catalog or department store clerk. When making a purchase through any of these channels, there is a risk that someone will use your number for illegal purposes.

Jaclyn Easton, contributing writer for *The Los Angeles Times,* producer, host of *Log On U.S.A.*, and author of the book *Shopping on the Internet and Beyond,* states, "I don't believe credit card fraud between online retailers and individual customers occurs. I have challenged all of my radio show listeners and other online devotees with a cash reward for the identity of one person who has experienced credit card fraud on the Net. No one has stepped forward."

PAY IT SMART

Using secure browsers like Internet Explorer and Netscape will help to protect your credit card information. These browsers inform you via icons that you're making a safe transaction: Internet Explorer displays a locked padlock and Netscape presents an intact gold key.

Through secure transactions, your credit card information is encrypted (transformed into unreadable code), which makes accessing your numbers difficult for anyone who's not supposed to have them. There is now a standard for secure transactions, which is supported by Microsoft, Netscape, Visa, and MasterCard among others, that makes shopping on the Internet all the more trustworthy. Learn more about it at the Internet Explorer (**www.microsoft.com/ie**) and Netscape (**www.netscape.com**) sites.

Hanging Out At The Cybermall

Ready to shop 'til your modem's content? Here are some malls you'll want to check out:

CyberShop
www2.cybershop.com/Cybershop/Online.f/Welcome.html

Purchase clothes, steamers, and luggage for your next trip at this virtual mall. Departments include gourmet foods, personal gifts, children's clothes and toys, and outdoor living. View color photos and read descriptive product details. Figure 4.9 shows some of their best sellers. Free shipping, too!

iQVC
www.iqvc.com

Beauty, books, and arts & leisure are departments you'll visit at iQVC, the Web site of the QVC Shopping Network (Figure 4.10). You can shop online for accessories, clothing, and for travel goods in the "personal care" department.

Figure 4.9   Browse through a wide variety of products on the Web.

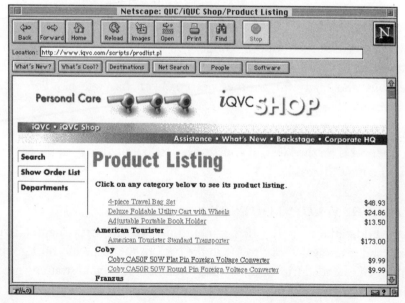

Figure 4.10   Useful travel items are sold at the iQVC Web site.

Viamall
www.viamall.com

Buy yourself a pair of sunglasses, a travel pillow, some luggage, and anything else you can think of for your next trip. Even buy some chocolate treats for the road.

New Quest
www.newquest.com/mall/index.htm

This site features more than 400 stores where you can browse for new clothes, health care products, sporting goods, and stationery for writing home.

Travel Byte

If you still can't find what you're looking for, visit the Shopping Direct Web site (**www.shoppingdirect.com**), where you can conduct one search for a particular product in more than 900 cybermalls and 20,000 individual cyberstores. Now that's the quickest and easiest shopping yet!

It's In The Bag

While you're in the shopping mode, you may want to take a good look at the condition of your luggage. Check the fabric, hinges, and handles. Is it durable, reliable, and ready for another beating from baggage handlers and airport conveyer belts?

If you think it may be time to buy some new luggage, a quick and easy place to shop for it is on the Web, of course. Here are some things to think about when buying new "luggables."

Go Easy On Yourself

The Eddie Bauer duffel bag I mentioned in the first chapter is great for weekend getaways—I just toss it in the back of the Jeep, and off I go. But if I'm taking an extended trip, or flying to my destination, I avoid straining my back and shoulders with bulky suitcases by taking my "pullable" luggage with wheels.

Luggage with wheels is less strenuous on your body and on your mind. From getting to and from hotels to maneuvering around airport terminals, wheeled luggage is as easy as it gets.

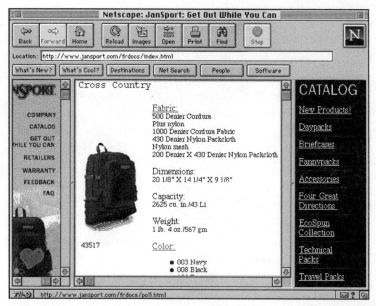

Figure 4.11   A large backpack, like this one from JanSport (**www.jansport.com**), is the luggage of choice for many travelers.

Strap It On

Another option for those of you who, like me, have an aversion to the traditional suitcase, is buying a great big backpack (Figure 4.11). For long trips, when I know I will be moving from place to place quite often, I strap my pack on my back and go. It's comfortable, easy on my back because of its support, and makes carrying my belongings hassle-free. While this may not be appropriate in some situations, like a business trip with the company CEO, it's certainly a good idea for casual traveling. Many backpacks sold today even easily convert to a suitcase for use in any situation.

Luggage Lifesavers

Most travelers know the number one rule of luggage packing: pack light. Those who follow the rule easily travel from one destination to the next because they don't have heavy baggage to lug around with them. They can keep their eyes on their belongings at all times because it can be carried with them in comfort. In addition, light packers may have less shoulder aches and back pains by the time their vacation comes to an end. Many travel experts advise vacationers to pack only the most essential items.

Here are some luggage-related tips to follow:

- When shopping for luggage, look for sturdy material. Also make sure it's waterproof. The last thing you want is to arrive at your hotel with soggy clothes.

- Buy a carry-on bag that can fit under the seat in front of you on an airplane. Over-head compartments are often packed with other people's things by the time you board the plane. Save yourself the worry.

- Make sure to fill out those address tags! If your luggage is lost, or winds up in Brussels while you're in Baghdad, you want to be sure the airline will know where to return it to you.

- Don't over-pack. Stuffing all your belongings in one bag strains hinges and stretches seams that may give way. Leave a few things behind, or pack another bag.

- Consider taking several small bags with you instead of just one huge suitcase. For many people, this is a lot easier than dragging along a 60-pounder.

If you find yourself in the position of having to cram ten pounds of travel gear into a five-pound bag, get another bag at a Web site, like Spiegel's (Figure 4.12).

Figure 4.12   Luggage shopping at Spiegel's Web site.

Pack It Up

Ever arrive in Florida without your swimsuit? Or without your sunglasses? Or without sunscreen? We all have forgotten one thing or another when we've gone on a trip. These slip-ups may mean making a trip to the hotel gift store and paying inflated prices for something you already have at home, or simply going without. Well, with dream vacations, nothing is forgotten, and, as you probably guessed, the Web can help you prevent this from happening.

There are lots of checklists on the Web that can help you make up your own personalized packing list. Or it may be even easier to just print a packing list right off the Web.

Some Packing Advice

In addition to the particulars of a packing list, here are some good general rules to pack by:

CLOTHES

Bring clothes that are dark colored. Light clothes show stains. Also, cotton clothes travel best because they wrinkle less than other fabrics, are durable, wash and dry quickly, and need little care.

FOOTWEAR

Wear sturdy, worn-in walking shoes. New shoes can give you blisters, which are no fun when you're doing a lot of walking.

Another lightweight and easy-to-pack item in the footwear category is flip-flops. If you're staying in youth hostels, or anyplace where you will share a shower with other travelers, it's smart to wear shower shoes to protect your feet. You depend on your tootsies when traveling, so show them the respect they deserve.

EAR GEAR

You may want to consider taking a Walkman or Discman on your trip. Listening to books on tape while watching the miles roll along by train, or listening to music on a long flight is relaxing and enjoyable. My fiancé Phil and I particularly like to take Garrison Keillor's *News from Lake Wobegon* tapes with us on road trips through rural America.

STASHING YOUR CASH

Keep your cash tucked away with a neck wallet, a small bag worn around your neck like a necklace. Keep your passport, flight tickets, traveler's checks, and currency inside, under your clothing, to make sure no one gets their hands on it but you. A neck wallet is much safer than carrying a purse, a pocket wallet, or a fanny pack. Even in "the wonderful world of Disney," pickpockets are lurking, so keep your money out of sight.

PLUGS AND OUTLETS

When traveling abroad, bring an adapter kit with you if you plan to use electric appliances like curling irons, razors, and hair dryers. Most countries use a different standard of alternating electrical current than the United States (the U.S. uses 100 volts; most countries use 220), as well as different outlet plugs. Your plug simply may not fit in a wall outlet overseas, so pick up a 50-to-1600-watt converter at your local hardware store before you go.

PACK THIS

Don't forget to bring along an open mind and positive attitude. Of course, when you're visiting a new place, things will be different and unusual. That is the point of traveling—to happen upon new experiences and see first-hand how other people live. Keep yourself open to new adventures, and enjoy. *Viva la difference!*

Travel Byte

Keep a journal to record observations, sentiments, and impressions of what you've seen and heard on your journey. Keeping a journal is a very personal way to commemorate your trip, and it makes a great read for years to come.

Travel Lists And Tips

Here are some great places to find packing lists and helpful tips from the Web.

Southwest Airlines
www.iflyswa.com/info/pack.smart.html

"Purchase travel-size bottles of shampoo, conditioner, and other toiletries, or place the amounts you will need of these items in small containers to take with you. Carrying around several big bottles can get awfully heavy; plus, they take up lots of space in your luggage."

ASTA
www.astanet.com/wwww/astanet/news/packtips.html

"Always carry your travel documents, medication, jewelry, traveler's checks, keys, and other valuables in your hand luggage. Items such as these should *never* be packed in luggage that you plan to check."

Embassy Suites
www.embassysuites.com/embassydocs./tips.html

"Don't over-pack. Limit packing time to one hour, or lay out all the clothes for the trip and then put half of those things back to prevent over-packing."

Travel Byte

After packing all the items on your checklist, pack one more thing: the list itself. It will come in handy when you pack up to return home. By going over the list, you'll make sure to leave nothing behind.

Some Opinions And Ideas On The Art Of Travel
members.aol.com/ddyment/travel.html

"Bundle folding involves the careful wrapping of clothes around a central core object, avoiding the hard folds that result in creases."

American Tourister
www.vacations.com/American_Tourister/Tips/index.html

"Pack a collapsible, lightweight bag if you plan to bring home more than you take."

A Sample Packing List

The Travel Kiosk Web site (**www.afn.org/~afn11300**) offers novice travel photographers suggestions for taking better pictures, including information on lighting, framing, and taking care of equipment while on the move. The site also provides travel tips, links to a number of related Web sites, and packing advice. The following packing list is excerpted from the Travel Kiosk Web site. You may find the list on the Web at **www.afn.org/~afn11300/ packing.html.**

❏ Carry-on—I use a carryon similar to the ones the flight crews use. I find that a carryon is sufficient on most trips. I don't worry about losing a bag and don't have to wait around for the luggage to be unloaded.

❏ Baggies—2 sizes. For laundry that hasn't dried, damp face cloth, and other wet items.

❏ Flight bag—I always carry a small extra flight bag because I may have bought more than I can bring back in my other bags.

❏ Clock, with alarm.

❏ Clothing—Carry half in carry-on, half in partner's bag if traveling with someone. If one of the bags is lost, we still have half our clothes. This should not happen if you have a carry-on, but someone *could* take off with yours by mistake.

❏ Electric plug adaptors—Different countries use different plugs, so carry adaptors if you have any electric appliances with you.

❏ Flashlight—I carry a small flashlight when I go on safari or to countries that might have erratic power. Also comes in handy during the night if I have to get up and don't want to disturb my traveling companion.

❏ Gifts—Quite often I take gifts to give to locals.

❏ Gloves—Cotton or heavy, depending on destination.

❏ Hair dryer—With dual-voltage capability. Take one only if there's doubt that one is available in the hotel.

❏ Hangers—A couple plastic hangers come in handy for drying clothing if there is no shower curtain rod, or not enough hangers in hotel closet.

❏ Laundry bag—Carry a hotel plastic laundry bag.

❏ Laundry clips—Have clips with hooks on end for hanging up hose to dry.

❏ Needle, thread, other related items.

❏ Night clothes (robe and slippers)—Can use plastic raincoat in place of robe. Can always slip on shoes in place of slippers.

❏ Plastic bottle—For purifying water to use for brushing teeth in certain areas of the world, or for drinking water when traveling on bus, or other day trip.

❏ Small purse—For times when I will not want to wear a hip pack.

❏ Raincoat, plastic with hood—Better than an umbrella, takes less space, and is excellent as a windbreaker.

❏ Shoes—Extra pair for walking.

❏ Silk spray—In warm countries, I take nothing but silk clothing. It takes so little space, is more comfortable than man-made fabrics, and dries quickly. And as silk clings, it needs spray.

❏ Soap—I carry a small hotel-size bar.

❏ Steamer or iron—I prefer a steamer with dual-voltage switch, as it's lighter in weight than an iron and easier to use.

❏ Sweater, light jacket—Comes in handy where air-conditioners are turned very low.

❏ Tights or long underwear—For very cold areas.

❏ Toilet tissue—Remove center core and press flat. Take very soft tissue and use it in place of Kleenex.

❏ Towels, bath and/or hand—An extra towel is always handy. Can use to squeeze moisture out of clothing after laundering. Some places give only one bath towel and I may need another for my hair. Take an old one that can be left at your last stop.

❏ Travel data—Flight scedules, hotel information, and other important papers.

❏ Underwear (two sets)—Insulated when necessary. If possible, carry nylon or silk. Even make my husband wear silk underwear on trips because it dries overnight.

❏ Vitamins.

Travel Photography

Unfortunately, dream vacations don't last a lifetime. We go, we see, we take some pictures. While those pictures are meant to remind us of happy and unique events in our lives, they often end up as just dull and lifeless images on film.

Taking good pictures takes practice. I have found that my photography skills improve with each trip I take. Here are some rules I have learned to shoot by:

• Take candid photos of people—shoot on impulse. Avoid staging your scenes.

• When taking nature and wildlife shots, be patient: Wait until the perfect moment.

- It's all about lighting. Use the warm glow of late afternoon or the pink of early morning to your advantage.

- Capture the particular details of a location. When in Arizona, make sure to incorporate cactus in your shots; when in Madrid, include Spanish architecture.

Travel Byte

When traveling in underdeveloped countries, film other than ASA 100, lithium batteries, and black and white film can be very hard to find. It's a good idea to bring your own with you.

Make photos from your next trip extraordinary and worthy of the events they capture. Your snapshots can be comparable to those of professionals by following great photography advice available to you on the Web. You'll find pointers that can make your pictures really mean something. From perspective and lighting to the film to use, you'll learn all that's needed to make your pictures stand out.

Fodor's Focus
www.fodors.com/focus

Follow this online photo guide to take travel photography 101. You'll find tips on taking shots of fireworks, celebrations, architecture, and how to shoot around campfires and in museums. You'll get lessons on lighting, techniques, and composition, as shown in Figure 4.13. Also learn the basics about purchasing a camera, film, and accessories.

Dan's Hangout
www2.superb.net/~beauvias/photo/travtips

There's lots of information at Dan's, from taking photographs in cold winter weather to snapping shots on the beach. Also read hints on when to shoot, and on buying and storing film.

Kodak
www.kodak.com/ciHome/photography/bPictures/specialSituations/travel/travelContents.shtml

Turn this vacation's snapshots into photographs you'll be proud of with a few tips from the pros at Kodak (Figure 4.14). Find insider information from the

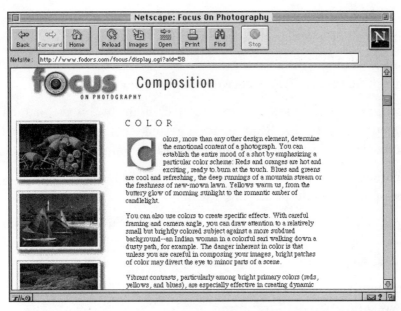

Figure 4.13 Fodor's Focus is a great resource for budding travel photographers.

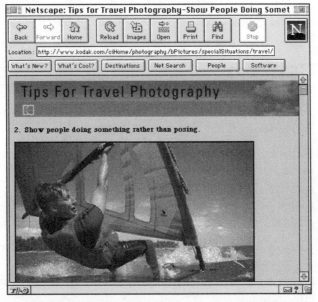

Figure 4.14 Learn how the experts take photos at Kodak.

professionals. Read photography tips and view sharp color-photo examples. Find hints on shooting close-ups as well as "picture-taking on the go."

Lonely Planet
www.lonelyplanet.com/road/witness/phot.htm

You'll read lots of photo how-tos and techniques at this site, named after the famous travel books. Read advice on what to take with you, from spare batteries to lens cleaning tissue, and how to keep your camera from getting stolen.

Photo.net
swissnet.ai.mit.edu/photo/index.html

Read tips and pointers, product reviews, and even a guide to photographing New England foliage. Also find suggestions for framing your photos and digital camera techniques, including scanning and Web posting.

Shutterbug
www.shutterbug.net/hints.htm

Get photo hints from *Shutterbug* readers who've learned from experience. Find handy tips, from using a plastic milk bottle as a light diffuser to using hotel shower caps as emergency camera protectors.

Hot Tips

National Geographic Photography
www.nationalgeographic.com/ngs/mags/ng_online/photography/0004.html

National Geographic doesn't just come in the mail anymore. The magazine's Web site lets you explore the ends of the earth in cyberspace. Find out how the experts call the shots in the National Geographic photography Q&A. Read bios on the staff photographers and find upcoming gallery events in your community.

National Geographic's "Hot Tips" is a valuable resource for amateur photographers. You can find the following information the Web at **www.nationalgeographic.com/ngs/mags/ng_online/photography/0092.html**.

Wildlife Photography
Do not be content to simply show what an animal looks like—to just create its portrait. A good wildlife photograph should also

show significant behavior. You must learn to anticipate the animal's behavior in specific situations and know the importance of different types of behavior. For instance, body language can indicate an animal's position of dominance or submissiveness within a group. Try to show the animal's environment as well. What obstacles must it overcome? How do weather extremes affect how and where the animal lives? How does it use natural surroundings to hide from enemies and stalk prey?

Photographs Of People
Photojournalism should leave viewers feeling that they know the subjects—not only what they look like, but also how they live and what their attitudes are. Photograph people being active, rather than merely posing, and take enough time to put the subject at ease. When a skilled photojournalist is working, a subject will often forget that a camera is present and go about his life with little self-consciousness.

Capturing The Scene
Aim to capture the soul of the place as well as its physical appearance. The viewer should feel what it's like to walk down a particular street or view a landscape that you've shot. Time is again a crucial element. You must first experience a location's moods—light, weather, smells—before you can convey them through photographs. The mood of a city street, for example, changes from night to day, from a sunny day to a rainy day. Many photographers favor the warm tones and directional qualities of late afternoon and early morning light. But do not discount noon light; its harshness can be used to convey its own, very different mood.

How To Improve Your Photography
Begin to look critically at the work of many photographers, and watch for opportunities to meet those whose work you admire. Many of the photographers who shoot for *National Geographic* participate in workshops; such informal settings are good opportunities to get to know photographers' work better, to discuss with them their philosophy of photography, and also to show your work. There are a number of such workshops annually, including the Missouri Photojournalism Workshop (run by the School of Journalism at the University of Missouri - Columbia), the Santa Fe (New Mexico) Photographic Workshops, the Maine (at Rockport) Workshops, and the Jackson Hole (Wyoming) Workshops.

Carrying Film On Planes, Airport X-Rays

It's always advisable to place your film, especially exposed film, in your carry-on luggage to avoid the possibility of loss. The best strategy is to carry the film in a see-through plastic bag or a clear refrigerator container and offer it for visual inspection, rather than allowing it to go through airport X rays. Newer X-ray machines are safe for film of moderate speed, but X rays have a cumulative effect; even these films can be damaged if taken through many times. Older machines, especially those used in Eastern Europe or in the former Soviet Union, should be avoided.

The Rules

It's easy to find rules about photography: "Keep the sun over your shoulder" or "Shoot only at sunrise and sunset" or " Shoot only around noon" or "Never let the horizon run through the exact center of the frame." It's fine to know the rules, but it's also essential to break them. Strictly adhering to the rules may ensure mediocre photographs. Top photographers break the rules as often as they keep them. Photography should be spontaneous, alive, and exuberant. If it works visually, do it.

Travel Byte

After developing your rolls of pictures from your trip, you may have one or two shots you are particularly proud of. Web sites of the Travel Channel, National Geographic, Southwest Airlines, and Outside Online host amateur photo contests. Put your picture-taking skills to the test by entering these competitions.

Photography Resources

To learn more, visit the home pages of professional photojournalists, such as the one shown in Figure 4.15. View photo collections and use them as examples to follow on your own travels. Find these sites through search engines' photography departments.

You can also browse electronic magazines to find useful articles on the ins and outs of photography. A few good ones include Sight (**www.sightphoto.com/photo.html**), and Photo District News (**www.pdn-pix.com/index.html**).

The following directories can connect you to other valuable travel photography resources on the Web.

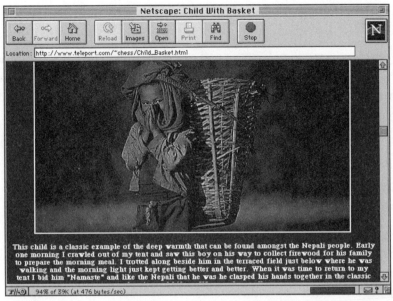

This child is a classic example of the deep warmth that can be found amongst the Nepali people. Early one morning I crawled out of my tent and saw this boy on his way to collect firewood for his family to prepare the morning meal. I trotted along beside him in the terraced field just below where he was walking and the morning light just kept getting better and better. When it was time to return to my tent I bid him "Namaste" and like the Nepali that he was he clasped his hands together in the classic

Figure 4.15 An online collection of travel photographs on the Web.

The Travel Photography Home Page
www.photosecrets.com/~ahudson/Bookmarks.html

This page will connect you to Web sites of personal photography collections and those of professional photojournalists. You can also find links to Web sites of photography travel tours, workshops, and schools. The site connects visitors to travel photography resources such as photo guides and newsletters, as well.

The Photo Page
www.Generation.NET/~gjones

Connect to hundreds of Web sites about photography, including home pages of clubs, online publications, online galleries, and associations. Amateur and professional photographers can link to mailing lists, FAQs, and sites about taking pictures underwater and in moonlight.

Weather To Go

As mentioned at the beginning of this chapter, many Web sites can tune you in to what the weather will be like on your vacation. A few years ago, this would have served me well. After arriving in Arizona with nothing but shorts, sandals, and T-shirts, I awoke the next morning to find a whirlwind of thick snowflakes falling. A blizzard in Arizona? I never would have thought it, but I would have known about it ahead of time if the Web was what it is today.

Worse yet, my friend Shannon had to drastically revise her wedding ceremony, which was to take place on a cruise ship, because of impending hurricanes in the Caribbean. While the wedding did go on (it was moved to Maui), it could have been disastrous had she not checked the weather before taking off for the high seas.

Like Shannon, you have the luxury of knowing before going. Here's a list of top weather Web sites to choose from.

The Weather Channel
www.weather.com/index.html

Read weather updates on U.S. and world cities, learn the hows and whys of weather conditions, peruse weather news, and check out special features, like Santa's weather at the North Pole and a "city of the day" update. Also look into the travel-weather department, and read weather history—a record of extreme weather conditions for the date of your visit.

Intellicast
www.intellicast.com

Here's worldwide weather forecasts, with a special department on ski conditions. Take a look at radar and satellite images (Figure 4.16) and read about "yesterday's extremes"—weather conditions from the previous day to make you cringe. Also read topical articles and ask Dr. Dewpoint weather-related questions.

CNN's Weather
www.cnn.com/WEATHER/index.html

Learn worldwide forecasts for more than 100 cities and view regional radar and satellite images. Also visit the storm center to get updates on current tropical storms and hurricanes, and read up on those of the past.

USA Today
www.usatoday.com/weather/wfront.htm

This site offers the weather of not just the U.S., but all over the world. Read forecasts, learn about earthquakes, volcanoes, thunderstorms, acid rain, and lots of other weather conditions. Find 5-day outlooks (like the one shown in Figure 4.17), and even examine ultraviolet forecasts to learn what SPF protection is best to wear.

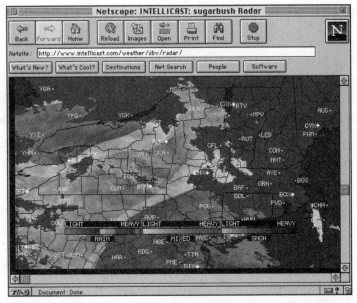

Figure 4.16 A real-time radar image on the Intellicast Web site.

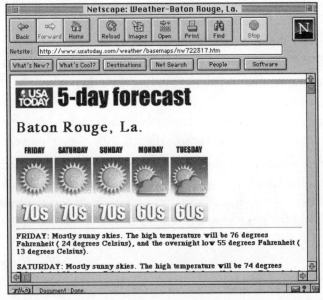

Figure 4.17 Check out the forecast of your destination with USA Today's weather pages.

Healthy Trails To You

Common health problems for many travelers include sunburn, altitude sickness, heat exhaustion, jet lag, and traveler's diarrhea. Everyone knows the last thing you want to do on a vacation is spend it on the toilet, and it's pretty hard to enjoy the outdoors when you've been roasted by the ultraviolet rays. So protect yourself and keep yourself healthy and happy on your trip.

- Sunburn—Wear your sunscreen! You can fry even on the cloudiest day on Padre Island, Texas. No matter where you go, slather it on. SPF 15 or above gives you the best protection. Wearing a hat also helps protect your skin.

- Altitude Sickness—From climbing Mount Kilimanjaro to visiting Boulder, Colorado, altitude sickness affects many people when traveling. To avoid the nausea, shortness of breath, and headaches experienced with reaching new heights, move to increased elevations at a gradual pace, climbing only several thousand feet in a day. Moving to lower altitudes often delivers swift relief.

- Heat Exhaustion—If you feel dehydrated, nauseous, are shaking, or are having trouble walking, you may be dangerously overwhelmed by the heat. To avoid heat exhaustion, drink lots of water, sit in the shade, or get into an air-conditioned building.

- Jet Lag—People may experience jet lag, excessive fatigue, or insomnia from changing time zones and altering their sleep schedules. To avoid jet lag, drink plenty of water and stay away from alcohol, which causes dehydration. Eat healthy and get exercise. It may be a good idea to just hit the hay for a few hours on arrival, and then follow the schedule of everyone else around you.

- Traveler's Diarrhea—Don't drink any water but pure bottled water. Also avoid using ice in drinks, and brush your teeth with bottled water. Local water may contain bacteria that can wreak havoc on your intestinal system. Also avoid foreign bacteria by eating only fruits you can peel, and steering clear of shellfish and raw foods, including vegetables.

Travel Byte

You know you should only drink bottled water when traveling out of the country, but make sure to check water bottles for sealed caps before you buy. Some people simply fill bottles with tap water and sell them to unsuspecting tourists.

Healthy Online Resources

The following Web sites can give you more details on these ailments, as well as specific diseases and other health hazards. Also learn about particular health concerns for your destination and preventative measures you can take to protect yourself.

Travel Health Online
www.tripprep.com/country/sp6.html

This Web site provides health profiles on featured destinations. You'll find information on recommended immunizations and disease risks, keeping the insects away, and safety on the beach. Pre-trip planning suggestions, a travel health overview, and official health data are also included.

MCW International Travelers Health Clinic
www.intmed.mcw.edu/travel.html

Learn what to pack in a medicine kit, get advice on traveling while pregnant, learn about common diseases and how to avoid getting them, and get advice on avoiding motion sickness and auto accidents. The site also offers numerous links to travel- and health-related sites on the Web.

Lonely Planet: Pills, Ills And Bellyaches
www.lonelyplanet.com.au/health/health.htm

Tips for staying healthy while traveling anywhere on vacation abound on the Lonely Planet Web site in Figure 4.18. You'll find a complete health checklist, comprehensive listings of precautions, ailments, and cures for those ailments and illnesses people may acquire while traveling.

In Case Of Emergency...

If you're planning on taking a trip to an adventurous destination, consider preparing a personal medical kit. Emergency first aid may prevent you from making an anxious trip to the doctor or having to cut your vacation short. You may want to include these items in your kit:

- Antiseptic towelettes
- Prescription medicine (in original containers)
- Antidiarrheals

- Sun block
- Over-the-counter pain reliever
- Insect repellent
- Foot powder
- Cough and cold medicine
- A water filter
- Soap
- Bandages
- Gauze
- Scissors
- Tweezers

World Health Organization
www.who.ch

Get briefed on worldwide health issues by reading the World Health Report, which includes facts about immunization and "disappearing diseases." Read about recent disease outbreaks and learn about vaccination requirements. The

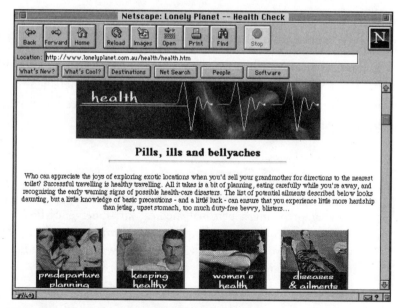

Figure 4.18   Health info from the Lonely Planet.

site also offers travel health information on possible heath risks and having medical examinations after your trip.

CDC: Centers For Disease Control
www.cdc.gov/travel/travel.html

Diseases around the world are listed, as well as lists of countries and the diseases you may encounter there. Read about prevention, symptoms, and remedies for ailments you may encounter in your particular destination. Extensive information is provided on required and recommended vaccines. You can also find out about recent disease outbreaks by visiting the site.

International Society Of Travel Medicine
www.istm.org

Browse the directory to find travel clinics operated by ISTM members in the country you plan to visit and get connected to their home pages. Read news articles and abstracts from the *Journal of Travel Medicine* and news items about diseases and epidemics including cholera, yellow fever, and diphtheria. Also peruse the ISTM newsletter.

Travel Health Information And Referral Service
travelhealth.com/index.htm

Learn where to get health care while traveling, especially if you know you might need such services. At this site you'll find areas telling you how to prevent health problems, find sources for further information, and participate in a travelers' forum. Find information on insect avoidance, politics, and safety, seafood-poisoning syndromes, and more. They also offer pre-travel checklists.

Keeping In Touch

Besides serving up cafe lattes and chocolate pastries, cyber cafes dish out access to the Internet and the World Wide Web. These cozy sanctuaries are located throughout the world, and more are opening every day. By offering email access, they allow travelers to keep in touch with family and friends for a lot less money than long-distance calls. You can receive email from others through Web sites that provide email boxes to travelers on the go, such as the Travelers e-Mail Web site (**www.backpackers.net**). In addition, cyber cafes can be welcome respites in a busy day of touring and sight-seeing—giving your feet, and your neck, a break. What better way to relax than to email others back home and make them jealous of your adventures.

You can also use cyber cafes to find information on the Web that you didn't think to take with you. While in Rome, you can stop by a cafe to pick up information about art museums in Florence—the next stop on your trip. (See Figure 4.19.) You can use the Web as a resource just as when you are sitting at your computer at home. A cyber cafe allows you to email and access info off the Web—with no hefty laptop computer to carry with you.

The following directories will help you locate cyber cafes in the country you plan to visit.

Cyber Cafe Guide
www.cyberiacafe.net/cyberia

Locate cyber cafes around the globe; just look up the country you plan to visit and check out where cyber cafes are located there. Read details about a particular cyber cafe's atmosphere, events, and the cost of a cappuccino. The Cyber Cafe Guide also lets you know about the computers, modems, and scanners available to you.

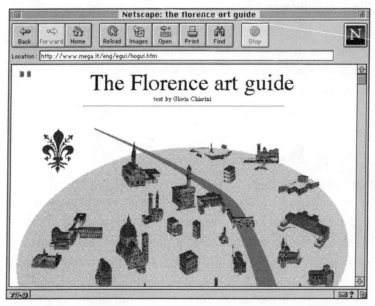

Figure 4.19 Find information about the next stop on your itinerary at cyber cafes.

Global Computing
www.globalcomputing.com/cafes.html

Connect to cyber cafes across the United States from this site. Names and location of numerous cyber cafes are listed. Click on a link and hook up to a cyber cafe's home pages. You'll get connected to Web sites like the one shown in Figure 4.20.

The Complete List of Cyber Cafes in Europe
www.xs4all.nl/~bertb/cybercaf.html

You'll link to numerous cyber cafes in Belgium, Italy, Ireland, The Netherlands, Austria, and other countries in Europe through this site. Web pages of the listed cyber cafes are linked to the site—and if a cyber cafe doesn't have a home page, email links are provided. You can send in your reviews of cyber cafes you've visited while on your travels.

Travel Byte

Why send an ordinary postcard when you can send one from cyberspace! While cruising the Web from a cyber cafe, visit The

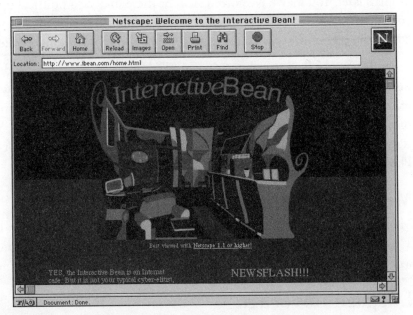

Figure 4.20 The home page of a cyber cafe in Chicago.

Electric Postcard Web site (**persona.www.media.mit.edu/Postcards**). You choose a photo from the "postcard rack," type in a message, and send it off to the email addresses of family and friends at home.

Insuring Your Dream Vacation

I'm no insurance salesman, but there are plenty of them on the Web. If you feel travel insurance is a good idea for you, search the Internet for a policy that suits your needs. If you need some enlightenment on the subject, keep reading.

Some people feel better traveling with insurance coverage, while some feel they don't need it at all. The choice is yours. Travel-insurance rates, deductibles, and premiums can differ depending on the company, so, as when shopping for anything else, it's smart to explore what's out there and to compare prices.

There are three types of insurance coverage most needed by travelers: trip-cancellation insurance, medical-evacuation coverage, and baggage insurance.

Trip-Cancellation Insurance

Nothing is definite. A trip you planned three months ago may not be possible two months later. You may have gotten sick, or there may be a political uprising at your destination that makes it unsafe to travel there. Trip-cancellation insurance covers the cost of the trip you've paid for that you may no longer take part in.

A good rule to follow is to buy trip-cancellation coverage from an independent insurance company—not from the tour operator you're traveling with. The reason is this: Let's say the cruise line you're traveling with goes bankrupt—they've lost all their money, including yours, and may not cover you. Your trip is canceled, but the insurance is worthless because the company can't cover it. Play it safe and go with outside insurance companies.

Medical-Evacuation Coverage

Medical-evacuation insurance covers emergency transportation to a hospital. This coverage is needed for people who are traveling to foreign countries and will be staying in remote areas without medical units or hospitals.

Luggage Coverage

Can you afford the replacement cost if your luggage is lost, damaged, or ripped off? If your answer is no, maybe baggage insurance is for you. Your homeowners insurance may cover personal property away from home, so check first before buying.

Home Safe

What could spoil a vacation more than to return home to find you've been burglarized. Tips on protecting your home may be found along with packing tips, or you may discover an article while perusing online publications. Here are a few of the tips I live by when my home will be home alone.

- Suspend newspaper and mail delivery. A pile of unread papers or an overflowing mailbox is a pretty definite sign to potential burglars that a homeowner is out of town.

- Put radios and lights on automatic timers to make your house look and sound like someone's there.

- Lock doors and windows.

- Move valuables away from windows.

- Water plants.

- Take in any hidden house keys from outside.

- Unplug electrical appliances. Power surges may damage appliances and can cause a fire.

- Empty the fridge. It's no fun to return to spoiled, smelly food. Yuck.

- Give a neighbor or friend contact phone numbers and copies of your passport if traveling abroad.

- Turn down the phone. An unanswered, continuously ringing phone is a sure sign no one's there.

Once your house is locked up tight, you're ready to set those travel wheels in motion. Chapter 5 provides you with Web site addresses and information that can help transport you to your dream location. Read about booking airline flights, reserving rental cars, and finding bus schedules online. In addition, you'll read airport survival tips and advice for the open road.

Planes, Trains, And Rental Cars: Getting Where You Want To Be

CHAPTER 5 TOPICS

- MAKE AIRLINE RESERVATIONS ONLINE

- GET GREAT DEALS ONLINE FOR YOUR FLIGHT

- SEE THE SITES BY RAIL

- RENTING A CAR ONLINE

- NET TRAFFIC REPORTS AND PUBLIC TRANSPORTATION INFORMATION

No matter how you go, make the Web your first stop when making transportation arrangements. Traveling by plane? Book your flight online to receive the lowest fares available and to experience the ease of ticketless travel. Riding by rail? Read up-to-date train schedules, choose your route and amenities, and purchase your tickets—all at one Web site. And if you're cruising by car, you can print out detailed maps, get directions to your destination, and receive the latest news on road construction in a snap.

The Web gives you comprehensive, real-time transit information you can't find anywhere else. So buckle up and get moving via the Web!

Flight Information

Flying is one of the most popular and easiest ways to get to your vacation destination; and the Web has lots of help for you frequent (and not-so-frequent) flyers. Read on to see how easy it is to find an inexpensive flight, book it, and find parking once you get to the airport.

Ticketless Travel

With the advent of the Internet, many airlines, such as Southwest, are offering customers the convenience of flying ticket-free. By booking your flight over the Internet, your reservation is confirmed and ready for you in an airline's database. There's no need for tickets because airline attendants can access your electronic ticket from their computer before you depart.

With ticketless travel, there's no need to pick up your tickets from an agency or wait for them to be delivered in the mail. And you will never worry about losing your tickets, or leaving them behind, again. Buying your electronic tickets is easy and fast, and gives you one less thing to be concerned about before your trip.

Here's how it works: First, you order your tickets over the Web by visiting airlines' Web sites, as shown in Figure 5.1, or sites that specialize in helping you make online reservations. Then simply follow the steps the site provides to purchase your tickets. You choose your destination, times, fares, and airline right from the site. Then, provide your credit card information, or if you'd rather, call the toll-free reservations number provided.

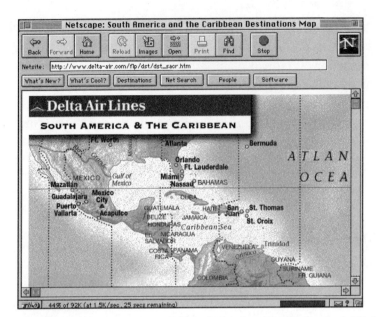

Figure 5.1 Book a flight to any of Delta's destinations from their Web site.

After purchasing your virtual ticket, you will receive a confirmation letter, a confirmation number, an itinerary, and an itemized receipt in the mail or via email. This may take a few days.

When it is time to leave for your vacation, all you will need at the airport is picture identification and your confirmation code. Show these two items as you check in for your flight and you're on your way.

Travel Byte

When flying ticketless, arrive at the airport early to receive your seat assignment.

Booking Online

Some airline Web sites already offer online booking; some do not. If the airline of your choice doesn't offer reservations over the Net, try one of the sites listed below. Many airlines are just getting on the ball and will offer online reservation services shortly. Lots of sites will book your flight for you, even if the airline itself does not.

Figure 5.2 Create your own personal flying profile at the reservations.com Web site.

Travel sites like reservations.com (**www.reservations.com**), shown in Figure 5.2, make reserving your seat a breeze and offer you information on deals. Take a look at these great booking sites, or visit the Airline Information On-Line site (**www.iecc.com/airline/airinfo.html**) to connect to other online reservation resources.

reservations.com
www.reservations.com

As the name implies, this site focuses on helping you reserve a flight to wherever you're going. You can also check airline schedules and flight availability, and even enter contests to win free tickets.

The Internet Travel Network
www.itn.net

This site uses the reservation systems of over 10,000 travel agencies in more than 50 countries to book your flight, hotel, and rental car. You can also participate in online travel discussions about vacation destinations and shopping for the best fare. You'll find lots of links here, too.

Microsoft Expedia
www.expedia.com

Set up your free Expedia travel account to reserve flights, hotel stays, and rental cars. To reserve your flight, simply enter your destination, airports, and desired flight times and the Flight Wizard will book it for you. Use the FareTracker feature to find the best deals.

American Express Travel
www.americanexpress.com/travel

The Web pages of American Express Travel (shown in Figure 5.3) keep you informed of special airline deals offered by major players like Northwest Airlines. Book your flight with ease using the real-time reservation system. And don't miss the great deals in the "last-minute travel bargain" section.

Travelocity
www.travelocity.com

Use Travelocity's secure server to purchase your flight tickets, in addition to making hotel and rental car reservations. You'll find complete fare listings and

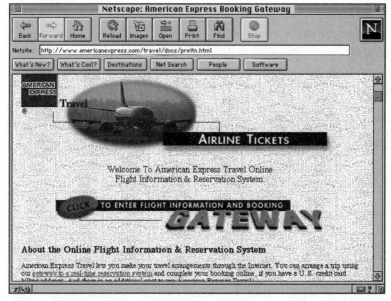

Figure 5.3 You can win free miles by booking your flight with American Express Travel.

timetables, and great offers from American Airlines and others. Get rock-bottom prices by using the "low fare search engine."

theTrip.com
www.thetrip.com

Make your airline reservations, gather specifics on your destination and departure airports, and even track your flight from this site. Also book your hotel rooms and rent a car, and get information on dining and lodging in specific cities.

Flifo
www.flifo.com

Visit this "Cyber Travel Agent" to schedule your flight. Find deals and steals with the FareBeater feature. You'll also discover discounts from major commercial airlines like Continental and TWA.

Instant Air
www.got.com/instair/instair.html

Make your real-time reservations from this site and get the lowest fares available with the "Low Fare Shopper" feature. Find available flights for approximately 30 different airlines (you can book car rentals, too) and discover special online offers.

Cheap Seats

You can save big bucks by shopping for your airplane tickets on the World Wide Web. Sites such as Epicurious Travel (**travel.epicurious.com**), Best Fares (**www.bestfares.com**), and Internet Air Fares (**www.air-fare.com**) provide up-to-date information on the lowest ticket prices available. The last-minute fares, special offers for Web surfers, and online auctions make the Web the best place to shop for a deal. There's just no better way to save.

First of all, comparison shopping is simple using the Web. Just click to visit Web sites of airlines you would like to fly and find out which one has the lowest rate available for your trip.

An even easier solution is to stop by travel reservation sites that have done the comparison shopping for you. Travel sites like Instant Air and others listed in the previous section give you real-time fares from numerous airlines all in one spot. In addition, these travel-reservation sites often have low-fare search engines that will find you the lowest fare offered on their Web site.

Last-Minute Bookings

Sites of airlines like American, Continental, TWA, and USAir offer last-minute travel bargains. To fill all their remaining empty seats right before a flight, many airlines offer reduced rates several days before departure. This benefits you because these seats are offered at reduced rates. The only catch is that the offered destinations and travel times are set, which may not fit into your plans. But getting up to 70 percent off a ticket price can make it worth your while.

A co-worker of mine looked to the Web to buy tickets for her daughter's flight home from college over Thanksgiving weekend. She bought last-minute, round-trip tickets from Orlando to Chicago for half the original ticket price. And that was over a holiday weekend!

You can find these short-lived fares on many airline Web sites, or you can become a member of a mailing list to get weekly reduced fare updates. For example, from American Airline's Web site you can become a member of their Net SAAvers email list. Each week, American sends out an email message letting you in on great last-minute deals that are valid through the upcoming weekend.

Only via the Internet can you receive such comprehensive information on these temporary deals. Last-minute booking is one of the best ways to save using the Web.

Read About Promotions

Lots of airlines advertise special promotional offers on their Web sites. For instance, if an airline begins a route serving a new region or city, you may be able to get low promotional fares on flights serving the new destination. Finding these deals is a piece of cake on the Internet and nearly impossible otherwise.

Travel Byte

Most discount tickets have restrictions. Read the fine print before you make your purchase.

ONLINE-ONLY FARES

Some sites offer deals exclusively to their cyber-surfing customers. Check out the sites of Alaska Airlines and Northwest Airlines to get special online-only discounts. What more could a Web traveler ask for—you're actually rewarded for making your vacation plans the easiest and fastest way possible. There's no better deal than that.

ONLINE AUCTIONS

Barter your way to great deals through online auctions of airline tickets. Airlines like Cathay Pacific have auctioned off seats for choice flights right from their Web sites. During these silent auctions on the Internet, seats are sold to the highest bidder.

For their third CyberTraveler auction, Cathay Pacific offered 18 first-class round-trip tickets, 56 business-class round-trip tickets, and 313 economy-class round-trip tickets between Hong Kong and Los Angeles or New York for travel during 1997. Visit their site, shown in Figure 5.4, to find information about upcoming cyber-auctions.

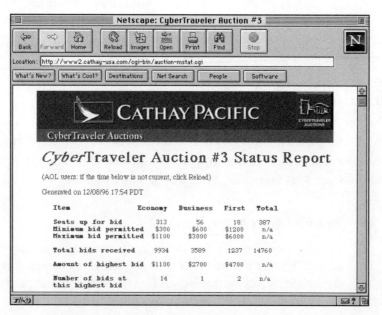

Figure 5.4 Participate in online auctions at Cathay Pacific's Web page.

Top Ten Ways To Save On Your Flight

1. Purchase your ticket either as far in advance or as last-minute as possible.

2. Choose small regional airlines—their fares are usually lower than those of the major airlines.

3. Fly round trip. Prices are less than if you book two separate flights.

4. Don't pay full-fare for the kids. Many international airlines allow children to fly at a lower cost than adults.

5. Stay at your destination through Saturday night. Low-priced flights often call for a Saturday night stay.

6. Air courier flights are the cheapest way to fly overseas. (For more information, look to Chapter 8.)

7. Travel in the late evenings. These flights are cheaper than at peak times of the day.

8. Check airline Web sites for flight specials and promotional deals.

9. Book your flight for a Tuesday, Wednesday, or Saturday. Traveling on these days costs less than other bustling days of the week.

10. Direct flights usually cost more than those with stopovers. Save money on your ticket price by changing planes.

Discount Agencies

Whether they're called discount travel agencies, consolidators, or bucket shops, they all mean the same thing: cheap tickets. Reserve your flight from a wholesale dealer and pay less than if you bought directly from an airline. Check into the following Web sites to find bargain-basement prices.

Travel Byte

Before purchasing a ticket through a consolidator, contact the airline that you plan to travel with and ask if the company is an authorized broker for that airline. If they are not, do not purchase any tickets from them. Move on to a different agency.

Online Discounted Air Fares And Flight Reservations
www.etn.nl/discount.htm

This site provides you with databases from discount travel agents to deliver the best buys to you. Choose from names like Air Discounter, Air Values, and Hot Fares. Locate deals on not only airline flights, but hotel rooms, too.

Travel Information Service
www.tiss.com

Visit this site, which is updated daily, to receive "20% to 70% off lowest published international airfares." Shop online and make your low-priced air, hotel, and car rental reservations on the Web.

Wholesale Travel Center
206.235.50.10/wtc/index.htm

This guide leads you to discount fares for more than 300 worldwide destinations. Conduct personal queries to reserve your flight, hotel stay, and rental vehicle.

Major Airlines' Sites

Many travelers have a favorite airline. If you have a favored airline in mind, you can use a search engine like WebCrawler, Yahoo!, or Excite to find its pages on the Web. Simply submit the name of the airline to conduct a search. You can also use one of the airline Web site directories found in the "Airport And Airline Resources On The Web" section of this chapter to connect to further airline Web sites.

To make it even easier, your preferred airline's Web site may be included in the following list.

Alaska Airlines/Horizon Air
www.alaska-air.com/home.html

Heading to Alaska? You can find flight timetables, book your seat online, get frequent-flyer info and even read about destination information on natural reserves and cities like Juneau. Surfers also receive special bonus miles just for booking an Alaskan adventure from their Web site.

Air Canada
www.aircanada.ca

Get flight schedules and fleet and performance stats, and sign up for the Aeroplan frequent-flyer program. Readers can check out the vacation packages, peruse photos, and find special fares. You may also read travel tips and get linked to hotels.

America West Airlines
www.americawest.com

Cyber shoppers can catch a "deal of the week" at America West's Web site. You can uncover particulars for specific types of travelers, from "senior saver" discounts to the scoop on traveling with your pet. Also read the latest news, FAQs, and destination information. Online booking is coming to this site soon.

American Airlines
www.americanair.com/aa_home.htm

At this site, you can go ticketless. In addition, cybertravelers may accumulate AAdvantage frequent-flyer bonus miles by purchasing flights online. You can check flight schedules, discover special seasonal schedules, peruse the online in-flight magazine, and catch last-minute steals.

British Airways
www.british-airways.com

Popping over the pond? Stop by British Airway's Web site for special ticket offers. There are also helpful Q&As and colorful photos at this site, as well as tips for traveling with kids. Visit the special travel clinics for safe and healthy travel.

Cathay Pacific
www.cathay-usa.com

By visiting this site, you can become a Cathay Pacific "CyberTraveler" to receive special bonus miles and access promotional fares and contests. As a special member, you'll even get to participate in online seat auctions not available to customers anywhere else. You can also get on the mailing list to receive CyberTraveler updates.

Continental Airlines
www.flycontinental.com

Stop by Continental's Web site to view flight schedules and terminal maps of various airports that Continental serves. You can also find system routes and information on group travel and in-flight entertainment. Interested travelers may read feature articles from *Profiles*, Continental's companion magazine, and subscribe to the weekly mailing list for travel tips and last-minute fares.

Delta Airlines
www.delta-air.com

You can make your reservations with ease by stopping at Delta's Web site. Before you book your flight online, enroll in *SkyMiles*, Delta's frequent-flyer program. Travelers may also take a look at airport guides and maps of numerous destinations.

Lufthansa
www.lufthansa.com

Visit the virtual airport of Lufthansa InfoFlyway, shown in Figure 5.5, to book your flight online. Commune with other travelers in the chat cafe (if you speak German) and peruse the Sky Shop for souvenirs.

Figure 5.5   A page from Lufthansa's Web site.

Northwest Airlines
www.nwa.com

The CyberSaver fares at this site are offered exclusively to Web site visitors. Also visit the site to find out about promotional discounts, gather flight information, and view airport maps and seating charts. Frequent flyers can find facts on the WorldPerks bonus miles program and check on the number of miles accumulated.

Qantas Airways
www.qantas.com

Not only will you gather flight information on international and domestic schedules, but you'll receive additional perks about the land down under: Get the story on things to do and resorts to relax at when in Australia.

Singapore Airlines Home Page
www.singaporeair.com

Travelers may read about in-flight services, entertainment, and travel packages. Seat plans, information about checking in, destinations, and in-flight services are also provided. Before you depart, look up the practical facts on Singapore's Changi Airport.

South African Airways
www.saa.co.za/saa/welcome2.htm

Sleek graphics make this site a must-see. Travelers may browse flight schedules, destinations served, and frequent-flyer information including discounts on hotels, car rentals, and safaris.

Southwest Airlines
www.iflyswa.com

At this site, you can look up flight schedules and fares, purchase your ticketless flight, and get info on airports, vacation packages, and the Rapid Rewards frequent-flyer program. And now that you have the basics, you can browse photos, past advertisements, and video clips to learn a little more about Southwest.

Swissair
www.swissair.com

This site offers standard flight information like schedules and fares, in addition to special low-rate offers. You can look into the special "destination of the month" and get the particulars on the Qualiflyer frequent-flyer program.

TWA
www.twa.com

Stop at this site to discover "hot fares of the week" and special deals for online shoppers. Not only can you enter contests to win bonus miles, but you can also view photos, seating charts, and destination maps. Find information about your vacation spot through links to cities and attractions, and take the Real-Time Global Flight Simulator for a test run.

United Airlines
www.ual.com

This "friendly" site, shown in Figure 5.6, offers information on schedules, routes, and flight status. Travelers may read about in-flight entertainment and grub, pick up some good travel tips, and get the low-down on several airports.

Figure 5.6 United Airlines' home page.

USAir/US Airways
www.usair.com

Join USAir's email list for "E-Saver" special last-minute rates and fares. You can gather practical information by viewing timetables and getting the particulars about in-flight entertainment. Travelers can find facts on frequent-flyer programs, too.

Travel Byte

Don't forget to reconfirm your international flight several days before you leave. Some airlines will give up your seat if you fail to reconfirm a specified number of days in advance. Ask the airline for details when you purchase your ticket.

Frequent-Flyer Programs

Despite the name, you don't need to travel often to join a frequent-flyer program. You accumulate miles each time you fly no matter what your pace. According to *Consumer Reports*, most flights give you "a minimum credit of 500 miles per trip no matter how short the actual flight." So no matter how long it takes or how short your excursions, when you compile enough miles, you're awarded a free trip.

Actually, you don't even have to travel at all to rack up those magnificent miles. That's because airlines let you earn miles by staying at specific hotels and renting from designated rent-a-car companies. You can even acquire miles by dining at certain restaurants.

The Web pages of airlines often provide information about their free frequent flyer programs. The Web pages of WebFlyer (**www.insideflyer.com**) brought to you by *InsideFlyer Magazine*, give you the scoop on popular frequent-flyer programs. At the site, you can read program reviews and sign up with programs online. WebFlyer provides information on bonus programs and how to accumulate lots of miles. You can also browse past issues of the magazine, read guest interviews with airline execs, and listen to archived simulcasts.

Flying In Comfort

Some people love to fly; some people never want to leave the ground. Either way, most people agree that spending several hours in an airplane can be uncomfortable and can cause claustrophobia at times. Here are some tips to make flying a little more agreeable. Visit the Healthy Flying Web site (**www.flyana.com**) for other ideas on how to make your flight more user-friendly.

Drink Up

Drink lots of liquids to keep your body hydrated on those long, bone-dry flights. Avoid drinking caffeine and alcohol, which can dehydrate you even more.

Get Moving

Get out of your seat and move around the aircraft. Get that blood circulating by walking the aisles, and give yourself a good stretch every hour or so. Even if the "fasten seat belt" sign is on, you can extend your legs and arms while in your seat.

Your Ears: Unplugged

Unpop those ears. Gulping fluids like juice or water equalizes the pressure in your middle ear. Holding your nose while swallowing works even better. The old standbys, chewing gum and yawning, may also help.

Stabilize Your Stomach

To combat motion sickness, gaze out the window toward the skyline. Keeping your eyes on a permanent focal point, the horizon in this case, helps to give you a grounded feeling and may ease your queasiness.

Comfiness Is Key

Baby yourself with music, a good novel, and airline-supplied blankets and pillows. Keeping yourself comfortable can have a lot to do with your frame of mind. Why not allow yourself to take it easy for a few hours and enjoy the ride?

Airports

Airports can be large and confusing, and parking is often an ordeal. The last thing you need as you're rushing to make your flight is terminal confusion. Visit these online airports to learn your way around ahead of time. You can even print out concourse and parking lot maps and take them with you. Find out about facilities and special services particular to your travel needs. You can also access timetables of connecting airlines.

BAA
www.baa.co.uk

Get practical information on major British airports such as Heathrow, Gatwick, Edinburgh, Glasgow, and Southampton. Retrieve flight information, find out about public transportation to and from the airports, and get facts on parking, car rentals, and baby-care facilities. Also take a peek at terminal maps.

Denver International Airport
infodenver.denver.co.us:80/~aviation/diaintro.html

Get directions to the airport, find where to park and how much it costs, and learn your way around (see Figure 5.7). Read about the runways, computer systems, and concourses A, B, and C. Also check into news, FAQs, and Colorado trivia.

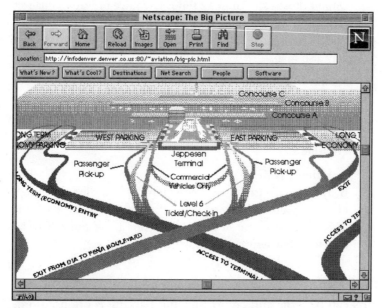

Figure 5.7 A parking map from the Web site of Denver International Airport.

Washington National Airport
www.metwashairports.com/National/index.html

View terminal maps at this site if you're flying into our nation's capital. Get details on facilities, from storage lockers to luggage carts, and pick up some fast facts about the airport itself. Also find lots of Web links to airlines.

Frankfurt Airport
www.frankfurt-airport.de

Check out beer steins and lederhosen at the duty-free shops and stroll the Frankfurt Airport art gallery. Get help checking in, finding your gate, and changing terminals. Read departure and arrival times and get assistance with checking your baggage.

Narita Airport
www.narita-airport.or.jp/airport/

If you'll be visiting Tokyo, you may want to visit this Web site. You'll gather detailed info on terminals, ground transportation to and from the airport, and boarding procedures. Also read up on services offered at the airport, such as the dental clinic and children's play room.

Travel Byte

Never carry a package or check in luggage for strangers. If they are smuggling anything or are transporting anything illegal, you will be held responsible.

AIRPORT AND AIRLINE RESOURCES ON THE WEB

As opposed to the earlier section of this chapter that presented major airlines' sites, this section provides directories containing a number of airlines, as well as sites dedicated to airports. Some of the directories in this section present useful facts, others provide links to home pages.

Airports International
www.airportsintl.com/betahome.html

Many U.S. and international airports are described at this site. Pick one to learn all about its features, including parking, flight information and time-tables, restaurants, shops, and nearby hotels.

Airwise
www.airwise.com

Click on "The Airport Guide" to get the skinny on airports worldwide. You'll find directions to the airport and information on parking, restaurants, and bars. Check for the airport you're interested in by geographical area.

Welcome To QuickAID
www.quickaid.com

Pick any airport listed on the site, browse the "Traveler's Yellow Pages," and gather information on ground transportation, connected airlines, and features of that particular airport. Look over floor plans and even find where ATM machines are located.

Airlines Of The Web
www.itn.net/airlines

Visit this site to link up to a vast number of airline Web sites. You'll also find related links to frequent-flyer programs, newsgroups, and airline stock quotes.

Airlines-online.com
www.airlines-online.com

Look up links to airlines and airports by airport code, city, or country. Choose among "official," "semi-official," and "unofficial" sites.

The Air Traveler's Handbook
www.cs.cmu.edu/afs/cs/user/mkant/Public/Travel/airfare.html

A stellar site for links to every aspect of flying you can think of. You'll get connected to airports, airlines, frequent-flyer programs, mailing lists, and more.

Suitcase Slip-Ups

You can help prevent your luggage from being misrouted. Follow these steps to see that your luggage arrives in the same place you do.

- Travel using only carry-on bags.
- Do not travel with expensive, name-brand luggage.
- Remove luggage tags and stickers from previous flights.
- Provide your name and address on study tags outside your suitcases.

- Check in as early as possible.
- Reserve a non-stop flight.

Right On Schedule

Before you head off to the airport, make sure your flight is running on time. You can stop by the Flyte Trax Web site (**www.amerwxcncpt.com**), shown in Figure 5.8, to see whether your departure will be tardy or taking off as planned. For any plane in flight in the continental United States, you can find the plane's route and see where it is at that time. All you have to do is submit the flight number, airline, and destination airport. You'll also receive the flight's expected arrival time.

Make sure your ride home has these URLs, too. Then everyone involved will have the most current information on your flight schedule.

Making Tracks

Whether you're planning to book the lowest coach fare possible or going first class, train travel is comfortable, effortless, and the safest way to travel today.

When traveling by train, there's no worry about staying awake at the wheel or feeling your ears pop on departure. As a matter of fact, train travel is so

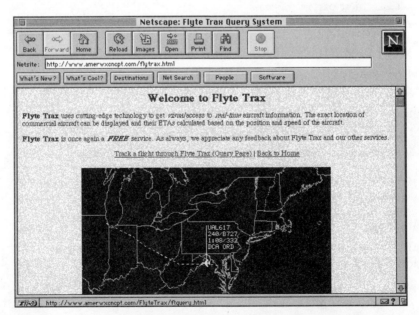

Figure 5.8 Check your departure time at the Flyte Trax Web page.

enjoyable that many people make a vacation out of a train trip itself—such as the numerous travelers who ride in luxury on the nostalgic Eastern and Oriental Express (**www.diethelm-travel.com/eastern.htm**), operated by the same company as the famous Orient Express, for their vacation. Whether the train is a means to your destination or the destination itself, use the Web as a resource when making your train travel arrangements.

Find out what facilities are available to you, such as your own compartment or cabin. Find out if there is a full-service dining car or if it's snacks only. Investigate schedules, and don't forget to look for promotions offering lower fares.

By stopping by the CTU Railway Page (**www.cvut.cz/home/railway.htm**), Railroad-related Internet Resources (**www-cse.ucsd.edu/users/bowdidge/railroad/rail-home.html**), and the Cyberspace World Railroad (**www.mcs.com/~dsdawdy/cyberroaad.html**), you can connect to Web sites on rail systems all over the world.

Travel Byte

Even if you're traveling just to get to your destination, check to find out about any scenic routes that may be offered. Amtrak and others offer many scenic rides across the country. Make getting there part of the fun.

North America

Many travelers opt for a rental car as their transportation of choice across North America. Train travel is often overlooked, although it's comfortable, inexpensive, and provides spectacular views of the United States and Canada. Stations are usually situated in city centers, so train travel is even convenient for city hoppers. Consider taking the train on your next trip.

Amtrak
www.amtrak.com

At Amtrak's Web site, shown in Figure 5.9, you can get particulars for your trip though route descriptions and schedules. Travelers may also find promotional discounts, participate in contests, or plan a combo-vacation through special Amtrak "Ski Amtrak" and "Rail-Sail" trips. Even make your reservations right from their Web site.

Figure 5.9 Amtrak's home page.

Rocky Mountain Railtours
www.fleethouse.com/fhcanada/rocky_hm.htm

If you want to climb the Canadian Rockies in comfort, visit this site. You'll get the details on rail excursions with names like "Rockies Roundup," "Blue Sky Spectacular," and "Western Rail Extravaganza."

BC Rail
www.mcs.net/~dsdawdy/Canpass/bcr/bcr.html

BC Rail's passenger service runs from North Vancouver to Prince George. View photos and read descriptions about the scenic views and services offered on the "Cariboo Propector" and "Royal Hudson" steam engine trains. You can look up schedules and find rates, too.

VIA Rail
www.viarail.ca

At the Web site of "Canada's Passenger Train Network," you can query for fare prices, use interactive rail maps, and book your trip over the Internet. Take a look at the electronic brochure to read trip descriptions and view photos.

Europe By Rail

If you're traveling through Europe, I strongly suggest you see it by rail. Europe has a seamless, cost-efficient rail service called the Eurail, which has flexible time schedules and passes that cater to different types of travelers. It's convenient, efficient, and you get to view historic sites from your window seat.

Europe by Eurail
www.eurail.com

Get information here on trekking through Europe by train. You'll find maps, like the one shown in Figure 5.10, articles, and chat rooms for communicating with fellow travelers. You can also get information on choosing a pass and keeping a budget. Download trip-planning software and order your Eurailpasses online.

Rail Europe
www.raileurope.com

You can look up rail fares and schedules by submitting your travel dates and departure and arrival cities, and book your train tickets online as well. Travelers may find details on rail passes, prices, and options to choose from. Info on national rail passes and those that include travel through numerous countries is provided.

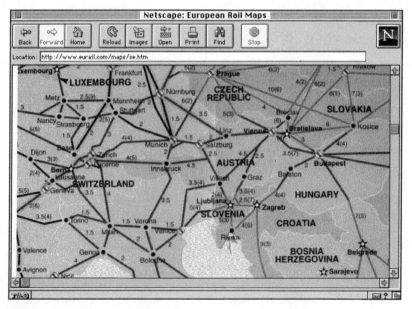

Figure 5.10 An online route map of the Eurail system.

Eurostar
www.eurostar.com

This site is for people who want to travel under-seas on the Channel Tunnel (also known as the Chunnel). The Eurostar offers direct service from London to Paris to Brussels. Its Web site will provide you with timetables, fares, special offers, and updates on new trains and expanded services. You can also find out how to book your ticket.

How To Travel Europe By Rail
www.starnetinc.com/eurorail/planindx.htm

Click on an interactive map to learn about rail lines throughout Europe. You'll find useful information about train stations and dining and sleeping as you ride the rails. Even get advice on choosing your seat.

Travel Byte

For train travel, summer is the busiest season. So book your trip as early as possible. Or better yet, try a different time of year. Imagine autumn in France....

Many individual countries in Europe also have easy-to-use rail systems, which may operate separately or as part of the Eurail system. These rail systems have Web sites of their own. Here are two examples.

BritRail
www.britrail.com

You can look over British Rail's maps for your train trip throughout the United Kingdom. Also choose among many variations and prices for BritRail passes and read about discounts for children, seniors, and students.

SNCF French Railways
www.sncf.fr/indexe.htm

Travelers can learn about interprovincial services for travel across the country-side, or look up services to Paris airports. You can view pictures of first- and second-class seating compartments and dining cars, and find out how to travel with your bicycle, or use the convenient "rent-a bike" service.

Travel Byte

When traveling by train, use a chain and combination lock to secure your bag to the seat while you're sleeping or in the bathroom.

Train Travel Across The Globe

In many countries, train travel is the least expensive way to get around. Ticket prices cost much less than the price of a car rental, gas, and tolls, which can be extremely costly overseas. Gasoline prices in Japan and Hong Kong cost approximately four times the price in the United States. Slash your budget by riding the rails.

RailPage Australia
www.com.au/railpage

Travellers can check railway timetables for New South Wales, Queensland, Victoria, Western Australia, and interstate services at this site. Read about current and upcoming events of interest to rail enthusiasts, view pictures of passenger and dining cars, and link other Web sites about riding the rails in Australia.

The China Railways Home Page
severn.dmu.ac.uk/~mlp/crsg.html

If you plan to travel in China, stop by this site to read about the thousands of steam locomotives you can ride while visiting. You can also view a rail map, look over a photograph collection, and read up on the history of China's rails. Travelers post stories and photos from their rail trips across the countryside.

Spoornet (South Africa)
www.spoornet.co.za

Passenger services include standard transportation services, day trips, luxury journeys across the plains, safari treks, and travel aboard restored vintage trains. You'll read about the "Blue Train," the "Union Limited," and the "African Train Safari." You can also view timetables and access information on current rates via email

Renting Your Wheels

If you plan on picking up a rental car on your vacation, stop by any one of the many Web sites of rental car companies to make your arrangements. You can peruse models, makes, and colors right from the sites of Enterprise, Hertz, and many other rental car Web sites.

On their pages you can look over photos, read vehicle descriptions, choose your amenities, and check prices. When you have decided which car you'd like to rent for your trip, fill out an online reservation form to submit your preferences, travel dates, and departure and arrival locations. At the Avis Web site (**www.avis.com**), you can even submit the time and date your airline flight is due in, so your rental car will be ready and waiting for you at the airport upon your arrival.

You will then receive a confirmation via email from the rental car company. Information on your itinerary, car availability, and rental price should be included. Print out your confirmation and bring it with you when picking up your car.

Some rental car Web sites give you useful extra information, too. The Web site of Alamo (**www.alamo.com**), shown in Figure 5.11, gives you the opportunity to correspond with other road warriors in chat forums and offers you directions to popular tourist attractions. Budget Rent A Car (**www.budgetrentacar.com**) provides city-specific driving guides for roads all over the world.

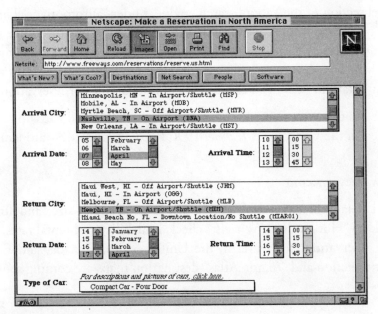

Figure 5.11 Rent your car online with Alamo.

Travel Byte

Check your rental car for scratches and dents *before* you leave the rental agency.

Rates of rental cars vary from agency to agency, according to model and included amenities. You can compare prices by visiting rental car company Web sites, just as you can with airline Web pages, as mentioned earlier in this chapter. When looking up prices, read the fine print. Find out what is included in the quoted price of your rental car. Check on mileage fees, damage waivers, cancellation fees, and included tax.

Travel Byte

If you're traveling in a group, renting a car can be a good choice. It can be an inexpensive way to travel if you split the cost of the rental car, gas, and tolls between the members of the group.

Rent-A-Car Web Sites

To find international, as well as national, rental car Web sites, look to the travel section of the Yahoo! search engine, under "automotive." The Guide to Airport Rental Cars (**www.bnm.com/rcar.htm**) is a great resource to connect with rental car companies at major airports all over the United States. At the site, you can view prices, click on home page links, and get tips and advice from "Travelin' Joe." You can also make your online car reservations there.

Here are the Web sites of a few of the top-rated rental car companies mentioned in the *Condé Nast Traveler* 1996 Readers' Choice Award issue.

Alamo
www.freeways.com

Read details of convertible, premium, mid-size, full-size, and luxury cars. Look up "Hot Deals on Wheels," check availability and rental rates, and make your reservations for travel in the United States, Canada, and Europe. An online auction and "Alamo Atlas" destination maps are coming soon.

Auto Europe
www.wrld.com/ae

At this site, travelers can look over and read information on rental cars not only in Europe, but in the Middle East, the South Pacific, the Caribbean, Africa, and North and South America. Current rates and feature information is posted on cars as well as campervans and motorcycles. You can make your reservations online and join the mailing list for a chance to win "free stuff."

Avis
www.avis.com

Visit "The Avis Galaxy," shown in Figure 5.12, to peruse the fleets offered in various countries. If you click on a car, you receive information on the make's features. You can also submit what you're looking for, and the site will offer suggestions to match your selected preferences. Renters can check rates and make reservations from the Web site. This site also includes road maps, special offers, and archived Avis ads from the 1950s and 60s.

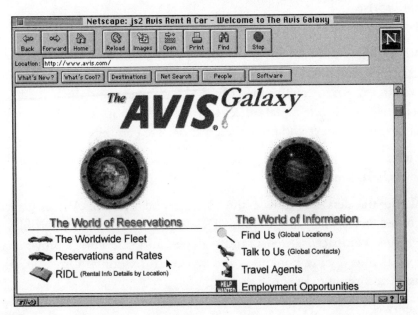

Figure 5.12 The Avis home page.

Budget
www.budgetrentacar.com

"From economy models to sport cars, recreational vehicles, and passenger vans," Budget offers a wide variety to choose from on the their site. You can look up what's available according to your destination in the U.S., Asia, Europe, the Caribbean, Latin America, and other locations. A special feature of the site is its detailed driving guides, which provide country-by-country information on speed limits, tolls, refueling, parking, road signs, and more.

Dollar
www.dollarcar.com

Browse the cars in Dollar Rent A Car's fleet and read about seating, trunk space, and features like air conditioning, power windows, and cassette players included in particular vehicles. Categories include minivan, convertible, luxury, standard, compact, and economy. Check rates, make your reservation (or cancel it) online. The site also provides details and maps on suggested scenic drives.

Enterprise
www.pickenterprise.com

View photos and read about the Enterprise rental cars available for your next excursion. Economy, compact, full-size, luxury, van, and sport utility vehicles are offered. An interactive map of the U.S., Canada, and the United Kingdom will help you locate rental offices in your destination. The Q&A may answer questions you have and online reservations are coming soon.

Hertz
www.hertz.com

World travelers can browse the Hertz rental fleets in Africa, Canada, the United States, and Europe online. Details are available on convertibles, station wagons, compacts, 2-doors, and 4-doors, and rate guides provide costs on special offers, early bookings, and weekend discounts. Office locations are listed according to region.

Kemwel
www.kemwel.com

Kemwel offers car rentals in over 1,000 locations worldwide—from small economy-sized mini-cars to larger, more luxurious models. Click on a world map and choose your vehicle according to the country where you'll be traveling. You'll find information on features and rates of various vehicles, too. Hotel and barge cruise program information is also provided, as are online motoring travel guidebooks that are worth a look.

National
www.nationalcar.com/index.html

Read about rental car service options, one-way rental service, and the benefits of joining the Emerald Club drivers' club. Enter contests in the "free stuff" section and check out special promotional deals, too.

Rent-A-Wreck
rent-a-wreck.com

On the Web site of this used car rental company you can access location information for offices in the United States and overseas. You'll also find giveaways and links to numerous travel-related Web sites. You can even download an audio clip of the company's jingle.

Thrifty
www.thrifty.com

At the Thrifty Web site, travelers can access worldwide office information and read about special promotions and holiday deals. You can browse through the online catalog of minivans, convertibles, Jeeps, wagons, and compacts, check on car availability and rates, and then book your reservations. You can also easily review your reservation at a later date or cancel it. The FAQ answers questions on car seats, additional charges, and what to do if the car is damaged.

Driving In A Foreign Country

The Budget Rent A Car Web site (**www.budgetrentacar.com**) provides information for travelers who plan to drive in specific countries. If you plan to rent a car to use overseas, visit the site and look up the drivers' guide for your destination. There you can access information on road signs, speed limits, and parking.

Drivers' Guide: Denmark

The following drivers' guide to Denmark was excerpted from Budget's Web site. From the home page, click on "Travelers' Tips," then on "Drivers Guides." You'll find a number of countries listed.

General Information
Drive on the right, overtake on the left. Most of the islands of Denmark are linked by bridge. A regular ferry service operates to the larger islands and those furthest away from the mainland. Cars are allowed on most ferries.

Speed Limits
Motorways: 110 kph (70 mph)

Towns/Cities: 50 kph (31mph)

Other roads: 80 kph (50 mph)

Motorways And Tolls
Motorways, or *Moiorvej*, are mainly two lanes in either direction. There are no toll roads in Denmark.

Refueling And Parking
Leaded (*Super Bensin*), unleaded (*Blyfri*), and diesel fuels are available. 98 ORT indicates 4-star leaded gas. Most stations accept major credit cards. Parking restrictions in most areas are clearly signposted. In the center of Copenhagen, a ticket system operates for parking. Tickets are purchased at machines.

Legal Requirements
Alcohol limit for drivers is 10 mg per 100 ml of blood. All passengers must wear seat belts at all times. Children should travel in the rear seats and must be securely belted in. You should always carry your driver's license with you. Police issue on-the-spot fines for a range of motoring offenses. These can he paid in cash and sometimes by credit card. Dimmed headlights must be used at all times, even in daylight.

Rental Car Safety

Car thieves prey on obvious tourists and distracted drivers. Motorists studying road maps at stoplights or on the side of the road are easy targets. It's smart to map out your route before you hit the road. Also, when stopped at a red light, keep your car in gear so you can quickly speed away if approached. You can also prevent theft by keeping your belongings stashed in your trunk—out of the sight of devious eyes.

Other safety tips include:

- Lock your doors and windows, both when you're away from your car and when you're in your vehicle.
- Do not stop for hitchhikers or anyone at the roadside flagging for assistance.
- Park your car in lighted parking lots.
- Wear your seat belt.
- Ask for directions from policemen, gas station attendants, and inside roadside restaurants.
- Locate hazard lights, spare tire, gas tank, and headlight and windshield wiper controls before you leave the rental car parking lot.
- Never get out of your car if you have to pull over to the side of the road. If something is wrong with your car, keep your doors locked, turn on your hazard lights, and wait for assistance from police.

Travel Byte

To save time on your travels, pick up your rental car in one location and drop it off in another.

Tools Of The Road

A number of resources exist on the Web that can help you get around in your rental car (or in any car for that matter). Interactive maps, a distance calculator, a road construction detector, and traffic monitors will help you navigate the best route to wherever you're heading.

INTERACTIVE MAPS

Interactive maps on the Web can give you detailed information on where you're heading and can even let you know how to get there. Give one of these maps, like one from Autopilot (**www.freetrip.com**), a test run by entering your street address and someone else's in your area, or try a landmark, like I did with Wrigley Field in Chicago. You'll see that these maps give accurate, detailed routes to take.

Some electronic maps, like the Lycos Road Map, even give you the choice of the shortest, fastest, and easiest route to take. Lycos road maps also give you smaller "maneuver" maps to show you exactly how to reach your destination en route to anywhere, from Austin to Wichita. Let any of the following interactive maps find you the quickest, best route possible. If you feel you'll need to make a pit stop for some food and 40 winks, MapQuest informs you of restaurants and hotels along your route.

Once you play with these maps, print them out for the drive to your dream destination. Or take them with you so you can easily find your way around your vacation spot when you get there.

Lycos Road Map
www.vicinity.com/lycos

Make your own personalized map at this site, shown in Figure 5.13. Just enter a street address with ZIP code, and X marks the spot on your electronic map. You can get detailed directions to that location with individual maps for each stage of the trip. You'll never get lost again.

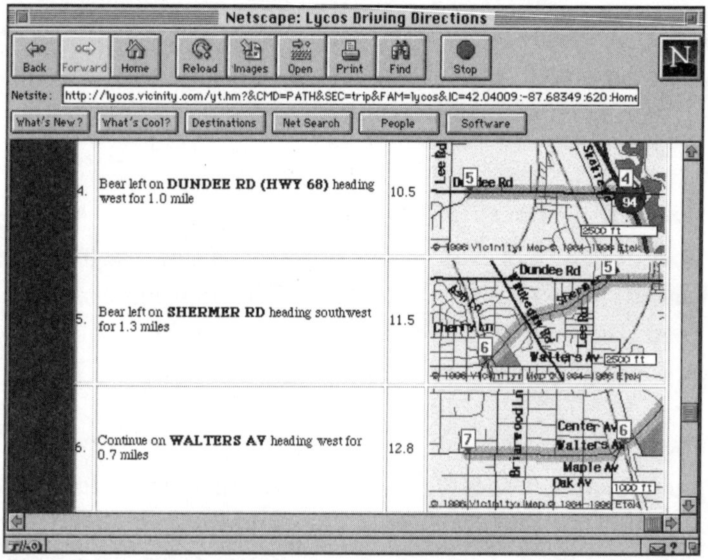

Figure 5.13 Personalized directions from Lycos.

Yahoo! Maps
maps.yahoo.com/yahoo/

Find your way to specific addresses or tourist attractions with a detailed map of any area in the U.S. Your personalized map can then be explored in any direction by using icons. You can also zoom in on your location for a closer look.

MapQuest
www.mapquest.com

You can view maps and locate a specific destination from anywhere in the world at this site. You can also access driving directions, calculate distances, and locate the hotels and restaurants nearest to your destination. You can even personalize your map with icons and field notes.

DISTANCE CALCULATOR

The How Far Is It? Web site (**www.indo.com/distance**) calculates the miles so you don't have to. Simply submit where you plan to leave from and where you're heading to find the distance in miles. The site also provides details of the locations you entered, including population, elevation, and the county in which it is located.

AVOID ROAD CONSTRUCTION

Before you leave to tear up the highways and byways, check to see where they're ripped up already. Look to the Rand McNally Web site (**www.randmcnally.com**) to find out which interstates, expressways, and thoroughfares are being worked on so you can plan your route ahead of time. It's no fun trying to follow detour signs in the dark, or any time of day for that matter, so give yourself early warning with this useful tool for the road.

CHECKING THE TRAFFIC

Before you venture onto the roadways with thousands of other travelers on summer vacation, check the current traffic conditions so that you can take the road less traveled. Use your search engine to find the traffic situation for wherever you're heading.

Traffic has definitely gone high-tech. Today, interstates may have electronic sensors built into the pavement so that the speed of traffic can be monitored and clocked. Web sites like that of Twin Cities Traffic Net (**www.traffic.connects.com**),

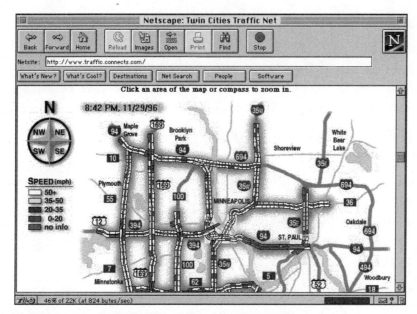

Figure 5.14 A real-time traffic map of the Twin Cities.

shown in Figure 5.14, use this information to bring you real-time traffic reports. Twin Cities Traffic Net presents an up-to-the minute electronic map to deliver easy-to-use traffic information to you.

Other Web sites use live Internet cameras, or webcams, to give you current status reports. The Arizona Department of Transportation/Freeway Management System (**www.azfms.com/Travel/camera.html**) delivers images of various freeways every five to eight minutes so that you can examine the traffic for yourself. You can even access real-time traffic information in foreign cities like Athens, Greece (**www.transport.ntua.gr/map/vcmap.html**).

Travel Byte

Attention speedsters: Check out the WWW Speedtrap Registry (**www.speedtrap.com/speedtrap**) to find out where you should lighten that lead foot. You can click on areas all over the world to locate potential speed traps. Even get an update on the Autobahn. (It's still speed-limit free.)

Public Transportation

If you plan on making a trip to a large city, you may want to avoid using a rental car to get around. Navigating your way along unfamiliar city roads in heavy traffic can cause a great deal of unwanted stress when you're supposed to be enjoying yourself. Parking is often extremely hard to find in large cities, and can be costly as well. Consider using a more convenient and inexpensive means of getting around town: public transportation. Many cities have easy-access transit systems that travelers can use to hop from museums, to parks, to beaches, to restaurants, and back to their hotel without a glitch. Subways, underground metro systems, buses, and ferries are available to urban explorers in cities all over the world.

City-Specific Information

Using the Web, you can access all sorts of information about local transit so that getting around a new city isn't such a mystery when you arrive. You can view maps of London's Tube, locate the stops of the Paris Metro, and get local train schedules for Boston. Listed are systems of a few major cities. Take a look at them to get a feel for this type of site, then, if you're heading to a different neck of the woods, simply conduct a Web search using words like "New York" and "subway" to find public transportation information specific to your destination.

MARTA (Atlanta)
www.itsmarta.com

If you're heading to Atlanta, don't pay for expensive cabs. Find public transit information and travel economically. You'll find ticket prices and schedules of bus and train services. Also take a look at the bus & train How-To-Ride guides.

MBTA (Boston)
www.mbta.com

Find your way around Boston by looking up bus, subway, commuter train, and ferry schedules. Conduct keyword searches, get directions to popular attractions, and even receive a history lesson on the city's transportation system. When's the last bus from Haymarket Square to Cambridge? Find the answer on the MBTA Web site (Figure 5.15).

Figure 5.15 Check Boston's local bus schedules from the MBTA Web site.

London Transport
www.londontransport.co.uk

After visiting this site, you'll know London above and below street level. Take a look at the London Underground map and receive updates on closures and alternate routes. Learn about special holiday services and get lots of advice for finding your way around the city. Even if you've never been to London, getting around once you're there is as easy as doing your homework at the city's transportation Web site (Figure 5.16).

New York City Subway Resources
subway.k2nesoft.com

Check out this site to find your way around the city that never sleeps. View photos and route maps of the city, from the Bronx to Coney Island, and read feature articles about the subway system, from abandoned stations to behind-the-scenes construction to recently discovered tracks.

Worldwide Transit Resources

To find public transportation information on the city you plan to visit, stop by the following directories, which contain links to a number of different

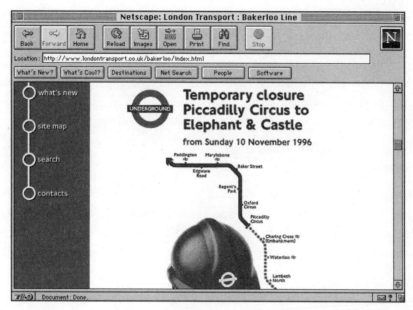

Figure 5.16 Get updates on London's Tube closures at the London Transport site.

cities. Maps, schedules, and routes for subways, metro systems, and buses in cities all over the world may be accessed from them. You'll also find links to city-specific Web pages.

The Subway Page
www.reed.edu/~reyn/transport.html

This site has plenty of links and system maps for almost every city worldwide. View images, live camera shots, and maps and get connected to route-navigation aids and local public transportation information.

The Subway Navigator
metro.jussieu.fr:10001

Whatever city you're heading to, stop by this site to make getting around a bit easier. You'll find subway, underground, and metro guides to 61 major cities. Just enter your starting point and destination to receive detailed directions on what trains to hop on. You can even obtain estimated travel times.

World Rail Transit List
home.cc.umanitoba.ca/~wyatt/rail-transit-list.html#CHN

Use this Web page to see if your destination city offers public transportation. At the site, you'll find a list of international cities, categorized by country. The type of transit offered within each city is provided, including commuter rail systems, shuttles, subways, and even restored trolleys.

Federal Transit Administration
www.fta.dot.gov

Locate links to public transportation-related sites of specific cities, which can lead you to details on bus services and routes, commuter rail schedules, and even trolley car rides in San Francisco. The FTA Web site (Figure 5.17) is a great starting point for checking out the transit systems of many cities nationwide.

Travel Byte

Information on ferry crossings, used for island hopping and for getting around in coastal regions, can also be found on the Web. Sites like that of BC Ferries (**www.bcferries.bc.ca**), which travels to 46 ports of call throughout coastal British Columbia, provide maps, schedules, and information on routes and fares.

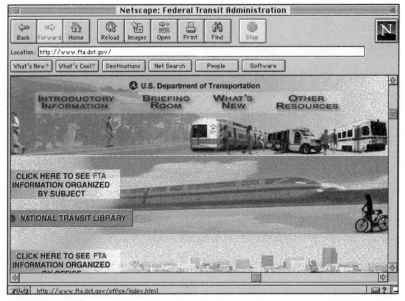

Figure 5.17 The FTA home page.

Traveling Safe

Many organizations, such as the National Highway Traffic Safety Administration and the U.S. Department of Transportation, strive to make sure you arrive at your destination safe and sound. Monitoring individual airlines and the automobile industry, investigating highway safety issues, and conducting numerous tests and investigations, these groups gather piles of public information for your use.

Want to fly the airline that has superior safety records? How about the one with the best on-time performance history? And wouldn't you like to know which car is the most reliable to rent for the road? Information like this is available to you so that you can make the best decisions.

Visit the following Web sites to read current transportation safety information, examine test data and conclusions, and get briefed on market statistics. Look the information over to choose for yourself the safest course of travel.

Airline.Net
www.radix.net/~fbavent/airline.htm

At this site, you can read records of filings made to the Department of Transportation or the Securities and Exchange Commission. Also find congressional testimony and Supreme Court decisions.

Office Of Airline Information
www.bts.gov/oai/oai.html

Gather information on the airline industry by reading about passenger trends, statistics on airports, and aircraft accident details. You'll even find overall performance ratings on the major airlines, including on-time performance records.

National Highway Traffic Safety Administration
www.nhtsa.dot.gov

Get your fill of highway safety information at this site. Gather lots of statistics, results of crash tests, and other consumer data you can use, such as product recalls and vehicle defect updates.

Advocates For Highway And Auto Safety
www.saferoads.com

This Web site is brought to you by a non-profit association of consumer health and safety groups. You'll find information on safety issues.

Travel Byte

For daily updates on the transportation industry, check out Transport News (**www.transportnews.com**), shown in Figure 5.18. You'll read articles on newly installed safety devices on the railways, hot issues in the airline industry, and other informative news.

Further Resources

Even more transportation resources exist on the Web. Chapter 13 details road trips across the country, Chapter 8 provides information on courier flights and air and rail passes, and Chapter 12 offers advice for traveling with the kids in tow.

If you found the transportation information you needed from this chapter, maybe it's time to book your accommodations. Web sites for hotels, motels, villas and B&Bs await you in Chapter 6.

Figure 5.18 Read about safety issues from the Transport News Web site.

Reservations Aside: Finding Accommodations

CHAPTER 6 TOPICS

- HOTELS, MOTELS, VILLAS, B&Bs, AND INNS ON THE WEB

- MAKING YOUR RESERVATIONS ONLINE

- HOW TO GET A GREAT ROOM RATE

- HOME EXCHANGES

No matter where you go, you'll need a place to rest your head. Whether it's to be the downy pillow of a five-star hotel or a woven bungalow hammock along the Mediterranean Sea, you can easily find the perfect place to turn in using the Web. Locate the home page of a specific hotel you have in mind, or gather information on various hotels in the area you're heading for. By visiting hotel home pages or online hotel directories, you can find current details on room prices, services, and amenities, and reserve your room in less than forty winks.

In this chapter, you'll learn how to use the Internet to gather information on hotel locations, facilities, and services; make your room reservations; and save money on your stay—in short, everything you need to choose the best hotel for your trip, all from hotel Web sites.

Choosing Your Accommodations

Every traveler has a different priority when choosing a place to stay. For some, cost is a key factor. Others find facilities, such as wheelchair access, the most important consideration. And still others may feel the proximity to historic monuments and museums is most significant. You can easily find whatever accommodations you're looking for on hotel Web sites. Popular hotel chains like Hilton, Marriott, and Westin, as well as small and large independently owned hotels, offer extensive information about specific hotels on their home pages. Visit these sites to see photos of guest rooms, check on services and facilities, and get a general feel for the accommodations.

Instead of just calling a hotel chain, browse the Web to discover other hotels in the area that are better suited to your needs and tastes. After all, where you stay and the service you receive can play a major part in the enjoyment of your trip. You'll be glad you took a few extra minutes on the Web to pick out the perfect accommodations for your dream vacation!

Location, Location…

Look for hotels located near the places you plan to visit on your trip. Take it easy on yourself by staying close to attractions or within easy reach of public transportation; a convenient home base will save you lots of time and money on long cab rides.

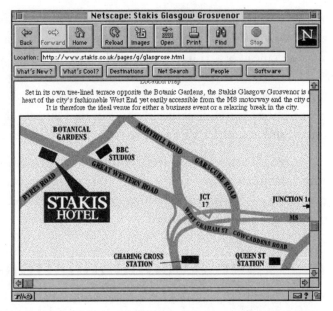

Figure 6.1   See where a hotel is located on an electronic map.

On most hotel Web sites, area maps like the one in Figure 6.1 show you exactly where your hotel is situated relative to local points of interest, state parks, bodies of water, city centers, and major highways. Many sites also offer lists of recommended attractions, shopping malls, restaurants, and nightclubs in the area. You might even discover great local watering holes you'd never have known about otherwise.

Travel Byte

Take your hotel's business card with you while sight-seeing, especially if you can't speak the language of the country you're visiting. You can always show the card to a taxi driver if you get lost.

Amenities And Services

Hotel Web pages are great resources for getting basic information on accommodations. Read details about the size of guest rooms. Find out if airport shuttle service is offered to and from the local airport. See if a fitness center is available on the premises, as seen in Figure 6.2 on the Web site of the Los Angeles Biltmore. If I plan to stay at a hotel during the winter, I use the Web to find

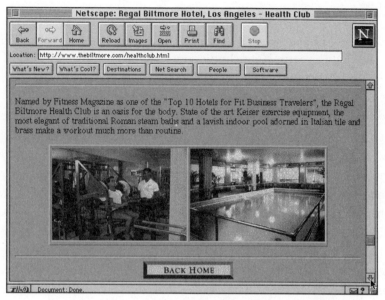

Figure 6.2 View photos and get information on fitness rooms.

one in the area that has an indoor swimming pool on the premises. I love to swim and taking a dip during the cold and frosty months is an added luxury when traveling on vacation or business. Other features to look for include "heart healthy" room service meals, laundry service, and on-site shopping.

Take care of the basics by checking numerous Web sites. Don't settle for a hotel that doesn't have concierge service if that's important to you. Make sure the hotel you choose for your dream vacation has the facilities that suit your needs.

To make your vacation as dreamy as possible, look for the extras many hotels offer for a more luxurious stay. From 24-hour room service to Turkish baths, these amenities can enhance your trip. At many hotel directory and chain hotel Web sites, you can search for a hotel with just the amenities you crave. Choose items like golf courses, gourmet restaurants, and on-site masseuses, or find out if a hotel offers your favorite vacation activities such as snorkeling, sailing, and daily sight-seeing tours.

As mentioned in Chapter 1, you can get lots of questions answered by email. Ask the hotel staff if supervised activities are offered for children. Get details on pool-side services, and find out if extended check-out is offered. Many hotels respond promptly to your inquiries—which makes email a very convenient way to get the information that's relevant to your needs.

Travel Byte

Look online to see if your hotel offers shuttle service to and from local airports. Hotel shuttles can save you more than 50 percent of the fares for lengthy cab rides.

Ratings And Stars

Not all hotels are rated equally. Rating systems, like the Michelin scale or the AAA diamond rating system, are provided to give travelers a feel for the level of quality, comfort, and service of a hotel. They let you know what to expect before you arrive. While many accommodations in foreign countries are rated with stars, keep in mind they are not all rated on the same five-star scale. Lodging standards are decided by individual countries and each monitors the rating system separately. For example, in France a three-star hotel may be considered top-of-the-line, while in the United States, a three-star hotel is considered just average. Also, in less developed countries, five-star lodging may not turn out to be nearly as sumptuous as a five-star hotel in the United States. A couple I know went to Egypt, and found their five-star accommodations below expectations.

Check out the Web sites of local tourist bureaus and organizations mentioned in Chapter 3. Many provide information on the standard hotel rating scale in a particular country or region. These scales can let you know what provisions you will receive according to the number of stars on the country's scale. Popular online travel books also offer their own hotel ratings; Fodor's (**www.fodors.com**), for example, reviews numerous hotels at their Web site and tells you which accommodations they recommend.

Hotel Directories

Online hotel directories offer easy access to information on numerous hotels that span the globe. Some directories offer details and critiques, others just provide links to individual Web sites. Either way, hotel directories lead you to information that can help you decide where to stay. Visit the following sites to find details on accommodations where you plan to travel.

Hotel & Travel Index Online
www.traveler.net/htio

Find information here on over 5,000 worldwide hotels, B&Bs, and resorts, including details on live entertainment, recent renovations, and swimming pools and pool-side bars. Read reviews, conduct quick searches, and look into exclusive offers, as well.

Hotels on the Web
www.traveler.net/two/twpages/twhotels.html

This lengthy list of hotel chains and independent hotels on the Web is brought to you by Travel Weekly Online. Sites are listed alphabetically, but you can use the "Quick and Chunky Alpha Index" to jump a few letters down the list. Brief descriptions of each site are included.

Hotel Net
www.hotelnet.co.uk

Locate a hotel in Europe by choosing a country from the list or clicking on the interactive map. At this site you can see hotel photos, take virtual tours, even sneak a peek at restaurant menus and find out about local attractions. Make your online reservation after choosing your hotel according to location, facilities, price, and/or size. Hotel amenities are indicated by symbols.

Accommodation Search Engine Home Page
accom.finder.co.uk

Get connected to hotels, motels, and bed and breakfasts worldwide by filling out a personal travel profile. With information on your preferred price range and the facilities and activities you're looking for, the Accommodation Search Engine will find the perfect place for you. You'll also find great deals, and you can book your reservation right from the Web site.

Hotel Discounts
www.hoteldiscounts.com

Find great deals through the "Hotel Discount System" and read up on hundreds of hotels. This site provides information on guest room amenities, as well as photos of the lobby, guest rooms, and hotel exterior. In addition, location maps will give you an idea of where the hotel is situated. Look up discounted rates, including deals of the week, check room availability, and make your reservations online. For extra speedy booking, use your Fastbook number, provided by this site.

Hotels Anywhere!
websites.earthlink.net/~hotelanywhere

You can get connected to numerous hotel Web sites and related travel information with Hotel Anywhere. Just click on your destination to get a list of hotel home pages to choose from, in addition to links to tourism organizations and other locally focused Web sites.

Web-Hotel
www.web-hotel.com

This site links you to Web pages of individual hotels around the world. Choose a continent on an interactive map, then narrow your search by country and city. When you find your hotel, follow the link to its home page.

All the Hotels on the Web
www.all-hotels.com

Choose your location on the interactive map to find out about hotels in the area. You'll be linked to independent hotels and chains throughout the world in seconds (see Figure 6.3).

Hotel World
www.hotelworld.com

At this online hotel directory you can make reservations at over 2,500 hotels worldwide. Search for accommodations according to your interests, including swimming, snorkeling, and tennis, and you'll find information on hotel services and nearby attractions. There's also news of festivals and events on this site.

Hotels & Travel on the Web
www.hotelstravel.com/hotels.html

You'll find connections to hotel Web sites with lots of specific information, and you can make online reservations. There are also links here to other hotel directories.

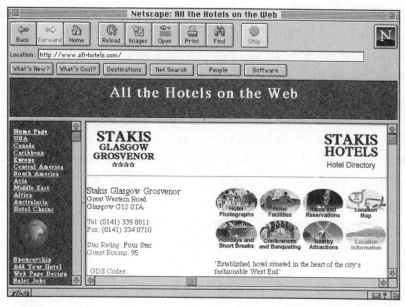

Figure 6.3 Find a hotel at your destination with All the Hotels on the Web.

Hotels on the Net
www.asiahotels.com

This site has up-to-date information on hotels and special promotional offers in China, Guam, Hong Kong, India, Indonesia, Japan, Korea, Malaysia, Macau, the Philippines, Singapore, Taiwan, Thailand, and Vietnam. You'll find details on the restaurants, services, facilities, and family packages at each hotel, and you can check current rates as well.

Travel Byte

Before unpacking, check the smoke alarm in your hotel room and test out the plumbing in the bathroom. If these two don't work, switch to another room. Do this first thing and you won't need to repack your belongings.

Chain Links

Do you have a favorite "brand name" hotel in mind for your trip? Many people develop a loyalty to a hotel chain after a particularly enjoyable stay at one of its hotels. If you prefer one line of hotels over all the others, simply visit that hotel chain's Web site. At the home page, you'll find links to all their locations world wide so you can get the details you need about lodgings at your destination.

For instance, visit the Web pages of Embassy Suites, shown in Figure 6.4, to find information about their hotels in the United States and all over the world. Choose your destination, then click on the hotel in the region where you will be located to read up on the guest rooms, special services, and recreational activities offered.

Many hotel chains maintain a consistent look and feel throughout their hotels around over the world. While you may not get a true feel for your cultural surroundings, you can count on consistent quality, and you'll have an idea of what to expect upon arrival.

Alp'Azur Hotels
www.nova.fr/alpazur

This Web site lists the locations of all Alp'Azur hotels and connects you to individualized information on each. Here you can view photos and read hotel

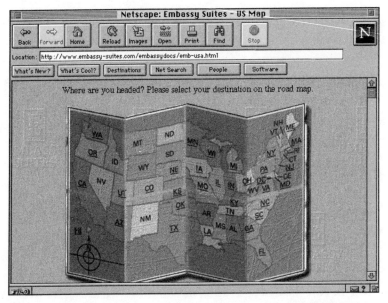

Figure 6.4 Locate the Embassy Suites throughout the United States.

descriptions, and you can also contact the hotel via email for additional information. This site also provides a good selection of links to other Web sites on France, and you can even choose to read it in French!

Amari
www.amari.com

This site has images of all eight Amari hotels in Thailand. Read about services, facilities, and restaurants; make your online reservations; and view a photo gallery about Asia.

Ascott
www.ascottres.com/ascott/prop.html

According to this site, Ascott hotels are "designed for the international traveler looking for a benchmark of excellence." Find information here on any one of the six Ascott hotels in Singapore, London, Bangkok, and Jakarta, and then make your reservations online.

Ashley House
www.ashley-house.com

The rooms of these three hotels, in Maryland, Virginia, and Wales, are decorated by Laura Ashley herself. At this site, you'll find photos of the guest rooms, as well as recipes from the head chef. Contact them via email, or fill out a response form to request a reservation.

Best Western
www.bestwestern.com

Brought to you by TravelWeb, this site provides information on Best Western locations worldwide. Find out about discounts for family trips and for seniors, and get information on the Golden Crown Club International and the frequent guest program as well.

Camino Real Hotels & Resorts
www.caminoreal.com

Read about Camino Real hotels in Mexico City, Cancun, Acapulco, Puebla de Los Angeles, and El Paso. At this site you'll view location maps, look at photos, and read about offered water activities such as snorkeling, wind surfing, and jet skiing. Make your reservations by email.

Canadian Pacific
www.cphotels.ca

Golf and skiing are the featured activities for adults at Canadian Pacific hotels throughout Canada; you'll also find information at this site (Figure 6.5) about the hotels' facilities for children. View location maps and read how to get around in each town where a hotel is located, and you can also get acquainted with the hotel chain's history and read updates on new hotel openings.

Choice Hotels
www.hotelchoice.com

This site links you to a number of hotel lines, including Comfort Inn, EconoLodge, Quality Inn, Clarion, Sleep Inn, Rodeway, Friendship Inn, and Mainstay Suites. Here you'll find special rates for Web users, and you can have your price quoted in over 40 different currencies. Click on "POI" and get a list of local points of interest within a 25 mile radius of the hotel you choose, including zoos, malls, ballparks, and restaurants.

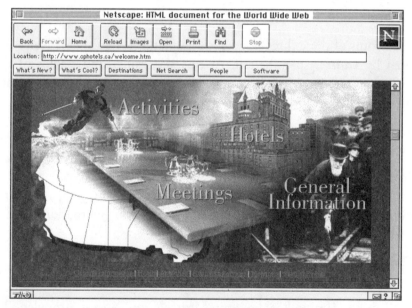

Figure 6.5 The Canadian Pacific Hotels home page.

ChinaTrust
www.chinatrust-hotel.com

Make your reservations here for any one of the six ChinaTrust hotels. Read room information, including rates, and view photos of guest rooms. There's also information on vacation packages, and you can find recommended attractions within 10 minutes, 30 minutes, and 1 hour from the hotel by car (Figure 6.6).

Crowne Plaza Hotels
www.crownepalza.com

Stop by this site to read hotel profiles (more than 100 locations in over thirty countries), find out about special rates, and make online reservations at the Crowne Plaza Hotel at your destination. Get practical information on locations, facilities like restaurants, and those special extras like squash courts, sun decks, and piano bars. Downloadable online brochures are coming soon.

Days Inn
www.travelweb.com/daysinn.html

Get an overview of the 1,700 worldwide properties of Days Inn. Because Days Inn is the official hotel of the International Hockey League, this site shows off different team logos; it also provides a customized search engine.

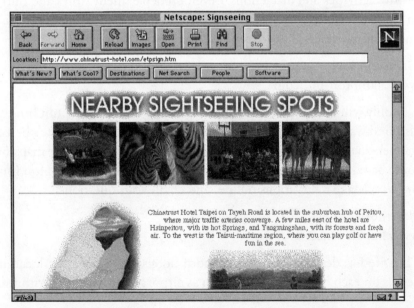

Figure 6.6 Get the scoop on local attractions at the ChinaTrust Hotels Web site.

DoubleTree Hotels
www.doubletreehotels.com/DoubleT/Home.htm

Use the interactive map to locate U.S. DoubleTree hotels, or conduct a site search to find a hotel near your destination. This site has descriptions of guest rooms and special services (like free chocolate chip cookies!), and facilities like golf pro shops and hair salons. You can sign up on the mailing list to receive updates as well.

Embassy Suites
www.embassy-suites.com

Click on the interactive map or choose from a destination list to locate Embassy Suites hotels all over the planet. You'll find information on individual hotels, as well as on the chain. You can check room availability and make your online reservations, too. There are great travel tips and online games here also.

Grande Hotels
www.grandehotels.com

Type in the Grande Hotel URL and find accommodation information from the Places to Stay hotel directory. The information even includes provisions like VCRs and mini bars found in the rooms. View photos and read up on nearby activities and attractions—even on department stores and outlet malls in the area. Get on the email list to receive "special information, discounts, and exclusive offers that are not available to the general public."

Hampton Inn
www.hampton-inn.com

Not only will you find details and locations on all the Hampton Inns, you can also find ways to save big bucks on your trip. Check out the site's best feature: the personal route planner, shown in Figure 6.7. This planner maps out your route based on parameters you set, and shows you all the Hampton Inns along the way. Make reservations online, and email your questions.

Hawthorn Suites
www.hawthorn.com

This site has descriptions of Hawthorn hotels in 18 different locations. Get details on each hotel's offerings, such as airport shuttles, suites with fireplaces,

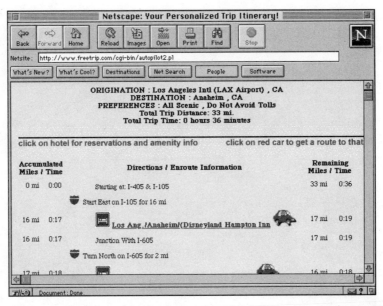

Figure 6.7 Easily locate hotels along your drive at the Hampton Inn Web site.

hot tubs, and complementary breakfasts. You'll also find directions to the hotels including area maps with nearby attractions.

Hilton
www.hilton.com

There are Hilton hotels all over the world, and you can make your reservations online. The Hilton site has lots of information on frequently visited cities, with "destination guides" for Atlanta, Chicago, Florida, Hawaii, L.A., and New York, as seen in Figure 6.8. Find special offers, read about guest programs, and join the HHonors program to earn points for staying at the hotels.

Holiday Inn
www.holiday-inn.comm

Take a look at the downloadable interactive brochures provided for individual Holiday Inn hotels, as shown in Figure 6.9. At this site, you can read overviews of worldwide locations, including details like check-in times and information about the hotel's location, such as distance from major airports. Find out about special discounts, and the Priority Club for frequent guests.

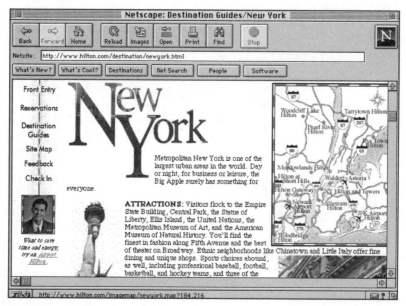

Figure 6.8 Get detailed information on your destination at the Hilton Web pages.

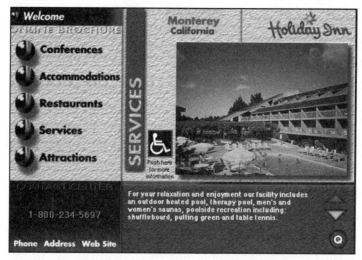

Figure 6.9 A downloadable interactive brochure from Holiday Inn.

Hyatt Hotels
www.hyatt.com

The majority of this site is provided by the TravelWeb hotel directory. As with most hotels on Travel Web, you can find detailed information on accommodations, such as the decor and number of non-smoking rooms. Get specific info on other facilities as well, like the hours for hotel restaurants. Read about the area where a hotel is located and find out about special deals.

Inter-Continental Hotels and Resorts
www.interconti.com

Locate Inter-Continental Hotels worldwide on this site and read overviews of each hotel's accommodations, dining facilities, and stores. You'll also find out about recommended local attractions to visit. Check room availability, and make your reservations online.

Loews Hotel
www.loewshotels.com

Use the location map to find the eleven Loews hotels. Make your reservations from the Web site and become a member of the Loews First program to receive upgrades and more. You'll also find up-to-date special offers, and you'll have a chance to submit any questions you may have.

Marriott
www.marriott.com

Gather information here on Marriott hotels, resorts, Courtyards, Fairfield Inns, Residence Inns, and Marriott Vacation Club International. You can search for locations worldwide and read overviews with maps and descriptions of restaurants and recreation facilities. Check room availability and make your reservations online, and use the "Marriott Concierge" feature for links to other useful Web sites.

Microtel Inns
www.microtelinn.com

This site provides rates, information on nearby restaurants and attractions, and location maps. You'll also find information about Microtel's pet policy and their "kids under sixteen stay free" program. Have some fun playing the "Micro P.I." online mystery game.

Novotel
www.cyberplex.com/welcome

Read up on the 300 Novotel hotels worldwide. You'll find overviews of accommodations, including such details as hairdryers and data hook-ups for your modem. Also find out about sights to see, as well as shopping and entertainment within 5, 15, and 30 minutes from your hotel.

Outrigger Hotels
www.outrigger.com

Making an excursion to Hawaii? Then visit this site not only for details on Outrigger Hotels, but for information on the islands as well. You'll find articles on "Hawaiian history" (shown in Figure 6.10) and "island culture," as well as travel tips and "Hawaiian factoids." Search for the hotels by island, find discounts, and make your reservations online.

Pan Pacific Hotels and Resorts
www.panpac.com

Interactive maps on this site guide you to information on Pan Pacific hotels throughout the Pacific and North America. You'll find descriptions of featured

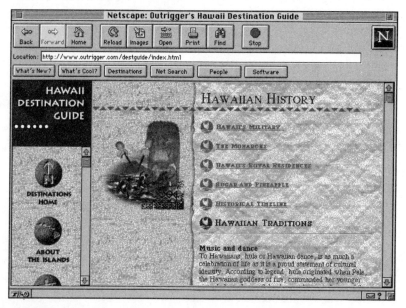

Figure 6.10   Read information on Hawaiian history at the site of Outrigger Hotels.

services, including the option to have fitness equipment delivered right to your guest room! View photos of accommodations and restaurants and catch things to do and see in the area.

Radisson
www.radisson.com

Create your personal travel profile to find a Radisson that suits your needs, or simply search the worldwide list of hotels. Read up on special programs and book your reservations on this site. And don't forget to check out their last-minute "Hot Deals."

Ramada
www.ramada.com/ramada.html

Find a Ramada hotel near your destination by interactive map, or via the search engine. When searching, enter a price range in which you would like to pay, and choose from a list of features, such as tennis, fishing facilities, free newspapers, pets permitted policy, and more. You'll also find information here about vacation packages and weekend specials.

Regal Hotels International
www.regal-hotels.com

Find out about special packages for the romantic or the "shop-aholic" in you. You'll find photos of accommodations here, as well as information about deluxe services such as complementary flowers and fresh fruit upon arrival. Check into area attractions including markets, parks, and gardens, and read about restaurant atmosphere.

Shangri-La
www.shangri-la.com

Use the electronic map to locate Shangri-La hotels in Fiji, Indonesia, China, Malaysia, Hong Kong, and Canada. On this site, you'll find rates and specials for each hotel, as well as contests and useful cultural information including advice on tipping.

Sheraton
www.sheraton.com

Gather information on the 420 Sheraton hotels in over 60 countries worldwide, and search for hotels by region, activity, and features. On this site you can read hotel overviews, learn about vacation packages, and follow links to TravelWeb's reservation service to book your stay. Be sure to visit the online lobby to find out about "Rising Star Chefs" and check out the featured recipes.

Sol Melia
www.solmelia.es/ihome.html

Search for any one of the 205 hotels worldwide by its proximity to local attractions, including museums, beaches, market areas, and historical sites. Make your reservations from the Web site, sign up for the frequent stay program, and take advantage of promotional offers.

Stakis Hotels
www.stakis.co.uk

Get a close look at the 50 Stakis hotels located throughout the British Isles. You'll find photographs and local area maps for each hotel. Read descriptions of guest rooms, services, and restaurants and find out about local attractions and haunts as well.

Westin Hotels
www.westin.com

Visit the "Travelers' Forum" to converse with other vacationers and acquire useful information about various Westin hotels. This site offers information on accommodations worldwide, as well as news on promotional offers and new hotel openings. Check out weekend specials and enter contests, and make your reservation via TravelWeb.

Woodside Hotels and Resorts
www.wlodging.com

Take a virtual tour of each of the six hotels in California. You'll get details of hotel highlights and guest room amenities, from the ceiling fans to the bathroom scales. Even hotel restaurant menus are available on this Web site! Register for weekend getaways, and make your reservation by email.

Travel Byte

If you are ever lost in a foreign city, look for large, Western-style hotels. They almost always have some English-speaking staff who can give you directions.

Independent Hotels

Both independently owned hotels and hotel chains can be found on the World Wide Web. Independent and chain hotels may offer many of the same facilities, but those that are privately owned and operated have individual character, providing you with a better taste of local flavor.

The hotel directories on the Web, listed at the beginning of this chapter, can lead you to the home pages of hundreds of independent hotels. On these sites, you'll find all the details you need to choose a place to call your temporary home.

In addition, if you're looking for an independent hotel in a particular area you can also use your search engine to find hotel directories for a particular country or region. Web pages like Hotels & Resorts in Indonesia (**www.indonesiatoday.com**), as seen in Figure 6.11, can lead you to information on many independent hotels according to city.

Figure 6.11   Get practical Indonesian travel information, in addition to hotel listings.

Tipping Tips

When to tip, who to tip, how much to tip? These questions plague many vacationers throughout their travels, leaving them feeling uneasy and unsure; not exactly what one wants to feel on a vacation. While tipping is up to you and should depend on the service you receive, here are a few general guidelines to follow:

If the bell man carried your luggage from the cab, shuttle, or car to the front desk or up to your room, tip him $1 per piece of luggage.

The maid should receive a $2 tip per day. You can total this up and leave it at the end of your stay, or leave the $2 each day. I've found that when I leave a daily tip, I get better service and have even received free turndown service in appreciation. In addition, this ensures that the right cleaning person receives the tip for a job well done.

If you request an ironing board, a hair dryer, a toothbrush, or any other item from housekeeping, tip the delivery person $1 for prompt service.

Check your room service bill for added gratuity before adding a tip to the total charge. At many hotels a gratuity is added to your total automatically. If this is has been done, there's no need to add any extra tip. If no gratuity is included, anything from 15 to 20 percent is a standard tip.

Tip the hotel concierge if he or she did extensive work to arrange transportation, tickets, restaurant reservations, and so on. Let them know that going out of their way for you was appreciated.

If you are traveling on foreign terrain, leave the equivalent of the appropriate tip in the local currency.

The Well Dressed Rest

If you're willing and able to go all out on your dream vacation, check out hotels converted from private manors, villas, palaces, and castles. These well-appointed lodgings are often decorated with antiques and period furniture, giving you a unique experience and the feeling you've traveled back in time—but with all the technology and plumbing of the present day! Your vacation becomes a fairy tale as you're waited on hand and foot in your ample accommodations.

You can stay in a plain old hotel anytime—make your visit extraordinary by staying someplace special.

Manor House Hotels
www.hotelnet.co.uk/hotelnet/eire/manor/home.htm

If you're planning to visit Ireland, look to this site for information on historic manors that have been transformed into guest hotels. You'll find photos, descriptions, and a history of each hotel. Online booking is available from the site.

Concorde Hotels
www.concorde-hotels.com

Make online reservations here for any Concorde grand hotel, including converted chateaus and palaces in Europe. You'll find brief descriptions of accommodations, including the location in relation to airports, and information on facilities like gourmet restaurants.

LaCURE: The Absolute Experience
www.villas.lacure.com

At this site you'll find details on over 250 villas in the Caribbean, Mexico, North Africa, Europe, and French Polynesia. Look over photos and read descriptions of the accommodations and their surroundings. You can check room availability and request a reservation by email.

Small Luxury Hotels of the World
www.slh.com

This site (shown in Figure 6.12), provides details on "country houses" with names like Thorngrove Manor, Keswick Hall, and Amberley Castle. These hotels are located in Australia, South Africa, France, Denmark, the United Kingdom, India, and even in the United States. You'll read descriptions, look at photos, and view location maps.

Langley Castle Hotel
dspace.dial.pipex.com/town/parade/ow51

Located in England, this 14th century castle was built during the reign of Edward III. Read about the castle's history and architectural features, and plan your visit according to the "forthcoming events and offers." You'll also find background information on guest room names, and details on amenities including

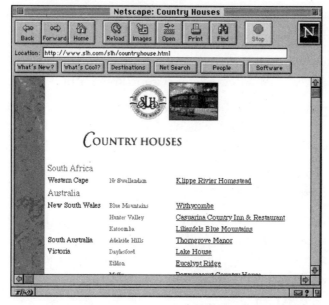

Figure 6.12   *Choose your palace at the Small Luxury Hotels of the World Web site.*

four-poster beds, spa baths, and 7-foot thick walls. This site also includes a currency converter and online booking.

Ashford Castle
www.commerce.ie/ashford/index.html

This castle hotel is situated on 350 acres of wooded parkland in Ireland. Read about outdoor activities such as fly-fishing, horseback riding, and duck shooting, and look into special fox hunting, holiday, and spa weekends. Online reservations are offered from this site.

Hotel Castle Mandawa
www.planetindia.net/CastleMandawa/facility.htm

This Web site offers descriptions of sword-bearing guards, guest-carrying camels, welcoming musicians, arched verandas, and other details on this fortress-hotel in India. You'll find information here on recreational activities like chariot rides, folk dances, and puppet shows, as well as pricing information and a location map.

Hastings Hotels
www.hastingshotels.com

Hastings Hotels owns and operates numerous castles throughout Ireland. On this site, you can read descriptions, view photos, and find out about rooms, restaurants, and pubs within each castle. Nearby attractions, upcoming festivities, and useful travel information are featured, and you can make your reservations online.

Travel Byte

Are you interested in renting a house, cottage, or cabin for your next vacation? If so, stop by the Cyber Rentals Web site at **cyberrentals.com/homepage.html**.

Homes Away From Home: B&Bs And Inns

Do you crave a cozy room with a plush bed and a downy comforter? Well, you're in luck—bed and breakfasts have their place on the Web. Bed and breakfasts, called B&Bs for short, are privately owned and operated accommodations, often run out of someone's home. Many travelers find B&Bs cozier, homier, and more comfortable than the large cookie-cutter hotels.

When I stay at B&Bs in the United Kingdom, where the concept of a bed and breakfast originated, I often get such a warm reception from my hosts that I feel as if I'm part of the family. I hear how the family garden is growing in the backyard, learn about the local ales and brew pubs, and listen to the youngest daughter practice her fiddle.

B&Bs are great places to learn about the area in which you're staying. By speaking with family members, you can learn about the local culture and history and get tips from those who really know their way around town. Local flavor, home-cooked breakfasts, and a personal touch you just can't get from a hotel are a few of the many benefits of staying at B&Bs.

While B&Bs can give you all the comforts of home, there are sometimes rules that may make you feel a bit restricted. For instance, meals may be served only at certain times, and at some homes you must share a table with other guests. In addition, you may not be able to come and go at your own hours because your hosts (understandably) lock up their house at night. But all this depends on the particular B&B: some houses have separate dining tables for their guests, and many hosts provide front door keys so visitors can get in and out at any time.

Keep in mind that American B&Bs, unlike European counterparts, can be very expensive. U.S. travelers pay for that down-home feel.

Travel Byte

On holiday weekends, or weekends during the peak travel season, many B&Bs and inns require a two or three night stay. Inform the proprietors if you plan to stay only one night.

A happy medium between a bed and breakfast and a hotel is an inn. Inns preserve the gracious feeling of a B&B, but have more guest rooms and operate similarly to a hotel. Inns generally give you more privacy than a bed and breakfast, and make you feel at home at the same time. You can find hundreds of inns on the Web, as well as bed and breakfasts, on the following sites.

The Inn Traveler
www.inntraveler.com

This site claims to be "where innkeepers look for inns." Locate country inns, country house hotels, and bed and breakfasts on the Web. You'll find specifics on over 600 inns at this site for locations worldwide. Descriptions of a different inn are featured every month.

Inns & Outs
www.innsandouts.com

This site provides information on 20,000 bed and breakfasts and inns (count them all!) throughout North America. Search the huge database according to your preferences and needs, and join in chat forums (Figure 6.13), try out recipes, and check out the calendar of events.

Bed and Breakfast Inns of North America
www.183.metronet.com

Find the perfect B&B for your trip in the U.S., Canada, the Caribbean, or Mexico. Learn about each inn's special features, including location, afternoon

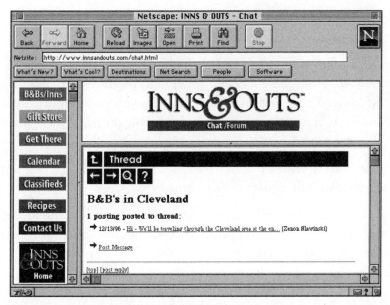

Figure 6.13 Communicate with other B&B enthusiasts at the Inns & Outs chat forum.

teas, and buffet breakfasts, and find detailed descriptions of accommodations. Look into the site's "favorite recipes" and visit chat rooms and message boards. You'll also find details on special events.

Bed & Breakfast Online
www.bbcanada.com/bbframe.html

If you're looking for B&Bs in Canada, stop by this site. You'll find over 1,100 up-to-date listings. Just search for the province and city where you're heading and find out about historic inns in the area.

Bed & Breakfast Encyclopedia Online
homearts.com/affil/ahi/main/ahihome.htm

Use the "Inn Finder" feature on this site to gather information on thousands of B&Bs and inns in the United States and Canada. Details available about specific inns include the date the structure was built, and the furniture and fireplaces found in the guest rooms. You'll also find out about local attractions and public transportation, and comments from other guests are available as well. Chat with other B&B enthusiasts in the chat forum.

Bed and Breakfast on the WWW
www.webcom.com/neatstuff/bb/home.html

This site links you to over one hundred bed and breakfast reservation services on the Web. From these services, you'll find specifics on thousands of bed and breakfasts in the United States and Canada; you can find just the right B&B according to your price range and tastes. You can also follow direct links to B&B home pages.

The Road Best Traveled
homearts.com/affil/ahi/main/rbthome.htm

This Web site provides archived information from The Road Best Traveled newsletter. You'll find descriptions of bed and breakfasts from past issues, or you can subscribe to the newsletter to receive information on bargains and package deals.

Travel Byte

While most inns don't serve meals between breakfast and dinner, many will gladly prepare a picnic lunch for you if asked.

Simply Sleep

Something to consider as a traveler is how much time you will actually be spending at your hotel. If you plan on sight-seeing all day, eating at local restaurants, and then dancing the night away, you may not want to indulge in luxury accommodations. If your hotel is simply used for a good night's rest, staying at more economical lodgings will leave you extra money in your neck wallet to spend out on the town!

Many inexpensive hotels offer lots of unexpected extras, such as complimentary continental breakfasts, saunas, swimming pools, and laundry service. For example, Comfort Inns offer exercise facilities, and Travelodge provides coffee makers in their guest rooms. These are great perks for the price you pay.

Foreign hotels, like those in Northern Europe, can be very expensive. I recommend staying in bed and breakfasts and pensions if you want to save money. You may also opt for budget hotels overseas for a cheaper nightly rate, but keep in mind that economy hotels abroad and those in the U.S. don't share a level playing field.

At many budget hotels overseas, guests may share bathrooms, and hot showers often require payment of an extra fee. In addition, you may find your room decor sparse by American hotel standards. While most bed and breakfasts and pensions overseas also require that you share a bathroom, they often offer more comfort for about the same price.

Another option is staying at youth hostels. Many hostels all over the world are very clean, safe, and offer basic dormitory-style lodging for a nominal price. One of the reasons I am able to travel frequently is because I save so much money staying at these basic, but comfortable, accommodations. You can read more about this type of inexpensive lodging in Chapter 8.

Staying Safe

Although you'll be on vacation, luxuriating in your big comfy bed, enjoying the wonders of room service, and relaxing in your Jacuzzi bath, it's always important to stay alert when it comes to your safety. While many hotels have tight security and you may feel safe and guarded, there's always someone out there who's ready and willing to take advantage of an unsuspecting traveler. Make sure you're not a victim by using your common sense, and keep in mind the following points of practical advice.

- Use your hotel's main entrance when coming and going; side doors are not as closely monitored. Also watch for loiterers on the hotel premises and in parking lots.

- Be attentive to your belongings when checking in and out of a hotel. Thieves often target the front desk because patrons have their valuables with them but are likely to be distracted.

- Avoid staying in a room on the ground floor. Outside access is much more difficult several stories above ground level.

- Stay at hotels with indoor walkways to your room. Hotels with outside corridors provide little protection against unwelcome visitors.

- Make sure your room has a dead bolt, chain lock, and peephole. Always lock your room door securely with all available locks.

- Hang on tight to your room keys. Keep them safe on your person so they won't be stolen. In addition, try not to let anyone see or overhear what room you are staying in.

- Never open your room door without first checking to see who is there. Verify uninvited hotel attendants by calling the front desk.
- When chatting with new acquaintances at local attractions or in restaurants, never reveal where you are staying. Many thieves break into rooms when travelers are out.
- Secure bags and briefcases in your room with combination locks, and lock your suitcase up as well.
- If your room ever looks disturbed or in disorder, ask the front desk for a security check before entering.

Booking It

Booking your accommodations over the Internet is as easy as booking your flight or rental car, discussed in Chapter 5. After you've chosen the hotel you'd like to stay at, visit the reservation domain on the hotel's Web site, usually designated by a highlighted link. There you'll be asked to enter the dates you plan on staying and what type of room you would like (deluxe suite, double occupancy, non-smoking, and so on), as seen in Figure 6.14. You may also be asked if you'd like a cot in your room and other miscellaneous information.

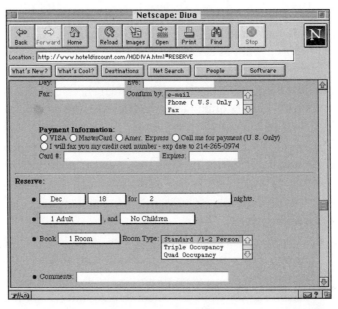

Figure 6.14 Booking a reservation at the Hotel Discount Web site.

At this point you'll be given the nightly cost of your room. If you'd like to reserve the room, enter your name, address, phone number, and credit card information (the same data that you provide when reserving a room by telephone). Send your reservation by simply clicking "return." You'll receive your confirmation via email, or by postal mail if you prefer.

If the hotel you want to stay at doesn't offer online reservations from its Web site, or has no Web site of its own, you can still reserve your room over the Internet. At sites that focus on booking rooms at thousands of hotels worldwide, you can easily find the hotel you've chosen and book your stay. These hotel directories list thousands of hotels, and are the reason some hotels don't have an Internet presence of their own. (Why do it yourself when someone else has done it for you?)

Sites like TravelWeb, HotelBook, and Places to Stay allow you to make reservations at hundreds of independent and chain hotels. You can even make your reservations at small mom-and-pop-style hotels and guest houses by visiting these online reservation sites. Simply browse the selection of hotels, or find a hotel by searching for your destination. When you've chosen a hotel, fill out and submit the reservation form, and your rooms are booked.

TravelWeb
www.travelweb.com

With TravelWeb, you can reserve rooms at over 40 hotel chains and over 8,000 hotels. You can conduct searches by city, room price, or type of accommodations, and specify such personal preferences as non-smoking rooms. Read brief descriptions and get information on check-in times and other details. Check room availability and book your reservation from this site.

Expedia
www.expedia.com

Visit Expedia's hotel directory to browse more than 25,000 hotels worldwide. Read brief descriptions of the hotels and find information on location, price, amenities, and proximity to airports and area attractions. View hotel location maps, check room availability, and reserve your room from this site. You must register for a free Expedia account before making your reservation.

HotelBook
www.hotelbook.com

Visit this site to make online reservations at any one of 6,500 hotels world-wide. Enter your preferences, including types of accommodations, such as cabin, chalet, or ski lodge, and find out about hotel promotional discounts.

Hotelreservation.com
www.hotelreservation.com

Search for your hotel of choice by city, or conduct a "GEO Search" to find one by interactive map. With this reservation service, shown in Figure 6.15, you can check availability for rooms at hotels, motels, and bed and breakfasts. You'll receive your confirmation number immediately when you reserve your room from this site.

Places to Stay
www.placestostay.com

Make hotel reservations in the United States, Europe, and the Caribbean. This site, shown in Figure 6.16, provides descriptions of each hotel, and reviews and rates them as well. View photos, enter contests, and after booking your stay, follow links to useful Web sites about your destination.

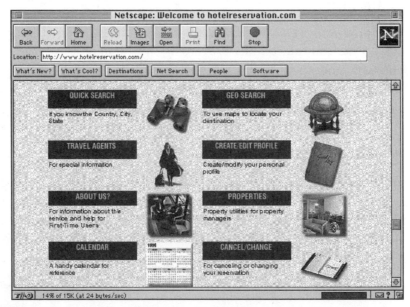

Figure 6.15 A Web page from hotelreservation.com.

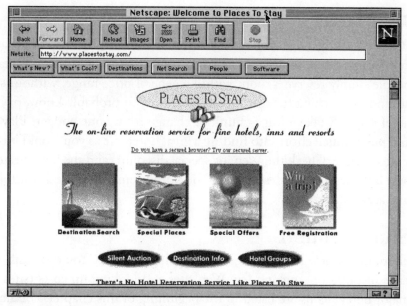

Figure 6.16 *The Places to Stay home page.*

TravelWiz
www.travelwiz.com

Find information here on over 80 hotel chains and make reservations for most of them. Get a closer look at hotels like the Essex House in New York: view 360-degree images of the lobby, an executive suite, a cafe, the bar, and the ballroom.

Travelocity
www.travelocity.com

Create a personal travel profile on this site to store your hotel preferences and participate in promotions, contests, and giveaways. With approximately 30,000 hotels listed, you can search by city, suburb, and other locations—even by the closest airport. Read descriptions of hotel property and rooms, and get info on dining, recreational facilities, nearby attractions, directions, and transportation to and from the airport.

Travel Byte

If you don't feel comfortable submitting your credit card data over the Internet, you can visit the Web site of your hotel to find other contact information, such as the reservation phone or fax numbers.

The Money Factor

When planning a vacation, many travelers concentrate on finding a low air-fare, but give little thought to getting a great bargain on their hotel stay. Often people simply reserve a room within a general price range, without shopping around or checking for discounted rates. As you probably know, paying for a hotel stay can take a huge chunk of change from your budget. Play it smart and put as much effort into finding a great hotel rate as you would into getting a great airfare. Check the Web for special discounts and the lowest rates for the best facilities at your destination. You'll find remarkable deals on top-of-the-line accommodations.

Shop Around

Shopping for low hotel rates is simple using the Web. You can easily compare rates just by stopping at a few Web sites and looking up costs (sites of many major hotel chains are listed in the beginning of this chapter). Because prices of hotel rooms vary according to location and season, you should specify exactly where and when you'll be visiting to receive the correct price.

Look for promotional specials and bargain deals you might never have known about otherwise. Some hotel chains offer low rates at newly opened hotels. Some have anniversary specials. These promotions are great deals for those who know about them; those who don't will probably miss out because most hotels don't mention these deals unless you ask about them. When you make your reservation, be sure to mention the special rate you saw on the hotel's home page—and just to be on the safe side, mention it again when checking in.

Information on discount weekend and week-long vacation packages can also be found on the Web. Many of these deals are offered by hotels in conjunction with restaurants, theme parks, and other attractions in the area. You can get a room, treat yourself to some wonderful cuisine, and get access to family entertainment for one low price. Get details about many different kinds of package deals by stopping by hotel home pages.

Many hotels offer special rates to qualifying individuals. For example, deluxe as well as economy accommodations may allow children under the age of sixteen to stay free of charge when accompanied by an adult. Discounts may also be offered to military personnel, seniors, and members of AARP or AAA.

These discounted rates are easy to find on home pages and can make a major difference in the cost of your stay.

Travel Byte

One way to keep your hotel costs down is by limiting your room charges. Room service, snacks from the honor bar, and pay-per-view movies are costly and add up quickly. Keep tabs on how much you're charging, and choose your charges carefully.

Weekly Discounts

Some hotels offer great last-minute deals on rooms all over the world. Similar to the short-lived specials airlines offer to fill up empty seats on impending flights, these deals are offered on hotel rooms that haven't been filled for the upcoming week. These specials are offered by the week and last for seven days.

You can find these weekly bargains on Web pages of hotels like Radisson, as seen in Figure 6.17. The one and only way to catch weekly low rates for Radisson and other hotels is by visiting the hotel's Web site.

Figure 6.17 *Weekly last-minute deals from Radisson.*

While you can get unbelievable bargains with these specials, they do have major restrictions. Keep in mind that they are temporary and can't be booked ahead of time. In addition, these discounts are available for a limited number of rooms—so if you're too late to book, you may miss out. Finally, you don't get to choose the destination. Only certain locations, designated by the hotel, apply.

Travel Byte

Thinking about purchasing a timeshare? Visit the Timeshare Users Group (**www.timeshare-users-group.com**) before buying.

Ask And You May Receive

Remember the adage "The squeaky wheel gets the grease?" Well, squeaky travelers get the deals. You may get a discount on your room rate just by letting your voice be heard. Simply send off an email message to a potential hotel stating when you'll be visiting a certain area, and ask for a discount and the lowest rate available.

In addition, always ask the desk clerk for a discounted rate or room upgrade upon arrival. I make it a regular practice to inquire when I check in, and found that these discounts and upgrades are usually granted during the off-season and on off-holiday weekends. You'll be surprised at how many hotels will accommodate you. Because a large number of guest rooms are left unoccupied on any given night, hotels are often willing to give you a bargain to fill the place up, even if these discounted rates are not publicized. You may get as much as 10 percent off your already discounted rate just by inquiring.

While it pays to be a squeaky wheel, don't squeak too loud. As with most people, hotel clerks don't appreciate rude customers. Those who are friendly are more likely to be accommodated than those who are impolite and pushy.

Frequent Stay Programs

Frequent hotel stay programs are similar to airline frequent flyer programs. Members like to stick to one hotel line so they get the benefits of the program, like guaranteed room availability, express check-in, and free use of fitness facilities. These programs are often offered in conjunction with frequent flyer programs from airlines, so you even earn miles on your overnight stay! When I stay at any Westin, Radisson, Hyatt, or Hilton hotels, I earn miles with American Airlines. I also belong to United Airline's frequent flyer program, and earn miles with that airline when I stay at a Holiday Inn, ITT Sheraton, Marriott, or at numerous other hotels and resorts. Details on these programs can be found on either hotel or airline Web sites, and you can often register for the program right from the hotel's Web site.

Travel Byte

If you need to cancel your room reservation, do so as far in advance as possible. If you don't, you may be charged for a night's stay.

National Hotel Brokers

Take a bite out of your room cost by visiting the Web sites of hotel brokers. Brokers can offer as much as 50 percent off standard room rates in selected cities by booking blocks of rooms at major hotel chains, then reselling them to you at a discount. Brokers are paid on commission directly by the hotels, so there are no membership fees or service charges to pay. These brokers simply deliver great rates to you. Be aware, however, that they may not offer a wide selection of hotel choices.

The following brokers were listed in *Diversion Magazine*, July 1996.

Central Reservations Service
www.reservation-services.com

Find rooms in numerous hotels throughout New York, San Francisco, Miami, Orlando, Los Angeles, and Boston. This site provides city maps with hotel locations, and information about location benefits, amenities, recreational facilities, and hotel restaurants. Make your online reservations and receive your confirmation via email. You can also put your name on the mailing list to receive news and updates. This free service requires no prepayment or minimum length stay.

RMC Travel
www.1travel.com

Browse approximately 1,300 hotels in locations throughout the U.S. and Canada. Enter the city where you'll be staying and the name of the hotel you have in mind, and follow links to other Web sites for information on accommodations. This site also includes selected B&Bs, villas, spas, resorts, and condos.

Accommodations Express
www.accommodationsxpress.com

Check availability at hotels in Atlantic City, Boston, Chicago, Las Vegas, New Orleans, New York, Orlando, Philadelphia, and Washington D.C. Accommodations Express will contact you with the current best deal in your particular price range and you can then make your online reservations on this site. You can also win free overnight stays and find information on discount rooms during conventions, flower shows, and sporting events.

Citywide Reservation Services
www.cityres.com

Find discounts at hotels ranging from economy to luxury, and everything in between, in Boston, New York City, Cape Cod, Montreal, Philadelphia, and Washington D.C. By email, specify what city you plan to visit, on what dates, and the number in your party, and the free Citywide service will contact you with available accommodations for your location and dates. You can also find promotional and package rates at this site.

City-Specific Brokers
Hot Rooms (Chicago)
www.hotrooms.com

Make your reservations any time, from the day you arrive in Chicago to four months in advance. You'll find deals and special promotional discounts at this site, as well as room rates, location information, and parking fees for each hotel. Book your accommodations by email; no credit card info is needed to reserve a room.

Express Hotel Reservations (New York)
www.express-res.com

Find discounts here for approximately thirty economy and luxury hotels in New York City. A color-coded map of the city lets you identify hotels by price range and location. Read brief hotel descriptions, submit the name of the hotel you're interested in to receive a quote, and make your reservation online.

There's also a New York City calendar of events and a Frequently Asked Questions list at this site.

San Francisco Reservations (San Francisco)
www.hotelres.com

Click on a city map to locate area hotels. Read about hotel amenities, accepted credit cards, and check-out times, and view photos of rooms, lobbies, and restaurants. Compare the discounted rates offered on this site with standard hotel rates, and check room availability. Hotels are also categorized by price range and type (exclusive, major, small, standard, or motor inn).

Capitol Reservations (Washington D.C.)
washington.digitalcity.com/sponsors/capres

Choose among convention, luxury, independent, and chain hotels at this site, which provides hotel highlights and pricing information, as well as links to Web sites for visitor organizations, memorials, museums, and restaurants in the Washington D.C. area. Email your reservation request and Capitol Reservations will contact you. Seasonal discount information is also available by email.

Travel Byte

Reserving your room with a credit card secures a discounted room rate.

Free Accommodations: Home Exchanges

The name home exchange says it all: you stay at someone's home and in exchange, they stay at yours. There's no fees to pay, and you get free lodging for an agreed-upon amount of time. Many Web sites unite vacationers who want to swap homes by providing descriptions and photos of houses and details on nearby stores, beaches, and playgrounds. Contact information is provided— it is up to the site visitors to contact the home owners to arrange an exchange. Web sites such as Home Exchange International (**www.west.net/~prince/he**), International Home Exchange Network (**www.homexchange.com**), Gateway Home Exchange (**www.GatewayExchange.com**), and the World Wide Travel Exchange (**www.wwte.com**) will help you get started.

Read All About It

To read the news on the latest hotel openings, promotions, industry issues, and announcements, tap into NewsPage at **www.newspage.com**. There you'll find daily updates on hotel travel packages, as well as newly added and canceled services and acquisitions. Just look under the heading "Hotels, Resorts, and Hospitality" to get the daily scoop.

Hospitality Net (**www.hospitalitynet.nl/**) and the online version of *Lodging Magazine* (**www.lodgingmagazine.com**) target people in the hospitality industry, but you can get the latest hotel news there, too. You'll find articles on what hotels are doing to keep their customers happy, safety and security measures and upgrades, and industry insights from those in the know. Where else would you learn that Hilton Hotels is working with the National Sleep Foundation to provide "ultimate sleep environments?"

Other Accommodations

You'll find more information on budget accommodations in other chapters of this book. Chapter 8 leads you to Web sites of youth hostels, a popular and economical lodging alternative. You'll also find advice on camping in the great outdoors, and guides to campgrounds all over the world, by looking in Chapter 12. To brush up on your sight-seeing skills no matter where you're staying, read the upcoming pages of Chapter 7.

Things To Do, Places To See

CHAPTER 7 TOPICS

- SIGHTSEEING ONLINE

- VIRTUAL MUSEUMS AND ART GALLERIES

- TRAVELLING SAFELY

- FINDING LOCAL EVENTS ON THE WEB

- REVIEWING RESTAURANTS

It's time to get busy planning the fun part of your trip—sight-seeing, attraction hopping, eating, eating, and more eating. In this chapter, you'll see how useful the Web can be for planning outings, excursions, and entertainment on your vacation. By visiting just a few Web sites, you can find out about local celebrations, sporting events, theatrical productions, and concerts at your destination—and order your tickets ahead of time online to reserve the best seats in the house. You can also visit sites of museums, art galleries, and restaurants to make the best recreational decisions in a yet-to-be-explored city.

Cyber Sightseeing

You can start planning what to do and see by stopping by Web sites of the tourist attractions you've always heard about, but never before had the chance to visit. Web pages like that of the Taj Mahal and the Acropolis (Figure 7.1) can be just as enticing as the real sight, and can provide you with all the information you'll need when you get there.

Find useful information on locations, fees, and hours of operation. Read about the history and significance of an attraction. Many travelers visit popular attractions just because they're popular, never taking the time to learn

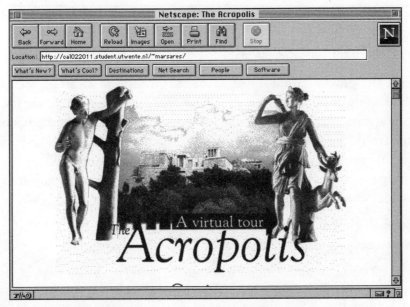

Figure 7.1 Visit the Acropolis without ever setting foot in Athens.

about who built them and why. Knowing the stories behind many interesting places can be inspiring, and can make the attraction more meaningful when you visit.

Always wanted to visit the Baseball Hall of Fame? How about Stonehenge? The following list will give you quick access to many major worldwide attractions.

The Acropolis
130.89.228.117/~marsares/tour/index.html

Take a virtual trip to the religious and cultural center of ancient Greece. Visitors to this site learn about the many temples of the Acropolis and the gods who were worshipped there, from Athena to Zeus. You'll see photos and read about Doric columns, friezes, and other architectural achievements, as well as the history of Athens from 3,000 B.C. to the present.

The Alamo
numedia.tddc.net/sa/alamo

Remember to visit this site before your trip to Texas. There's lots of information here on the Alamo, including a chronology of the events surrounding the site. You'll read about the cavalry, attack forces, and the number of lives that were lost, and about the life and times of famous frontiersmen like Davy Crockett, Jim Bowie, and Sam Houston.

Alcatraz
199.106.87.9/~heather/alcatraz

This site provides photos and a concise history of Alcatraz. You can learn about early construction on the island and get a background on its role as a military fortress, a federal penitentiary, and its current status as a national park open to the public. There's also information about the Native American occupation, the origins of the name Alcatraz, the costs of building the various structures, and other interesting facts. You can also get information about fees, holiday closings, and contact information to help you plan your visit.

Baseball Hall of Fame
www.enews.com/bas_hall_fame

Make a virtual visit to Cooperstown by stopping at the Baseball Hall of Fame online, shown in Figure 7.2. Read the latest news about new inductees, as well as all the information and stats on historic members. You'll also find photos,

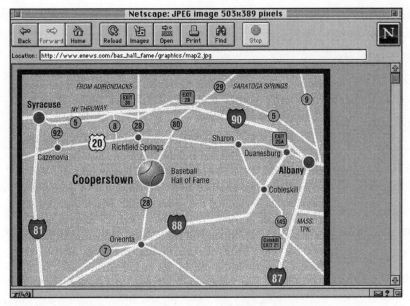

Figure 7.2   Find directions on how to get to Cooperstown.

quotes from baseball legends, contests to enter, coupons for admission, and details on the Hall of Fame elections. Special museum exhibits are high-lighted, on such topics as the champions of the World Series. Print out a map to help you get there, with directions from nearby cities and airports. You'll also find links to baseball team home pages.

Buckingham Palace
www.londonmall.co.uk/palace

This Web site provides simple background information and the history of Buckingham Palace. A stately picture and painting are included, as well as information about admission charges so you can have your currency ready when you arrive at any of the three nearby underground stops.

Eiffel Tower
www.paris.org/Monuments/Eiffel

This site provides lots of interesting facts on Paris's most famous landmark. There are statistics on the amount of paint on the structure, how many steps it takes to get to the top, its weight, and the unusual stunts performed by visitors over the years. Find out about the tower's construction for the International

Exhibition of Paris in 1889, and how it was almost torn down in 1909. You can also find useful information for your trip here, such as the best bus routes to get you there.

Ellis Island
www.ellisisland.org/index.html

Before you visit Ellis Island to get in touch with your immigrant heritage, stop by this Web site. You'll find practical information here on daily hours, as well as museum highlights. Read about the American Immigrant Wall of Honor, the Family Immigration Center, and other projects "in the works."

Empire State Building
www.nypl.org/research/chss/spe/art/photo/hinex/empire/empire.html

This site concentrates on the construction of the Empire State Building in 1930. A photo gallery of construction workers swinging beams, screwing in bolts, and securing rivets is provided. Get the facts on the building's height, cost, and the total time it took to build (7 million man hours). Read about Lewis Wickes Hine, the photographer who captured the images of the men who built what was, for a long time, considered the tallest building in the world.

Golden Gate Bridge
www.camerica.com/mousing_around/gatecam.ssi

Stop by this Web site for a live view of the Golden Gate Bridge. There's also a gallery of bridge photos, archived for your viewing. You can also follow links to Web sites about San Francisco and other attractions in the Bay area.

Graceland
www.elvis-presley.com

Any Elvis fan can get their fill of "Elvisology" at this site, shown in Figure 7.3. There's lots of trivia, and you can read all about the life and career of the king of rock and roll. If you're planning to be one of the 700,000 annual visitors to the mansion, you can gather information on Graceland tours and other associated attractions, such as The Elvis Presley Automobile Museum, which houses "vehicles enjoyed and owned by Elvis." Also check out the events calendar and the memorabilia department.

Figure 7.3   The Virtual Graceland Web site.

Great Barrier Reef
www.lonelyplanet.com/dest/aust/gbreef.htm

This Web page is a good starting point if you're interested in the Reef. Links at the site detail Queensland, the principal coastal state of the Great Barrier Reef, and there's lots of information on the popular diving sites and drop-off points. You'll also find photographs here of many underwater marvels, as well as of surfacing whales.

Great Wall of China
zinnia.umfacad.maine.edu/~mshea/China/great.html

For an interesting account of the Great Wall, check out this personal travelogue. The narrator's account begins with the fascination and wonder that comes from seeing firsthand the only manmade structure visible from space. She then shares her investigation into the history of the wall, explaining how its construction began in the 2nd millennium B.C., and how it was finally fortified in the Ming dynasty (1368-1644).

Hearst Castle
www.hearstcastle.org

Pools, terraces, gardens, guest cottages, and other structures of William Randolph Hearst's mansion are described at this site (Figure 7.4), where you'll read all about the history of this "American castle." Learn about Hearst, as well as those associated with the media mogul. There's information here about the Hearst art collection, and lots of statistics about the building—everything from the number of fireplaces (41) to the number of bathrooms (61). Take a look at the online brochure for useful information, including tour descriptions, schedules, and prices, as well as places to stay in the area.

Hoover Dam
www.hooverdam.com

"Virtual tours" show the ins and outs of the Dam and how it works to produce electricity, replete with pictures and easy-to-understand information. Educational links are provided, as well as links to government electricity sites and other dam and regional sites. The historical information at this site details not only the Dam and the Dam project, but also the history of the region in the form of a timeline.

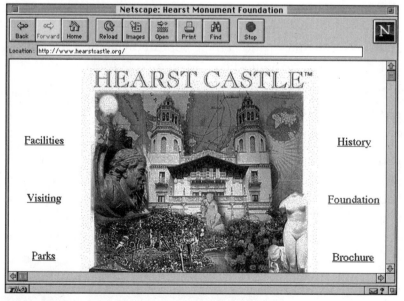

Figure 7.4 Visit the Hearst castle online.

Machu Picchu
www.tardis.ed.ac.uk/~angus/Gallery/Photos/SouthAmerica/Peru/IncaTrail1.html

Take a virtual hike along the Inca Trail to reach your final destination: the ancient ruins of Machu Picchu. You'll find descriptions of the trail and the local terrain, as well as photos of ancient structures; learn why they were built and what purposes they served. There's lots of information about the Incas and their extensive empire at this informative site.

The Mayan Ruins
pages.prodigy.com/GBonline/tikal.html#stela11

If you're traveling to the ancient city of Tikal and the Mayan Ruins, check out this site for a preview. You'll find captioned photos of the ancient ruins, as well as links to other Web sites about the Mayan people and their way of life.

Niagara Falls
www.iaw.com%7Ebberketa/everyt.html

This site covers not only the Falls itself, but also facts on gorges, ice bridges, and whirlpools formed by the river. Take a look at geology maps, get information on ferry services, and get directions to the many attractions in the area. Be sure to stop by the Daredevils Hall of Fame to read about people who have challenged the Falls throughout history with tightrope crossings, barrel jumps, and jet ski stunts.

Space Needle
spaceneedle.com

View a live image of Seattle's 605-foot wonder at this site. You can learn about its construction, tour the observation deck, browse the virtual souvenir catalog, and read interesting trivia about the needle: its heaviest visitor, how many lightning rods it's equipped with, and how many people have jumped from it. There's lots of useful visitor information on what to see and do, with a map and directions to get you there. Look over menus from the revolving restaurant and make your dinner reservations online.

St. Louis Gateway Arch
www.nps.gov/jeff/arch-home

The Gateway Arch, along with the Museum of Westward Expansion and the Old Courthouse, is part of the Jefferson Expansion Memorial in St. Louis. Find information on all three attractions at this site, including information on the arch's construction, tram rides, accessibility, daily hours, and entrance fees. You can also read about video kiosks and films, in addition to special events and festivals happening throughout the year.

Stonehenge
www.britannia.com/history/h7.html

This informative Web page provides you with the history of Stonehenge, as well as modern theories about its construction and the transport of stones to the site. Learn about local legends of the Druids and King Arthur. This is a good Web page to print out and take along with you instead of carrying a guide book.

Sydney Opera House
www.sydneyoperahouse.nsw.gov.au/about.html

Learn how one of the world's most recognized performance halls was designed and constructed, from its beginnings as an entry in an international design competition in 1957. This site describes the styles, decor, and acoustics of venues within the opera house, including the Concert Hall, Opera Theatre, and Drama Theatre, and has details on backstage tours and other guided tours. There are links to information on current and upcoming performances, too.

Taj Mahal
ans.edu.au/student.projects/tajmahal/home.html

This site whets the appetite for a trip to the Taj. You'll find extensive historical information on the area and country, including biographical sketches of the dynasty that produced the creator of the structure. View a layout of the estate with links to five different areas of the monument, each described in detail with photos. You'll find many legends and stories, images of Taj-inspired artwork, details on architects and often-overlooked features, in addition to comprehensive studies using maps and photographs.

Temple of Abu Simbel
www.ccer.ggl.ruu.nl/abu_simbel/map.map?169,20

This site allows you to explore the Egyptian temple that was built in dedication to pharaoh Ramses II. You can view a map of the inner chambers, learn about statues adorning the temple, and view close-up photos of facades. Interesting facts on the architecture and lighting of the temple can also be found here.

Tower of London
www.voicenat.com/~dravyk/toltour

You'll receive a detailed walk-through of the Tower on this informative Web site, as well as a historical background of many of the structures within the tower, including why they were built, and where their names came from. There's information here on the unusual habits of past kings and queens, the important historical events that took place there, and the people who were imprisoned at the Tower throughout the years.

Victoria Falls
www.africaonline.com/AfricaOnline/travel/zimbabwe/vic_falls.html

Natural wonders are always worth a look, even at a Web site. This site includes photos, and details the area surrounding the falls; useful information can also be found on items such as sundown cruises to view the local wildlife. The more adventurous traveler can find information about white-water rafting downstream.

Wall Drug
www.state.sd.us/state/executive/tourism/adds/walldrug.htm

If you've made a pilgrimage to Yellowstone, you've certainly seen the signs along the road for Wall Drug. Basically a tourist trap, Wall Drug carries all the western "souvenirs" and even has a giant Tyrannosaurus Rex. Pictures on this Web site preview what you'll see when you get there, and there's also an explanation of the Wall Drug phenomenon.

The White House
www.whitehouse.gov

Tour the White House by clicking on the room of your choice from a diagram, as shown in Figure 7.5. Learn about the history of individual rooms, including decorations, and the events that have taken place within them.

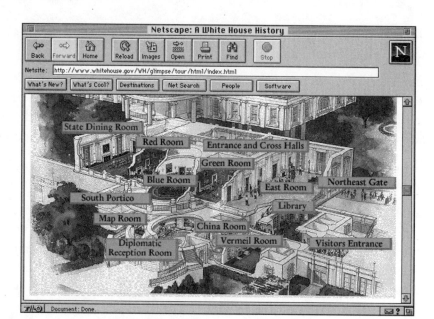

Figure 7.5 A virtual tour of 1600 Pennsylvania Avenue.

You'll find photos and details on furniture and art work here, and you can also read up on current events, look over recipes from White House chefs, and send the president an email message.

Planning Ahead

Kay Lite, a travel agent and travel correspondent for WLUP radio in Chicago, advises that travelers bypass tourist attractions on the weekends to avoid large crowds. "Plan around the busiest times. Avoid touristy spots on Saturdays and Sundays; the last place you want to be is Disney World on a Saturday."

In addition, Lite suggests that travelers avoid spending all their time at highly touristed areas. "Sightseeing does not necessarily mean visiting hot tourist attractions. It may mean hopping in your car and taking a ride to view the scenery around you."

Cyber Happenings

Even the most gung-ho, camera-equipped tourist needs to take a break from the sightseeing circuit. Plan to do something unique—participate in local events taking place in your destination city. These events may include holiday festivals, performances, state fairs, local art exhibitions, cultural celebrations, or parades. Special activities like these provide rare experiences and allow you to become involved with the local community, not only as an observer, but also as a participant. They give you a chance to become familiar with local traditions, beliefs, and rituals.

You can gather information on special events happening in your vacation spot by visiting entertainment directories on the Web. These sites feature databases filled with current and upcoming happenings in cities, towns, neighborhoods, and parks all over the world.

Sites like Festivals.com can provide you with all the information you need to include exciting and unusual events in your vacation agenda.

Festivals.com
www.festivals.com

Looking for a good party? You can find celebrations taking place the world over. This site clues you in to jazz festivals, ethnic seasonal festivities, and state fairs, as well as information on sporting events such as boating, marathons, auto racing, and rodeos. You'll get details on itineraries and performers, and useful contact information. The site provides details on each event, such as the types of music you'll hear, and offers a good general feel for the celebration itself.

FreeTime Guide
www.ftguide.com

Discover what's going on in approximately 2,700 cities in the United States. The information on this site is gathered from Chambers of Commerce and Visitors Centers across the country. Enter the month and the week you'll be in town, and search using keywords describing your interests for special events or all-year-long attractions. This site provides only basic information; you'll need to make a phone call for details on the event.

CultureFinder
www.culturefinder.com

For classical music, opera, and dance lovers, this site locates upcoming performances in the United States and Canada. Search by city, date, or organization to scan the database of year-round schedules for 580 performing arts organizations, or read the weekly update to learn what's new for the week. (But remember, updates are added to the site on a daily basis.) There are numerous weekly articles and editorial features on dance, opera, and "New York Scenes," or you can visit the library or the artist showcase. Stop by the Culture Shop virtual store to buy CDs, books, and T-shirts.

Ticketmaster
www.ticketmaster.com

Search for concerts, sporting events, and family shows happening at your getaway place by name or artist, or simply click on a state map. Look to "Best of Broadway" and "Best of Off-Broadway" for theater events, where you'll find descriptions of each show and details about the theater in which it's running. You can also see what tickets are on sale at your destination each week, for last-minute arrangements. Find out what other event-goers are seeing by perusing the list of most popular events (generated daily by the number of inquiries in the database), view seating charts to get the best seat in the house, and order your tickets from the site.

The Official Guide to the Phat Planet
streetsound.com/phatplanet

Get the skinny on the night life in your destination by reading postings from those in the know—other club goers on the Net. You can gather info on clubbing around the globe, or check up on local bands and DJs. This site covers music, from hip-hop to acid jazz, disco to experimental, at "wicked" clubs in the U.S., U.K., Central and South America, Africa, and other world-wide locations.

Top Ten Tourist Tips

1. Keep your mind open to new experiences.
2. Make an effort to learn about the culture and history of wherever you are.
3. Be sensitive when taking photographs, especially when capturing pictures of people and religious objects. Photographing spiritual ceremonies is often frowned upon or expressly forbidden.
4. Enjoy your vacation. Don't let mishaps or unexpected glitches get to you.

5. Remember you are visiting someone else's home. Respect the etiquette and property of others.

6. Don't let the bad behavior of one person affect your opinion of an entire population.

7. Use all five senses—sight, smell, taste, touch, and hearing—to take in your new surroundings.

8. Break out of your shell and get to know the local people of the area you're visiting.

9. Be a safe tourist, but don't dampen your trip with excessive anxiety and mistrust.

10. Remember, being a visitor doesn't mean you should receive special treatment.

Where To Find What To Do

Tourism bureaus can provide you with information on happenings in your vacation spot. Many of these local organizations have Web sites, as mentioned in Chapter 3; visit them to get updates on events, concerts, and festivals. Just use your search engine to locate your tourism office online, or visit the Tourism Offices Worldwide Directory (**www.mbnet.mb.ca/lucas/travel/tourism-offices.html**) where you'll find links to Web sites, email addresses, and other contact information for numerous tourism offices.

In addition, visit the following Web sites for suggestions and recommendations for what to see and do on your trip. These sites keep you current on the goings-on in popular travel destinations.

Good Times Guide
travel.epicurious.com

Read reviews online from the critics at Condé Nast Traveler on theater and dance performances in major U.S. cities. Browse critiques of concerts, symphonies, and operas, and read descriptions about restaurants near the performances; get the scoop on popular drinks and the decor of "hot hotel bars." You can also brush up on city architecture with descriptions of buildings worth a look (directions included), and follow links to other relevant Web sites.

EW Metro
pathfinder.com

Peruse current and past issues of EW Metro, brought to you by Entertainment Weekly Online, to read articles on music, theater, and night life throughout the United States. The monthly issues of this online publication provide recommendations on a variety of performances to see, with theater information, ticket prices, and show times included.

Internet Vacation Guide
www.whitehawk.com/vacation

Looking for attractions to take in on your trip? This site will link you to Web sites of numerous points of interest in the United States. Search for links by state, or by listed category; topics include gardens, curiosities, and museums. You'll find links here to sites of music festivals, theaters, and opera companies, and state government Web sites are also listed.

Where Magazines
www.wheremags.com

Find recommended sites to see and daily itineraries for Chicago, New York, Toronto, London, Paris, New Orleans, and other major cities. You'll receive monthly updates on music, theater, dance, museums, bars, concerts, and gallery and museum exhibitions, find recommendations on performances and restaurants, and get tipped off to free attractions. You can also search for your interests—choices include searching by store name and an extensive list of categories including books, furniture, music, optical, salons, malls, swimwear, and more. Zero in on city neighborhoods by viewing online maps.

Museums Online

The Web is a valuable resource for information on museums to visit on your trip. Not only will you find out about hours, access for the disabled, and admission charges, you can also take part in interactive online exhibits. Play games, toy with puzzles, view displays through live Web cams, watch video clips, and discover a whole lot of interesting facts. You can take virtual tours of museums at your destination to see if they look interesting to you and your travel companions, and learn a thing or two along the way!

Visit the following Web sites for quick access to the most popular museums online.

The Smithsonian
www.si.edu

Just click your mouse on the Smithsonian map to visit any one of its numerous buildings and galleries, including the Postal Museum, the National Museum of American History and the Ripley Center. You can find out about current exhibitions covering American history, space, art, design, and numerous other topics you'll want to explore when you visit the museum. Information on films, lectures, workshops, performances, and demonstrations is also provided, including ticket prices of special exhibits. This site also provides virtual 3D tours of exhibits and online magazines.

Exploratorium
www.exploratorium.edu

At this site, online exhibits on science, perception, nature, and other topics give you an idea of what's currently on view at San Francisco's Exploratorium (Figure 7.6). Get glimpses of exhibits through live Web cameras, 360-degree panoramas, and audio clips. The schedule of special events, information about

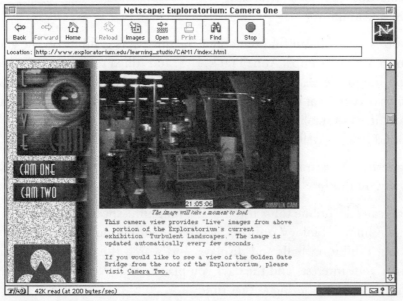

Figure 7.6 Take part in interactive online museum exhibits at the Exploratorium.

upcoming workshops and lectures, and interior maps will all help you plan your visit.

National Air and Space Museum
wwww.nasm.edu

Visit online exhibits about early flight, jet aviation, moon walks, World War II aviation, and more, and find out about aircraft on exhibit at the museum in Washington D.C. The museum floor map will help you find what you're looking for when you get there, and the Web site also provides a way to post your questions.

The Natural History Museum
www.nhm.ac.uk

Web surfers of all ages will enjoy exploring London's Natural History Museum online. Learn through interactive exhibits on dinosaurs, fossils, the galaxies, and earth science. Look over the "science casebooks," view photos, and even examine specimens through virtual reality. You can also read about what happens "behind the scenes" at the museum. And don't forget to check out the visitor information on the many galleries, special events, daily schedules, and directions to the museum.

Holocaust Memorial Museum
www.ushmm.org

At this site, you can find out about the museum's exhibits on the ghettos and concentration camps, Anne Frank, U.S. and Allied response to the Holocaust, and life in the years after the Holocaust. Also read about presentations and films occurring at the museum, located in Washington D.C., and learn about how it was established. Hours, pass information, and directions can all be found here, as well as a historical summary and an FAQ.

American Museum of Natural History
www.amnh.org

You can take online tours through the museum's special collections and exhibits on human biology, animals, gems, meteorites, ocean life, and more. Read about exhibition halls and displays, and search the calendar of events—just enter your interests and the days you plan to visit New York City to see what the museum is offering at that time.

Henry Ford Museum & Greenfield Village
hfm.umd.umich.edu

Visit the Web site of "the largest indoor-outdoor museum in North America" and learn about American innovation and famous inventors including Henry Ford, Thomas Edison, and the Wright brothers. Explore images of museum and village highlights, and find out how some of the exhibits were created. The events guide will help you plan your trip, and provide information about educational programs, classes, and behind-the-scenes tours taking place on the museum campus, located in Michigan. You can take part in the online exhibit, too.

Colonial Williamsburg
www.history.org

At the Colonial Williamsburg Web site you'll find photos and descriptions of characters of the time. For example, Thomas Jefferson describes his personal ties to Williamsburg, and explains how you can bump into him at the museum, located in Virginia, and talk about the issues and events of his time. Browse areas and buildings of the park, brush up on American history, and zone in on your particular interests with the historical almanac.

Travel Byte

Keep your feet happy and blister-free. Wear your most comfortable walking shoes when seeing the sights.

Virtual Art

Sure, you can appreciate a work of art without ever knowing about its history or creator, but wouldn't a little knowledge help you be even more insightful and appreciative? Thousands of art galleries and exhibits are now appearing online to deliver historical information about important works of art. Visit world-renowned galleries like the Louvre, the Prado, and the Metropolitan Museum of Art to see and learn about masterpieces that have been admired throughout time. Read about accomplished artists like Monet, Michelangelo, Picasso, and their talented peers you may never have heard of.

Visiting online art galleries is like taking a history class, without the yawn-filled lectures. Learn about the artwork you're interested in, prepare for your visit to the classics, and get the practical information you need on daily hours, discounts, special exhibits, and workshops.

Here are some of the numerous art galleries you can explore online and then visit in person.

Guggenheim Museums
math240.lehman.cuny.edu/gugg

From this site you can access information on the four affiliated Guggenheim art museums: the Guggenheim Museum in Bilbao, Spain; the Solomon R. Guggenheim Museum in New York City; the Guggenheim Museum in SoHo; and the Peggy Guggenheim Collection in Venice, Italy. You'll find information on the life and works of artists like Kandinsky, Picasso, Ernst, and Mondrian. Learn about current exhibits, view photos of sculptural works and paintings, read bios of artists and reviews by art critics. You'll find practical information here as well, including descriptions of free tours, and workshop and lecture schedules.

Louvre
mistral.culture.fr.louvre

The home page of the Louvre contains images and information on artistic works throughout history, including the Middle Ages, the Renaissance, and modern times. Not only can you see famous paintings like the *Mona Lisa*, shown in Figure 7.7, you can also learn about Egyptian antiquities, Islamic art, sculpture, prints, drawings, and more. Find out how collections were formed, learn about the museum's past, and find visitor information, including daily hours, tours for disabled persons, and audio guides. This site can be viewed in English, French, Spanish, or Portuguese.

Kyoto National Museum
www.kyohaku.go.jp

At the home page of the Kyoto National Museum in Tokyo, you can learn about East Asian Art through descriptions of the museum's permanent exhibits of scrolls, ink paintings, sculptures, and ceramics. Museum theater hours, upcoming lectures, and admission fees are also available. The site calls its museum dictionary a young person's guide to Asian art basics, but it's great for adults as well.

Things To Do, Places To See

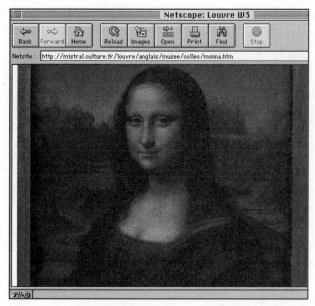

Figure 7.7   The Mona Lisa online.

Uffizi
fortuna.italia.com/televisual/uffizi/index.html

Visit the virtual Uffizi, the online version of the gallery in Florence, Italy (shown in Figure 7.8), to get a lesson in art history. You'll find extensive information, including photos, on the museum's numerous paintings and the artists who painted them, from da Vinci to Rembrandt, from Flemish to Florentine masters. Learn about famous works such as the *Baptism of Christ* and the *Birth of Venus*, and brush up on your art vocabulary through the interactive glossary—visual examples included.

Travel Byte

If you plan to visit temples, cathedrals, churches, or mosques, wear long sleeves and full-length pants or skirts. Many religious centers prohibit entrance to visitors not wearing proper attire.

Museum And Gallery Online Directories

Visit the following Web sites for connections to hundreds of online museums and art galleries from all over the world.

Figure 7.8 Brush up on your art history at the Uffizi Web site.

World Wide Arts Resources
wwar.com/towns/index.html

Click on any of the numerous U.S. or foreign cities listed on this site and find links to art galleries, museums, and exhibitions spanning the globe, as well as Web sites for art festivals at your destination. You can also search for museums by type, such as classical, contemporary, or native art, or by the name of the gallery you're interested in.

Hands-On Science Centers Worldwide
www.cs.cmu.edu/%7Emwm/sci.html

This page will direct you to the Web sites of science museums, with an emphasis on interactive education. You'll find links to numerous museums in Asia, Australia, Europe, and North America, including the Singapore Science Center, the Israel National Museum of Science, the Calgary Science Center, and the Pacific Science Center in Seattle.

Impact Guide to Museums on the Web
www.sils.umich.edu/impact/Museums

At this online directory, you'll find links to museums of archeology, architecture, art, history, natural history, and science and technology, located all over the world. Find the Web sites of museums at your destination by using the World Map Locator, or by browsing a regional list. This site uses icons to let you know which museum Web sites offer online exhibits and virtual tours.

Virtual Library Museum Pages
www.icom.org/vlmp

This site will connect you to the Web sites of numerous children's museums, art galleries, aviation museums, planetariums, and more. You'll also find links to regional and topical directories. Icons signal recommended online museums, and while new museum links are added to this site almost daily, there are also lists of museums in many locations that don't yet have an Internet presence.

Museum Online Resource Review
www.okc.com/morr

This guide to museums on the Web will connect you to botanical gardens, nature centers, planetariums, science centers, art galleries, and more. You'll find Web sites for museums of history, archeology, paleontology and geology, art, and aquatics. Search by keywords in a museum's description and find links to newsgroups and email lists as well.

Museums Around the World
www.museumca.org/usa

This site is chock full of links to Web sites of museums worldwide. The exhaustive list of links is organized by country, and by state within the U.S. From the most famous museums in Paris, to small, out-of-the-way *museos* in Chile, the search engine will link you to the museums you'd like to visit on your trip.

Travel Byte

Many museums and galleries are open late at least once a week. Visit during the evening hours to avoid crowds.

Playing It Safe

Nothing puts a damper on a vacation like having a run-in with a pickpocket and having all your belongings stolen by a grade-A thief. Protect yourself on your travels by staying aware of your surroundings and keeping a sharp eye on your belongings.

If you plan to travel abroad, visit the Web site of the U.S. State Department (**travel.state.gov**) for information on common crimes targeted at tourists in the county you plan to visit. Besides public announcements on bomb threats and anti-American violence, you'll find out about dangers that are not considered severe but should be kept in mind when you're visiting. You'll find information on the locations and types of crimes known to occur in your particular destination, such as where pickpockets frequently target travelers, and if car theft is a common occurrence. Road safety tips and other useful travel information can also be found here.

Here are some other ideas on how to stay safe no matter where you're headed:

- The number one way to protect yourself is to avoid looking like a tourist. Thieves know that tourists are often carrying expensive cameras, traveler's checks, passports, and lots of money. Try to blend in with others around you so you're not an obvious target (no plaid shorts).

- Brand name and expensive luggage is an eye-catching item for thieves— don't buy it at all, or keep it at home.

- Hide your belongings. Expensive cameras and purses swinging in the breeze are tempting objects for pickpockets and thieves. Wallets bulging in back pockets are also easy targets. Hide your camera strap and camera under your clothing, and wear a neck wallet (as mentioned in Chapter 4) as you would a necklace to hide your important documents and money under your clothing.

- Keep a small amount of money (in small bills) in your front pockets for cabs, entrance fees, and so on. Then when you buy something, you won't have to reveal where most of your money and valuables are hidden.

- Never count your money in public.

- Never leave your bags unattended.

- While small backpacks come in handy to hold water bottles, maps, and extra socks or jackets, avoid storing valuables in them. Their accessible back pockets are easy for thieves to get to, and you may not notice the tampering until it's too late. Once when traveling in Italy, a friend had the bottom of her backpack cut open and her wallet taken; she didn't know until she went to pay for something and found her money gone.

- If you're a traveler on the move, carry a few small but sturdy padlocks with you. You may want to store your luggage in airport or train station lockers for the day while you're exploring, and these lockers often require you to provide your own lock.

Travel Byte

If you are pickpocketed, have your bags stolen, or are accosted in any way, go straight to the local police station. If you are in a foreign country, go to the nearest U.S. embassy or consulate.

Theater On The Web

Do you plan on taking in a Tony-award-winning drama on your trip? How about a musical or two? Many travelers attend theatrical performances for evening recreation, others make it the focal point of their entire trip. Whatever your interest, viewing live performances is worthwhile and enjoyable entertainment. And sitting in a theater will keep you off your tired feet for a few hours!

A visit to the Web can provide you with information on what shows are running in London's West End or on Broadway in New York. But you don't need to visit these playhouse meccas to attend encore-worthy performances. Traveling troupes visit cities all over the world with experienced and skilled actors, directors, and technicians, so celebrated productions can be enjoyed by theater lovers everywhere. You can find out about specific plays and musicals through their individual sites on the Web: Search by the name of the show you want to attend, as in *Sunset Boulevard* (**www.sunset-tour.com**), seen in Figure 7.9, and you can find out if it will be showing at your destination.

Many cities house top-notch small theater companies and community theater groups. Attending these performances supports the community and local artists of your destination, and gives you a chance to experience theater native to the area. In college towns and cities with universities, you can attend exceptional productions that feature budding actors and playwrights, and often you can participate in lively discussions about the performance afterward. These small-scale productions are great bargains and definitely worth the ticket price, which can't always be said for many of the shows running on Broadway.

Whether you plan to attend an Andrew Lloyd Webber runaway hit, a small experimental performance in Seattle, Washington, or a Shakespeare festival in Stratford, Ontario, you can find information about them through the Internet's

238 Chapter 7

Figure 7.9 Virtual Broadway on the Web.

interactive theater directories. Find out where certain productions are running, or look up your vacation spot to see what will be showing while you're there. You'll find plot summaries and reviews from top critics in the business, practical information on show times and ticket prices, and details about the venues, such as seating plans so you can choose the best seat in the house. You can even purchase your tickets on the Web. Find all this and more on the sites listed below.

Playbill On-Line
www.playbill.com

To get the big picture on the theater world, visit this site, shown in Figure 7.10. You'll find news on opening productions, rising stars, and new hires. Photos and audio clips of cast albums are available here, as well as interviews and profiles found in Playbill programs. Make online reservations for performances, everything from Off-Broadway to experimental shows, at more than 1,400 theaters. Get interactive—chat with other theater-goers, participate in online polls, and join the Playbill Club, which extends discounts and exclusive advance ticket offers to members.

Figure 7.10 The Playbill On-Line Web site provides news on theater productions worldwide.

Theatre Central
www.theatre-central.com

While Theatre Central is primarily a resource for actors, playwrights, and other theater professionals, you can use this site to connect to useful Web links for your trip. Find links to numerous Web sites for theaters, professional theater companies, and Shakespeare festivals, and conduct searches for events using Peekaboo, a network for theater and music events.

Broadway
eMall.Com/ExploreNY/Broadway/Bway1.html

This site provides you with *The New York Times* reviews to Broadway and Off-Broadway performances. Read rants and raves on long running shows like *Cats*, newly launched performances such as *Rent*, and current revivals like *Show Boat*. The extensive articles cover everything from story lines to individual performances. You'll need to register for The New York Times on the Web (linked to the site) to read the critiques. There's no charge, and it's worth the extra effort.

The London Theatre Guide On-Line
www.londontheatre.co.uk/online/index.html

To select the performances you want to attend while in the heart of the theater world, visit this site on London theater. There's info here on West End shows, and you can take your pick of "at a glance" summaries or detailed performance reviews. Lots of theater information can be found, including seating plans and photos of numerous theaters and productions. You can also find helpful information on disabled access, performance dates, and box office prices. Reserve your tickets from the site, and get details on theater museums and backstage tours for your trip as well.

TheatreNet
www.theatrenet.com

Read about London's theater scene at the TheatreNet Web site. Productions in-the-works and currently running performances are covered, as well as news about individual performers, producers, and production teams. You'll also find useful details on performance schedules and ticket prices, as well as background information on plots and themes.

Concert Finders

If it's the music scene you're into, you'll enjoy browsing the abundant information on hot clubs, cool jazz festivals, resounding operas, and rocking concerts on the Net. Get the scoop on any music genre that interests you, from classical to jazz, from regional symphonies to the Rolling Stones.

If you're interested in local music of the area you're visiting, find out about popular venues by searching the Web using keywords for the city where you'll be and words like "symphony," "orchestra," and "concert." The Boston Symphony Web site shown in Figure 7.11 was found when I searched with Yahoo! using keywords "Boston," and "symphony." Pretty easy.

There are numerous ways to find out about concert events for wherever you're heading. Online tourism offices can provide you with information when you inquire by email. Look up popular venues in or near your destination city like Carnegie Hall or Chicago's Ravinia Festival, shown in Figure 7.12, or look up a particular roadhouse you have in mind. Search with keywords specific to the

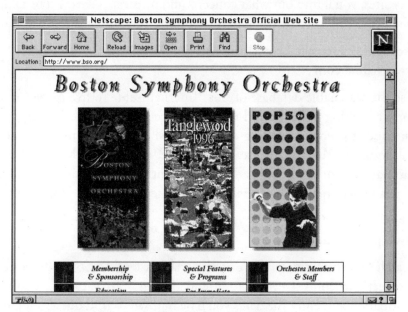

music you're looking for; for example, looking up "jazz" and "New Orleans" will get you information on numerous popular clubs in town.

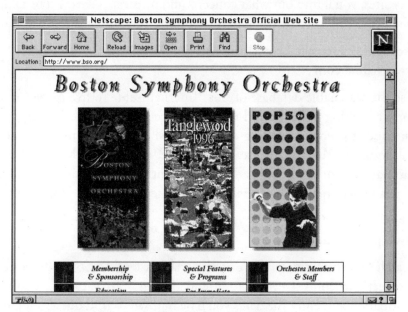

Figure 7.11   The Web site of the Boston Symphony.

Figure 7.12   Find out what's playing at the Ravinia Festival in Chicago.

In addition, you can find out about local concerts and tours heading to your vacation spot by stopping by just one or two Web sites. At these concert directory sites, you'll find out what concerts and musical events will be taking place when you're in town by just entering your destination and your vacation dates.

Worldwide Internet Live Music Archive (WILMA)
www.wilma.com

Use the searchable database of this "Internet guide to live music" to discover concerts taking place around the world (see Figure 7.13). You can get details on concert events, including dates, venues, and Yahoo! maps of the concert hall location. You can also search by artist, read "spotlights" on touring performers currently on the road, and gab with other music lovers in the chat forum to get opinions and reviews. You can even send out electronic postcards.

The Concert Hotwire
www.pollstar.com

Search by artist or venue in this site's database of 14,563 different events to discover live concert events to attend during your vacation. Look up your destination and enter the dates you'll be in town to find out about concerts by artists from Phish to the Monkees. Read the industry buzz in weekly columns, and check into the Internet's most requested concert tours.

Online Restaurants

Is pondering all this sightseeing and concert-going making you hungry? Then visit virtual restaurants to get a taste of eateries all over the globe. Many restaurants have created Web pages to offer potential customers information on their menus, atmosphere, and location. In addition, some Web sites act as restaurant directories; you enter the city where you'll be and the type of cuisine you'd like to nibble on, and the site will provide information or links to Web sites that fit your criteria.

Sites like the Zagat Dining Guide, shown in Figure 7.14, lead you to restaurants in your destination and also provide ratings and reviews on each particular dining spot. You can read critiques on the meals, the decor, and the service at restaurants in all price ranges.

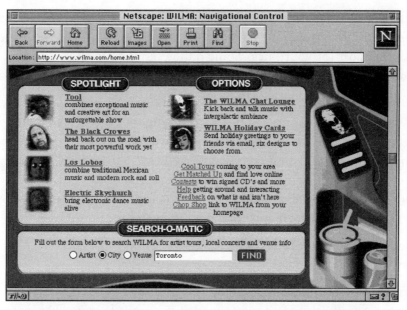

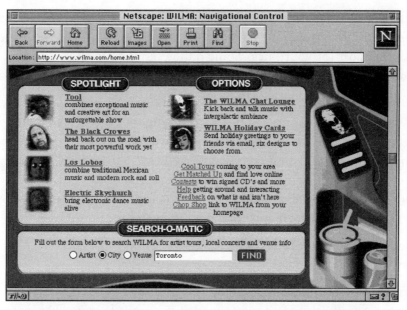

Figure 7.13 Find concerts to attend on your vacation at WILMA.

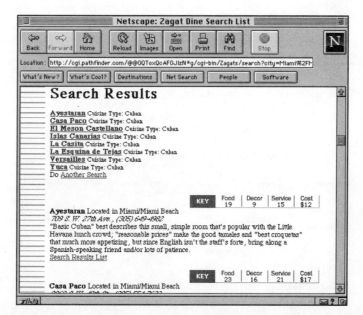

Figure 7.14 Read restaurant reviews online at the Zagat Dining Guide.

These restaurant Web sites are great for helping you find the perfect dining place in your destination. They enable you to choose the best places to dine to get the most for your buck. Some online restaurants also allow you to make your reservations from their Web sites, like you can for the restaurant in Seattle's Space Needle, shown in Figure 7.15.

While chain restaurants can be found throughout the United States, in major cities abroad, and on the Web, they can't give you a taste for the regional cuisine that locally owned restaurants can. Venture away from restaurants near highly touristed attractions to eat at local authentic eateries—you'll avoid the high prices often charged to tourists who don't know any better. These Web sites will help you locate an authentic restaurant to suite your tastes.

Fodor's Restaurant Index
www.fodors.com/ri.cgi

Visit this resourceful site to locate and read reviews of restaurants all over the planet. Specify a city and view a map of the urban layout. Then choose from a number of neighborhoods or nearby attractions to distinguish the vicinity in which you'd like to dine, or choose a restaurant by price range. You'll find

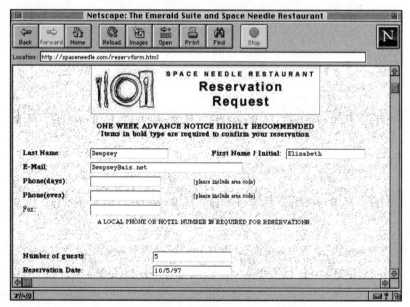

Figure 7.15 *Make your dinner reservations from the Web.*

detailed descriptions of location, atmosphere, and food; a red star denotes those restaurants that Fodor's highly recommends. Practical information, such as weekly schedules and whether reservations are necessary, is also available here.

Zagat Dining Guide
pathfinder.com/@@GQToxQcAFGJIzN*g/travel/Zagat/Dine, or go to **www.pathfinder.com**, and click on "Travel," and then "Zagat Dine."

Review ratings from the 1996 editions of the Zagat Survey books and the "Zagat Survey of America's Best Meal Deals" to find top-notch restaurants. Meals, service, and decor of each restaurant are rated on a scale of 0 to 30, and the commentary provides personal details. Find practical information for your trip including hours, accepted credit cards, and phone numbers of restaurants located in major U.S. cities, such as Boston, Honolulu, New Orleans, Los Angeles, and Miami.

Travel Byte

While seeing the sights, take time out to sit on a park bench and watch the people go by. You can learn a lot about a city or culture just by observing the men, women, and children of the region. A people-watching picnic lunch, with provisions bought from a local market or deli, is inexpensive and relaxing, and can provide the entertainment for a whole afternoon.

CuisineNet
www.cuisinenet.com

Visit the Restaurant Central department on this site to browse lists of restaurants in Boston, New York, San Francisco, Seattle, and Chicago. Search by neighborhood; food style, from barbecue to Californian; and type of eatery, including diners, brew pubs, and coffee shops. You'll find information on everything from dress codes to daily hours, as well as descriptions of atmosphere and ambiance. The site sorts your search results by ratings for food, wine, and value, and you can donate your own two cents: rate restaurants you've visited in your travels by filling out a survey. Columns from gourmet chefs and chat forums are also available.

Gayot's Guides
www.gayot.com

Read reviews of suggested restaurants in New York, Chicago, Los Angeles, Washington D.C., and New Orleans. Search by restaurant name, or by your dining preferences—select a preferred neighborhood, cuisine type, price range, and accepted credit cards; then read the recommendations, which detail atmosphere and choice items on the menu. Location and contact information is provided. You can even be a food critic and contribute restaurant reviews from your travels.

Dining Out on the Web
www.ird.net/diningout.com

This extensive list of links connects you to Web sites of restaurants around the world. These sites, sometimes in other languages, are for individual restaurants, and provide menus, prices, and location information. You'll find links to other, more specific, directories, including the Worldwide Sushi Restaurant Reference and the Kosher Restaurant Database. Links to restaurant reviews can be found here also.

Dine Site
www.dinesite.com

Dine Site can link you to thousands of restaurants throughout the United States. Search by restaurant name, or by the type of meal you'd like to eat, to read menus and reviews. Food, service, atmosphere, value for your dollar, and an overall rating are provided on a scale of 1 through 10, as well as exterior photos and reviews from other Web surfers.

eaTneT
www.eatnet.com

"America's Restaurant Directory" locates numerous restaurants in the United States, as well as a few overseas. Locate restaurant information by selecting from a list of cities and cuisine type, including American, Mexican, Greek, Deli style, and Thai, or conduct a keyword search to find basic information on restaurants such as address and phone numbers.

Diner's Grapevine
www.dinersgrapevine.com

This database can connect you to information on more than 6,000 restaurants in the United States and approximately 1,000 international restaurants. Look over menus, read reviews, and view interior and exterior photos for everything from five-star restaurants to pancake houses and every type of eatery in between. Search by atmosphere (festive, elegant, very European), price range, entertainment (singing waiters, live music), and type of cuisine. Location maps are available, and you can also check out the featured restaurant of the day.

Richards Restaurant Ranking
www.lagerling.se/rest.html

Want to dine out in style? This site directs you to some of the best restaurants in the world. Find reviews and ratings, browse the menus, and read the history of these fine establishments. There are details here on atmosphere and entrees, including suggested appetizers, soup, sauces, and wines; in addition, find out what meals the house chefs recommend, and read about their careers.

Souvenir Shopping

From bargaining at bazaars to searching out souvenir shops, one of the favorite pastimes of many travelers is shopping. When visiting new places, you'll pick up unique items that will remind you of your trip for years to come. Don't waste your money on expensive plastic trinkets sold outside of tourist hot spots; it's a good practice to buy quality authentic merchandise made by the local people. The Web can help you find out where goods and crafts are sold, and may have the information to help you make smart buying decisions. Using keywords, such as the name of the city and the items you're looking for, you can search the Web for authorized and reputable dealers of the products you're interested in.

The following list contains popular souvenir suggestions for shopping-savvy travelers. Look for Web sites on these products to find stores that sell genuine mementos from wherever you're going:

- Austria: wooden crafts, knitwear, ski gear
- Denmark: pewter, linens

- France: perfume, clothing
- Germany: clocks, wooden crafts, ceramics
- Greece: jewelry, rugs, pottery
- Hungary: porcelain, leather items
- Israel: religious objects, carpets
- Italy: glassware, leather goods
- Morocco: copper jewelry, carpets
- Spain: lace, pottery
- Switzerland: chocolate, music boxes, watches
- Turkey: carpets, perfumes, copper objects
- United Kingdom: whisky, crystal, tweeds

If you would like to purchase a souvenir from your virtual travels, stop by Web sites that sell authentic merchandise online. Web pages of stores and catalogs often sell imported goods from foreign countries, or regional products made in the United States. The Sovietski Collection (**www.sovietski.com**), seen in Figure 7.16, sells authentic goods from the former Soviet Union.

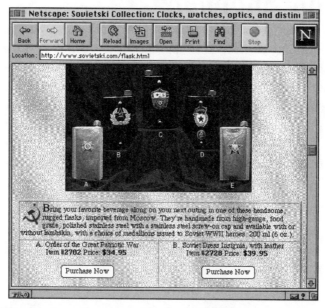

Figure 7.16 Purchase imported goods on the Web.

Travel Byte

Try to purchase souvenirs that you can carry home with you. Shipping merchandise home often results in broken mementos and a large bill. If you must ship your souvenirs, it's a good idea to purchase insurance on the shipment.

More For Your Travels

There are plenty of other Web resources for tourists to use to plan their trips and bypass hassles. Discover ways to save while on the road in Chapter 8. For information particular to those who are traveling to foreign countries, details on traveler's checks, passports, and exchanging currency can be found in Chapter 9. If you're still hungry for more on eating out, look to Chapter 13, where you can find out about America's time-tested diners.

Dollars And Sense: Traveling On A Budget

CHAPTER 8 TOPICS

- STRAP ON A PACK AND GO

- LAST-MINUTE TRAVEL BARGAINS

- PREPARING A BUDGET

- FLYING COURIER AND STAYING
  AT HOSTELS

- VOLUNTEER TRIPS, WORKING ABROAD,
  AND STUDENT TRAVEL

Whether you need to save a few hundred dollars on a trip to Cairo, or you only have a few hundred to spend on a trip to Yellowstone, there are a vast number of Web sites that can help you save. This chapter is tailored to those who want to spend the minimum, but still have the desire to see the world.

It can be done—and it doesn't mean you have to give up cleanliness or risk your safety to do so. In fact, traveling for less has many other benefits besides saving cash. You're more likely to meet local people at provincial restaurants, on park benches, and riding public transportation, than in exclusive restaurants and on guided tours. And staying in hostels gives budget-conscious explorers a chance to meet other travelers from all over the world.

In this chapter you'll learn more about shoestring travel, in addition to finding out how to spend less no matter where you're going or what your travel style happens to be. Web sites of hostels, courier flight organizations, and global volunteer programs can help make traveling on a budget easy to arrange.

A Pack On Your Back And The Open Road Ahead

You see them wandering city streets with maps in hand, hiking boots laced up, and large, colorful backpacks strapped on: Travelers across the globe have turned to backpacking for flexible, inexpensive travel. To accommodate these world stompers, budget travel companies, youth hostels, and travel gear stores, not to mention related Web sites, are popping up at an unprecedented rate. Once considered vagabond travelers, backpackers are now thought of as the average tourist. People of every age group have taken this economical approach to seeing the world, realizing that less can actually mean more when it comes to spending money on vacation.

If your idea of experiencing a foreign country doesn't include observing its people and places through a tour bus window, backpacking may be for you. A communal outlook comes with the territory of shoestring travel: from sharing a room with six other travelers at a hostel in Santiago, Chile, to chatting with the owners of a mom-and-pop cafe in Naples, Italy, there's a "let's get to know you" feeling about this easy-going style of globe-trotting.

The Web is a great resource for learning about the ins and outs of backpacking. There are Web sites, including the one in Figure 8.1, with information on

Figure 8.1 One of the many sites about backpacking on the Web.

hostels, new travel products, and features on everything from doing laundry in the sink to buying rail passes. Check out the following Web sites to learn more:

Backpackers.com
www.backpackers.com

Keep in touch on the road by registering with Backpackers.com. This site offers a free email box to each backpacker who stops by the site. This enables you to send and receive email messages from wherever you are (great for use in cyber cafes). You'll also find links here to Bazaar, an online magazine featuring intriguing first-hand accounts of backpacking trips throughout the world.

Izon's Backpacker Journal
ourworld.compuserve.com/homepages/izon/e-mail.htm

This site is brought to you by Lucy Izon, writer of the syndicated column "Backpack and Budget." Here you'll find budget travel information, including helpful advice on trip preparation, and updates on travel gear, hostels, and budget tours. Read contributions from backpackers on wonderful and not-so-wonderful travel experiences. You'll find information on locations and services of cyber cafes worldwide, as well as links to Izon's columns in the *L.A. Times* and the *Toronto Star*.

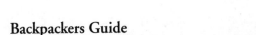

Backpackers Guide
www.geocities.com/Yosemite/6241/backpackers_guide.htm

Follow lots of useful links from this site to help prepare for your trip. You'll find links to cybercafes, online guides, budget travel info, and Web sites for backpackers. The site also lists youth hostels, including links, and provides brief but information-packed summaries of accommodations.

Backpackers Index
www.ozemail.com.au/%7Ebackpack

This site provides lots of links for backpackers heading to Australia. Click on links to hostel affiliations, maps, magazines, and other sites of interest. Communicate with other backpackers on the message board. You'll hook up with travel companions and find budget travel ideas, hostel recommendations, and information on trails in and outside of Australia.

Ro's Essentials of Backpacking
www.edu.yorku.ca/~tcs/~sjacobs/bp-ing.htm

Are you a backpacking newbie? Then read the author's personal account at this site to learn more about it. You'll find information on good times to travel, places to visit, and how much money to take with you, as well as sleeping and eating along the way. The site also offers links to other backpacking sites.

Eurotrip
www.eurotrip.com

This site caters to budget travelers planning to tour "the continent." Abundant tips, recommendations, and travel stories are provided from backpackers who have traveled the world. Read useful advice about sleeping at hostels, saving your money, and staying safe on the road. Post your questions on the discussion board and after your travels, vote for your favorite "happening hostel." You can also subscribe to the Eurotrip newsletter to receive budget travel information via email.

Tap Online
www.taponline.com/tap/travel

Plenty of travel information is packed into this site, shown in Figure 8.2. You'll find hostel listings, including a special pick, and featured topics such as spring

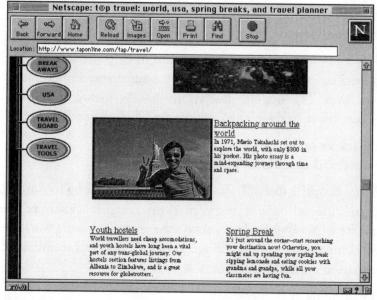

Figure 8.2 Read accounts from other travelers at the Tap Online Web site.

break getaways. Firsthand recommendations on what to do, what to eat, where to stay, and how much you can expect to spend are provided. Visit the message board to hear from others about accommodations, recommendations, and destinations.

Backpacking in Australia
www.ida.com.au/backpackers

Find extensive information here on what to see and do while backpacking through Australia. This site provides details on zoos, gardens, and harbors, as well as places to stay, and there's a search engine to help you find hostel and location information quickly. Backpacking in Australia also provides useful tips on such subjects as getting a visa and dialing Australia from the United States. "The Wall" message board lets you post messages and arrange travel plans with others.

Campus Traveler
www.campustravel.co.uk

You'll find articles at this site written by backpackers on a budget. Topics include treks through Bolivia, Havana, and Africa; hitchhiking experiences; and saving money. You can view photos taken during these adventures in the site's library, or place an ad for accommodations or travel companionship if you need to.

Travel Byte

If you plan to carry a backpack, carry as little in it as possible. It may seem light now, but it won't after you've lugged it with you for a week! Before you leave on your trip, remove half of the items you packed in the first place. Otherwise you'll end up doing just that in a foreign trash can, never to see your hefty belongings again.

Budget Building

When planning a budget, it's good to be ambitious, but be sure to be realistic as well. Worrying about running out of money when you're only halfway through your itinerary can put a damper on your trip. A good rule of thumb is to take 20 to 25 percent more money with you than your budget suggests, in case you run into unexpected expenses (and just to keep your mind at ease).

Don't forget to include pre-trip costs in your budget, like that new ski jacket you just can't go without or the sunscreen you need to pick up at the drug store. Any costs associated with acquiring your passport, hostel membership card, or other similar items should also be factored in. And watch out for impulse buying in anticipation of your trip; on top of the costs of absolute necessities, this can empty out your pockets before you even get to the airport.

Travel expenses, a critical item in your vacation budget, can be estimated by checking out the Web sites of airlines and auto rental companies found in Chapter 5. Let's consider a hypothetical spring trip to California. Looking up the airfares to San Francisco from a few airlines or airline consolidators can give me a rough idea of how much it will cost to get there, as shown in Figure 8.3. I'd then add that ballpark figure into my budget.

To estimate the daily expenses I'll incur on my journey, I'd check out the nightly rates of hotels and hostels at my destination and multiply the estimated cost of a nightly stay by the number of nights I expect to be on the road.

Don't forget to include the entrance fees for museums, or the ticket prices of sporting events, theater performances, or whatever, in your budget. These can all be found by visiting the Web sites mentioned in Chapter 7.

Doing all this research gave me the information shown in Table 8.1, so I could better budget my trip.

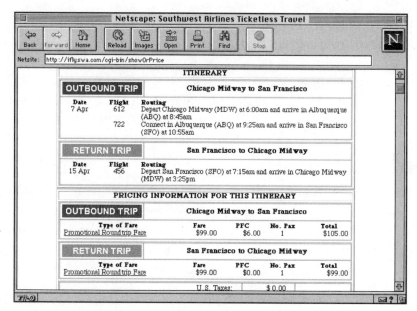

Figure 8.3 Use the Web to plan your travel budget.

Table 8.1 Vacation cost comparison chart—Chicago to San Francisco—Tuesday, April 7–Wednesday, April 15.

Airline	Fare
Southwest Airlines (www.ifltswa.com)	$204.00 (Promotional Fare)
Delta Airlines (www.delta-air.com)	$438.55

Accomodations	Nightly Rate
HI Hostel at Fisherman's Wharf (www.hostels.com/hostels/hostel.menu.html)	$13-$15
Marriott at Fisherman's Wharf (www.marriott.com)	Lowest rate available $179

Things to Do	Cost
Afternoon in Golden Gate Park	Free
Check out Golden Gate Bridge	Free
Visit San Francisco Museum of Modern Art (www.sfmoma.org)	$7 (Thursday 5P.M.-9P.M. 1/2 price = $3.50)
Tour Alcatraz (www.nps.gov/alcatraz)	$12.00
Explore Chinatown	Free

(continued)

| Table 8.1 | Vacation cost comparison—Chicago to San Francisco—Tuesday, April 7–Wednesday, April 15 (continued). |

Things to Do	Cost
Visit the San Francisco Zoo (www.sfzoo.com)	$7.00
Stroll Haight-Ashbury	Free
Investigate San Francisco's Exploratorium (www.exploratorium.com)	First Wednesday of every month is free; other days: $9.00

How much you can expect to spend day-to-day varies with each person and individual travel style. Daily expenses also depend on where you'll be—a jaunt through Jakarta costs a whole lot less than a visit to Venice. To get an idea of what other travelers have spent on their visits to your chosen destination, visit the travel-related newsgroups listed in Chapter 2.

Check out these Web sites to get tips on how to hang on to your change during your vacation:

Shoestring Travel
www.stratpub.com

This "e-zine of inexpensive travel," shown in Figure 8.4, is jam-packed with useful travel links. Read articles on budget travel and excerpted clips from travel news groups. You'll read about restaurants, hotels, and things to see and do, and find recommendations of campgrounds, information on walking tours, and listings of hostels.

European Travel Network
www.etn.nl/index.html

This non-profit organization offers links to Web sites of numerous consolidators, tour operators, and discount travel agents. You'll find connections here to bargain air fares, discount accommodations, and cheap cruises. Order an ETN discount card online.

Tips for the Shrewd Traveler
www.travelsecrets.com/tricks01.htm

The advice offered at this site ranges from preventing Montezuma's revenge with Pepto-Bismol, to "Getting the best for less at hotels." Find tips on safety,

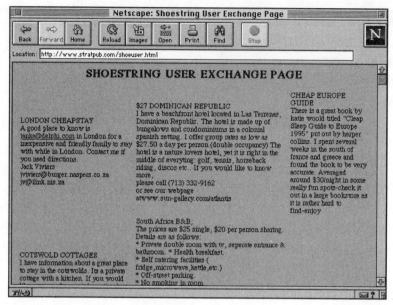

Figure 8.4 Advertise your bargains on the Shoestring User Exchange Page.

shopping at duty-free stores, and getting the best deal on air fares, and read the "Traveler Beware" section to find out what *not* to do on your vacation. You can also find out what discounts may be available, such as the many bargains offered to seniors.

Traveler Savings Site
home/sprynet.com/sprynet/inetmktg

Useful links can be found all over this Web page. From here you can connect to sites about student travel, budget accommodations, discount clubs, and "hot deals." This site has articles on air consolidators and last-minute travel clubs, and you can also subscribe to the free Traveler Savings Ezine.

Down To The Minute

Last-minute bargains from the Web just can't be beat. As mentioned in previous chapters, unsold hotel rooms and airline seats are offered for well below standard prices—up to 70 percent off the lowest rates. Hilton (**www.hilton.com**) and Radisson (**www.radisson.com**) hotels offer Web surfers weekly deals on rooms. TWA (**www.twa.com**) and Northwest Airlines (**www.nwa.com**) offer similar discounts on flights—and US Air (**www.usair.com**) and American

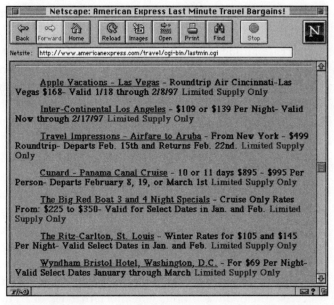

Figure 8.5 Discover last minute travel bargains at the American Express Web site.

Airlines (**www.americanair.com**) will even send you their weekly specials via email. General travel sites, like American Express (**www.americanexpress.com/travel**), shown in Figure 8.5, offer weekly last-minute deals on airline flights, cruises, hotels, and even travel packages. Check these sites to see if the specified travel times and destinations fit into your travel plans.

Top Ten Ways To Spend Less On Your Trip

- Choose low-cost destinations. In countries like Mexico, India, Indonesia, and the Czech Republic, the U.S. dollar is strong, so you'll get more for your buck.

- Travel during the off-season and save 25 to 50 percent on airfare, hotel stays, and cruises. Visit Colorado's ski country during the summer when ski slopes become hiking wonderlands, instead of during the expensive peak winter season, or travel to Europe during the winter to avoid the summer's tourist invasion and inflated prices.

- Watch for price hikes during highly popular events. Hotel proprietors in Pamplona, Spain know tourists will pay almost any price for a room during the festival of "Los Sanfermines" and the running of the bulls.

- Purchase airline tickets on the Web either 30 days or more before your vacation, or just a day or two ahead of time, in order to receive more than 50 percent off standard fares. Another way to save up to 50 percent is to purchase your tickets through a travel consolidator or fly with a discount airline like Reno Air or Southwest Airlines. To save even more, fly to overseas destinations as an air travel courier. See the section "Courier Flights," later in this chapter.

- Ask for the lowest price available. Inquire about discounted rates, promotional deals, and special packages when booking your airplane tickets, hotel room, and rental car. The traveler who is too embarrassed to inquire will end up paying more than the person who has the chutzpah to ask. Low and discounted rates are out there—you just have to be proactive to receive them. In addition, remember that it's okay to walk away from a price that you think is too expensive, or is more than you had included in your budget.

- Use discount brokers when booking your hotel accommodations to save up to 65 percent off of standard room rates. To save even more, stay at youth hostels, or spend your nights beneath the stars at a campground (more on camping in Chapter 12).

- Avoid tourist traps. Attractions with costly extras, like a boat ride in Amsterdam during which your picture is taken and sold to you at the end of the cruise for a hefty sum, can lure the foolish, and suck your neck wallet dry.

- Restaurants and hotels with flashy signs promoting an English speaking staff and acceptance of major credit cards often charge high rates to unsuspecting tourists. Go local to get the best deals— choose restaurants and hotels in untouristed neighborhoods.

- Bypass the perfect location and spend your nights out of town; room rates decrease the farther you travel from popular locales. Bed and breakfasts can be expensive in tourist towns like Williamsburg—staying in a neighboring town can reduce the cost of your accommodations by up to 15 percent.

- Cut the cost of getting around town by using public transportation. Rental cars and cab rides are pricy. Ride for less on buses, ferries, commuter trains, and underground metro systems. It can save you a bundle by the end of your trip.

Budget Travel Guides

Many location-specific guidebooks have been written especially for the budget backpacker. Series of books like Let's Go, Lonely Planet, The Berkeley Guides, Europe Through the Back Door, and The Rough Guides, have been staples of travelers' journeys for years. But you no longer need to buy them to read much of their information: These online guidebooks provide helpful tips, point out great attractions to visit, and clue you in to cheap places to stay, right from their Web sites, such as the one shown in Figure 8.6. Some of these sites even reprint the exact text from the guidebooks.

Specific details on each individual Web site are provided in Chapter 3; I'll list the URLs again here for your convenience:

- *The Berkeley Guide to Europe*—**www.tripod.com/bin/travel/browser/europe**
- *Europe Through the Back Door*—**www.ricksteves.com**
- *Let's Go*—**www.letsgo.com**
- *Lonely Planet*—**www.lonelyplanet.com**
- *The Rough Guide*—**www.hotwired.com/rough**

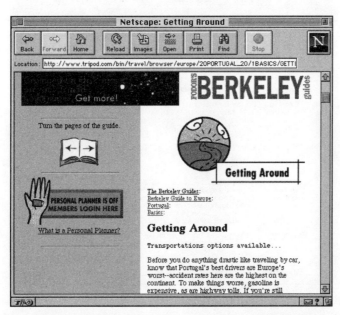

Figure 8.6 Read reviews and recommendations from online budget travel publications.

Travel Passes

While renting and driving a car through Europe can be extremely pricy, travel by train using a Eurail pass, as shown in Figure 8.7, is very reasonable—a great option for the budget-minded traveler. In addition, British Rail, German Rail, and France Rail also offer rail passes for economical travel.

These bus and rail passes have been so successful that major airline companies are offering similar options to travelers. Now you can purchase books of flight coupons that let you hop from destination to destination without paying an exorbitant price.

The EuroFlyer pass provides discounted travel within Europe on airlines such as Air France. Transbrazil offers the Brazil Airpass, Scandinavian Airlines sells a Visit Scandinavia Pass that covers flights within Denmark, Sweden, and Norway, and Quantas Airlines offers The Australia Explorer pass.

These passes have rules and regulations that you need to understand before you buy. Air passes, as with rail passes, can only be used with a certain time frame, ranging from three weeks to a month or two. These passes are only

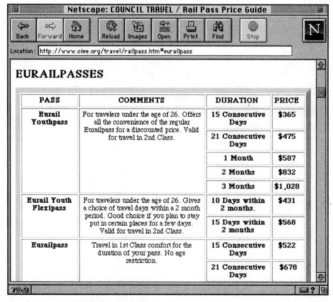

Figure 8.7 Find out about cheap ways to get around town from travel Web sites.

available to U.S. citizens. Find out about these exclusive offers and take advantage of them!

Email airlines for more information on overseas passes. For more information on rail passes, look under "Train Travel" in Chapter 5, or contact the rail companies directly.

Courier Flights

One of the biggest items preventing budget-conscious travelers from exploring the world abroad is the expensive plane ticket. A great way to get a cheap seat overseas is by traveling as an air courier. International express delivery companies hire couriers to check priority shipments through as luggage, instead of sending them as cargo. It's cheaper for a courier company to do it this way, and it prevents the shipment from sitting in customs for days.

As a courier, you check shipping documents on international flights in exchange for an inexpensive ticket price. Couriers can receive up to 85 percent off of standard airline fares. In fact, couriers may fly for free if they've been hired at the last minute!

Couriers fly with major airlines like British Airways and United Airlines, and fly like any other passenger in a standard coach seat. One drawback is that your luggage may be severely restricted—at most you will be allowed to check only one suitcase. Carry-on bags are allowed, which is great for those who are smart about packing light.

You are not liable for the documents being shipped by courier companies. Most of the time representatives of the company check the shipment at the airport and pick it up after the flight.

Nearly every assignment provides a round trip ticket, and you are allowed a stay of 7 days or more at your destination. You can arrange to fly with a non-courier companion on the same flight, or arrange to fly as couriers on consecutive flights so you both get bargain-basement deals.

When I had a week of vacation time coming to me, on a whim I decided to pop over the pond and make a visit to London, one of my favorite cities in Europe. I arranged a round-trip courier flight from Chicago's O'Hare Airport to London's Heathrow for $350. I received a contract and airport information via fax from the courier broker and a week later I showed up at the airport at my scheduled time, met with the courier representative, and off I flew for an exhilarating week exploring the city of Beefeaters, double-decker buses, and Big Ben. When I'm done writing this book, I plan to fly another courier flight—this time to Hong Kong!

The following Web sites will link you to information on becoming a courier.

International Association of Air Travel Couriers
www.courier.org

The IAATC provides visitors to its Web site with lots of information on flying as a courier. Read the FAQ for details on logistics, benefits, and regulations, and find out what other travelers have to say about their courier experiences. If you're interested in becoming an IAATC member, fill out the online registration form. You can also find out how to get daily information on last-minute bargain flights.

Worldwide Courier Association
www.wallstech.com

This Web site answers such common questions as "Where can I fly?", "Do I have to fly alone?", and "From what U.S. cities do courier flights depart?" Visitors can listen to an audio clip or a watch a video clip of what Robin Leach has to say about the company, and you can become a member of the Worldwide Courier Association from the site.

The Air Courier Association
www.aircourier.org

Visit the Web site of The Air Courier Association, as shown in Figure 8.8. Get a rundown of what's expected of couriers, restrictions, and how to get started. The site provides examples of last minute specials on flights to Bangkok, London, Milan, Rio de Janeiro, and more. You can also read information on becoming a member.

IBC Pacific, Inc.
www.ibcpac.com

If you're interested in courier travel to Asia, visit this site. You can fly cheap to Thailand, the Philippines, Korea, Hong Kong, Singapore, and Japan. Read about the company, and take a look at the FAQ for ticket prices and the length

Figure 8.8 The home page of the Air Courier Association.

of time you'd be allowed stay at a particular destination. You'll also find specifics on what you'll need to know as a courier, such as how much baggage you can take with you, and the logistics of checking the company's documents.

FAQ

The Air Courier Association, discussed earlier, locates available air couriers for the international freight industry, and keeps members informed about travel opportunities and discounted fares. The association's FAQ answers common questions regarding air courier travel. It can be found on the World Wide Web at **www.aircourier.org**. The following questions and answers are excerpted from their FAQ:

Q. What does an air courier do?

A. A freelance air courier is a person who accompanies time-sensitive business cargo that is checked as excess passenger baggage on international flights. This is how a majority of overnight international mail and parcels get to foreign countries. The big name freight retailers that pick up from businesses do not have enough cargo to justify sending a jetliner to a foreign city themselves.

Q. What exactly am I expected to do?

A. Show up at the airport on time, meet the courier company representative at a predetermined airport location, usually the gate where your flight leaves, and deliver the On Board Courier Pouch to the courier company employee in the customs area of your arrival airport. Then you are on your own.

Q. Any restrictions?

A. You must be at least 18 years old, have a valid passport, wear nice casual clothes or business attire and be punctual. Blue jeans are allowed if they are pressed, clean and not torn or faded. Drinking while on courier duty is frowned upon. Children are not allowed to accompany onboard couriers.

Q. What kind of people fly as freelance air couriers?

A. Our members come from all walks of life. There are no hard rules concerning who can or can't fly as a freelance courier. Many of our members are students, retirees, teachers, outdoor enthusiasts, hobbyists, business owners, entrepreneurs, adventure travelers, and people in freelance occupations such as travel writers, importers, exporters, photographers, and persons exploring overseas markets.

Q. When are my courier duties over?

A. As soon as you deliver the On Board Courier Pouch you are finished. You do not have to make any deliveries. Sometimes you will act as courier on the return flight to the U.S. Once you clear through customs, you are on your own.

Q. Is there any chance of being caught with an illegal shipment checked as my baggage?

A. Absolutely not. Courier freight companies have been in business for many years and are well known by customs officials. All shipments are inspected before departure. In fact, you are never allowed to handle the freight. The entire operation is aboveboard. A freelance courier just carries the paperwork, a job that doesn't exactly require a Ph.D. in nuclear physics.

Travel Byte

Sleep the night away on overnight flights, bus rides, and train trips to save extra cash.

Hitching A Ride

I don't recommend hitchhiking. In fact, I think it's a really, really stupid thing to do. But lots of travelers do it, despite the potential risks of having your belongings stolen and being assaulted, among other things. That said, there are Web sites that provide advice on hitchhiking for those who want to risk it. One of them is:

Hitchhiking Abroad
www.umich.edu/~icenter/hitching.htm

This guide to hitchhiking provides advice on how to carry signs, what to bring with you, and basic hitchhiker etiquette. Information on staying safe is included, with advice such as "keep luggage close at hand." The site also lists the best and worst countries in which to try thumbing it.

Hostels

For basic accommodations at the right price, stay at hostels, often referred to as youth hostels. They are found the world over—in Japan, Israel, Zimbabwe, even the good ol' U.S. of A. And despite the name, they are open to people of all ages.

Communal living is the standard at hostels. Most rooms are shared with other guests—you could be calling six to twenty other travelers "roomie" for the night. Men and women are often housed in separate quarters, but some hostels do offer double rooms or provide a room for a family to share.

Many hostels have kitchens, complete with cooking utensils and pots and pans, for preparing nearly-home-cooked meals. Others serve inexpensive meals to overnight guests. Large comfortable common rooms give guests a place to relax, chat with other travelers, and play cards.

Hostels come in all shapes and sizes. Converted windmills, lighthouses, and dude ranches make these budget accommodations unique and much more than just a roof over your head. While exploring Scotland, I stayed at a hostel at the foot of Ben Nevis, the U.K.'s highest peak. The cozy lodge was a welcome respite after a long day of hiking up and down the mountainside. Hostels are filled with bohemian travelers, with a spirit for adventure that just can't be found at private hotels.

There are a few conditions to staying at hostels that you should keep in mind. Hostels close up shop during the day. They open in the evening for travelers to check-in and settle down, but close again at curfew, which can be as early as 10:00 pm. While pillows and blankets are provided, you are often required to purchase sheets (about a dollar per night) or use your own. Valuables should be watched and locked up tight—theft is often a problem in overcrowded rooms.

Having a hostelling membership card with you will reduce the cost of your stay, but is not required for most hostels. The Web site of the Internet Guide to Hostelling (**www.hostels.com**) can provide you with information on hostel affiliations, networks, and discount organizations, as well as contact information for hostels throughout the world. More detailed information on the pros and cons of hostelling can also be found at the site.

Independent Hostels

You can also use a Web search engine to locate independent hostels at your destination. Sites like the following provide details on rooms, facilities, nearby attractions, and more. Many hostels, whether independent or members of a network, have Web sites so travelers can find out about facilities and room rates before an expedition.

Hostal Lopez
Madrid, Spain
www.pair.com/navarro

This Web site describes the location (two blocks from the Prado), features (a renovated 19th century building), and nightly costs (including current exchange rates) of the Hostal Lopez. Read the FAQ, look at photos of the hostel and the plazas of Madrid, and print out a map of the Madrid Metro, as seen in Figure 8.9. You'll find links to other Web pages about Spain, as well. Email your reservation request, including the number in your party, the type of room needed, and your arrival and departures dates.

Hostal Las Colinas Inn
Lima, Peru
ekeko.rcp.net.pe/COLINAS

Check out what this hostel has to offer, then fill out the online reservation form to set aside a bed for your trip. Read about the city, nearby attractions,

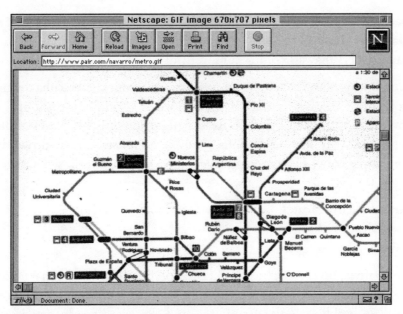

Figure 8.9   *Find the quickest route to your hostel with online maps.*

and features such as laundry facilities and refrigerators. They'll even pick you up at the airport!

Happy Valley Backpacker's Hostel
Sandton, South Africa
www.backpack.co.za

Detailed descriptions of the hostel grounds, reception area, and kitchen facilities are provided at this site. You can read about the outdoor *braai*, or barbecue, where guests mingle; view photos of gardens, the pub, and the pool room; and reserve your accommodations from the Web site. For your safety, the hostel will arrange transportation from Johannesburg for you.

Greenmont Farms Hostel
Underhill Center, Vermont
homepages.together.net/~aquila//greenmont.html

This hostel is a refurbished 19th century barn situated on a working farm. The Web site describes the farm's history, as well as the barnyard animals you'll be calling "neighbor;" nightly rates and directions are also provided. Links to Web pages of nearby activities are included, as well as an email link to submit your reservation request.

Backpackers Vacation Inn and Plantation Village
Haleiwa, Hawaii
backpackers0hawaii.com/accomod.html

Stop by this hostel's Web site for information about cheap scuba diving (shown in Figure 8.10), bike rentals, hikes, and whale watching expeditions, as well as room and board at the hostel. Read descriptions and look over photos of the three buildings: the Beach House, the Main House, and the Brown House; as well as photos of Plantation Village. Stay a week at this hostel and get the 7th night free.

Grand Pacific Hostel
San Diego, California
www.1link.com/gph

Keg parties, no curfew, free breakfasts, and beach barbecues make this hostel a haven for travelers who want to let loose. Read the history of the hostel's 100 year old building, look over photos, and check out nearby activities through Web site links. Email your reservations.

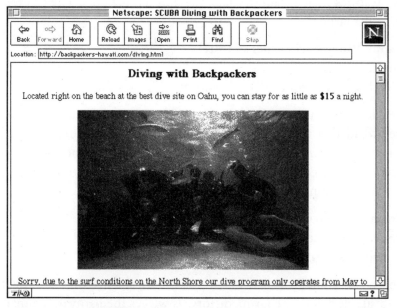

Figure 8.10 Use the Web to find out about inexpensive vacation activities.

Travel Byte

Save money at hostels by carrying a sleep-sack with you instead of renting sheets. Take a standard bed sheet, sew up the side, and *voila*!— you have your own easy-to-carry bed linens!

Hostel Directories

Use hostel directories to quickly find a hostel at your destination.

World Wide Hostel Guide
www.hostels.com/hostels/hostel.menu.html

This directory, brought to you by The Internet Guide to Hostelling, is a must-see for the world traveler needing cheap accommodations. You'll find information on hostels in Africa, Central America, Europe, and other continents. Contact information is provided, and hyperlinks connect you to hostel home pages.

Go Hostelling Online Magazine
hostel.com/~ebarnett/gohosteling.html

This online publication, produced by the co-owner of a California hostel, provides feature articles on hostelling culture and "hostel-hopping." You'll find information and links to sites about traveling along the West coast, including a list of the author's hostels of choice. There are also links to other hostels in the area and to outdoor travel pages.

Hostels Europe
www.eurotrip.com

This guide to budget travel in Europe provides information on hostels, listed according to location, with descriptions from travelers who've stayed there (including details like whether or not the showers are hot). You can also follow links to Web sites about budget travel in a particular area. Visit the discussion board for notes from other travelers about locating hostels, attractions to visit, and cycling across the countryside. Read the travel tales, and join the mailing list.

United Hostels of Europe
www.webcom.com/hostels

Visit this Web site to read up on hostels throughout Europe. You'll find informative descriptions of each hostel's atmosphere and cost, the best time of year to visit, and the advantages of the location. Check out the "Famous Five

Hostels," which include a converted three star hotel in Amsterdam and the oldest hostel in Switzerland. Your additions are welcome.

Hostelling Affiliations And Networks

While many exemplary hostels operate independently, others belong to networks or affiliations. Networks are made up of individual hostels in a particular region that associate and assist one another. Other hostels are members of affiliations that supervise their overall operations and set standards. Web pages of hostelling networks or affiliations can provide you with information on membership discounts and hostels within their association. You'll find specifics on accommodations and nightly rates.

Banana Bungalow Hostels
www.bananabungalow.com

This Web site has information on hostel location, safety, meal services, activities, and facilities such as sun decks (shown in Figure 8.11). Look at photos of room interiors and exteriors, find out the cost of accommodations, read about the company history, and get general information on hostelling. Email your questions and comments.

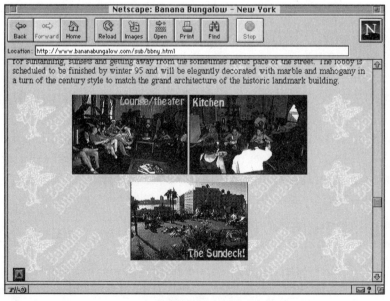

Figure 8.11   View photos of a hostel's interior and facilities.

Hostelling Russia
www.spb.su/ryh/ryha.html

Founded in 1992, Hostelling Russia gives backpackers a cheap sleep in St. Petersburg, Moscow, and other cities. This site provides lots of information for the hostel in St. Petersburg, including rates, location, and amenities, like included breakfasts and nightly movies. View pictures of the hostel, read visitor reviews, and get an online discount if you book your reservations from the site.

Budget Backpacker Hostels in New Zealand
www.backpack.co.nz

Check out numerous BBH hostels from this site, listed by the four main islands: Cook Island, North Island, South Island, and Stewart Island. Hostels include converted historic villas, general stores, lodges, farms, and hot spring resorts. Visitors can read descriptions of hostel interiors and find out about activities in the area. Check out the nightly rates, and reserve your bed via email.

Travel Byte

For news on hostelling, visit the Hostelling News page at www.hostels.com/news.

Pacific Rim Hostelling Network
hostel.com/~pacrim/pacrim.html

This network includes hostels located along the Pacific Northwest from San Diego to British Columbia, Canada. Names include "Rain Forest Hostel," "Eel River Redwoods Hostel," and "Spa International Hostel." The site offers information on eco-touring, cycling, and "hostel hopping" the area. A listing of hostels, area activity suggestions, and discount coupons can be emailed to you.

The Australian Youth Hostel Association (YHA)
www.yha.org.au

This site of one of Australia's largest hostel networks provides location information for numerous hostels on the continent. Booking information is also included, in addition to notices about YHA special-interest activities, including sailing excursions. You can also follow links to hostels around the world.

Travel Byte

Budget hotels, guest houses, pensions, family homes, monasteries, temples, and university dorms also provide inexpensive accommodations. Ask to see the room before you pay. If you feel uneasy about safety or cleanliness, move on and check out other options nearby.

Pacific Coast Hostels
www.HiHostels.com

Heading out West? Find information on hostels located in San Diego, Portland, Seattle, Vancouver, and other locations. You'll read about location, meals, activities, and facilities such as barbecues and parking. Look at the quick reference chart to see what each hostels offers its guests, and find tips for making your stay enjoyable.

Hostelling International
www.iyhf.org

This Web site of one of the largest hostel organizations offers information on hundreds of hostels. Locate national hostel offices in the part of the world you plan to visit, anywhere from Poland to Pakistan. There's also news here about new hostel openings and discount travel opportunities.

Hostelling International—British Columbia
www.virtualynx.com/bchostels

For trekkers heading up north, this site is worth a look. Find basic information on seasonal rates, guest capacity, location, and email addresses through the hostel directory. Read the FAQ, learn how to become a member, and read up on ski packages. You can also sign the guest book to join the mailing list.

Inexpensive Edibles

You don't need to spend a fortune eating out three times a day. There are plenty of easy ways to cut your spending by eating decent meals at prices you can afford. Check out these shortcuts to eating for less:

- Avoid restaurants near tourist attractions and main thoroughfares that are crowded with tourists. Look instead for eateries filled with locals for low-priced traditional meals.

- Check average meal prices by perusing menus posted in restaurant front windows.

- When dining out, order a *prix fixe* meal, which often includes bread, an appetizer, an entree, and a bottle of wine. Avoid dining "a la carte."

- Eat lunch at restaurants instead of dinner. Meal prices are often higher in the evening.

- Buy local produce, bread, cheese, and other food items from neighborhood markets for inexpensive snacks and makeshift meals. You can even picnic in a local park.

- Watch for extra charges. Sitting outside along the Avenue des Champs-Elysées can cost more than sitting inside the café. In addition, some cafés charge more for sitting at a table than they do for snacking while standing.

Freebie Finding

Many tourist attractions cost a pretty penny (or *franc*, or *peso*, depending on where you are). A gondola ride in Venice is every traveler's dream, but they're extremely pricy. An inexpensive and equally enjoyable option is taking public transportation. (I'm not kidding!) In Venice, motorized open-air canal boats, called *vaporetti*, wind along the Canale Grande. My fiancé Phil and I hopped on, leaned back, and enjoyed the city's romantic waterways, for a lot less money.

As a traveler on a budget, look for alternative activities that cost very little, or even nothing at all. Visit free attractions like the Coliseum in Rome and Speakers Corner in London's Hyde Park, and keep your eye out for freebies like a tour of Parliament's chambers in Copenhagen. Attractions like zoos, fountains, botanical gardens, and beaches are often free to visitors.

Check the Web sites of tourist attractions (see Chapter 7) to find vacation freebies.

Volunteer Excursions

Working overseas may not exactly be a vacation, but it does give you the opportunity to see the world for practically nothing. Most often, room and board are provided at the site and you pay only for your travel expenses, such as the cost of your round-trip flight. Volunteers are needed for environmental or community service projects; archeological excursions, restoring historic landmarks, and building houses in third world countries are just a few experiences that may be available. Programs vary in length, ranging anywhere from two weeks to a few months, and may require knowledge of a foreign language or project-related skills.

Beth and Mark Smith are currently teaching students in Sotik, a small village outside Nairobi, Kenya. Taking a sabbatical from their teaching jobs in Iowa City, Iowa, they left their familiar lives behind to explore the cultures, customs, and beauty of Africa. In their letters, they express how rewarding their experiences have been so far. Learning Swahili, making new friendships, and seeing the children use what they have learned is compensation enough. They've even created a Web site documenting their experience (**www.avalon.net/ ~cmissen/markbeth**).

Global Volunteers
www.globalvlntrs.org

This non-profit U.S. corporation offers one- to three-week programs to work on human and economic development projects all over the world. The site provides program information, including goals of the projects, and what's expected of volunteers. You can read retrospectives from past volunteers, and look over the FAQs such as "Is this right for me?" and "Do volunteers have any free time?"

Global Service Corps
www.earthisland.org/ei/gsc/gschome.html

The Global Service Corps offers two- to three-week project trips in Kenya, Costa Rica, Guatemala, and Thailand. View photo galleries from past programs and look into upcoming trips. You'll find specifics on dates, where you'd be staying, travel during the project, what you'd be working on, and why. You can find out how to register for a trip and read the free quarterly newsletter from the site.

Earthwatch
www.earthwatch.org

Earthwatch expeditions, based in more than 20 U.S. states and 50 countries, range from caring for chimpanzees to saving Borneo's rain forest. Search for

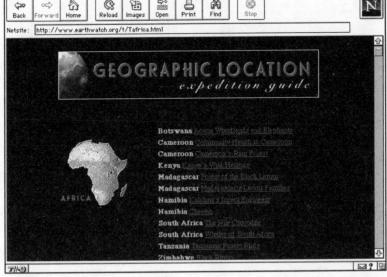

Figure 8.12 Volunteer programs are offered in locations all over the planet.

projects by location (as seen in Figure 8.12), your skills, the time of year, and the cost. Learn about research opportunities on animal behavior, archeology, ecology, endangered species, coral reefs, and more, and gather information on prices, the research area, logistics of the expedition, and the tasks you'd be involved in. You can also read accounts from others who've participated, and reserve your space on a team from the Web site.

Peace Corps
www.peacecorps.gov

If you have some extra time on your hands and want to see the world, join the Peace Corps, whose Web site is shown in Figure 8.13. Programs average two years in length, and volunteers are needed to work in agriculture, education, forestry, engineering, health, and other areas. Overseas opportunities are offered in more than 90 countries. The Peace Corps Web site includes application information, and you can contact a recruiter in your area.

Volunteer In Parks
www.nps.gov/volunteer

Learn how to be a VIP (Volunteer in Parks) at the Web site of The National Park Service. VIPs are needed in almost every one of the United State's 360

Figure 8.13 The Peace Corps home page.

parks, from Maine to Hawaii. Learn about the individual parks at this site, and find out how to apply for a position. A downloadable application is in the works.

Get A Job

Why not earn some cash while you're overseas? Immerse yourself in a foreign culture and come as close as it gets to being one of the locals. Working overseas gives you a perspective the average tourist will never get to appreciate. The following Web sites can help you in your job search in a foreign country:

Overseas Jobs Express
www.overseasjobs.com

Get linked to over 700 employment resources in approximately 40 countries, including jobs for the summer only. This online newspaper includes columns on international employment, questions to the editor, and easy search tools to find a job that's right for you. Check out the hot employment site of the week and visit the TravelLink section to meet other travelers interested in working abroad.

Cool Works
www.coolworks.com

Whether you want to volunteer your services or make some cash, abundant job opportunities (more than 21,000) await you at this site. Find the type of job you're interested in, including employment at national parks, on cruise ships, in campgrounds, and on the ski slopes. The site provides specifics on benefits, pay rates, room and board information, and recreation opportunities. Check out the slide show to see where you could wind up.

Summer Jobs
www.summerjobs.com

This free service may help you land a job in your dream location. You can search for summer employment by country and city, or conduct a keyword search to specify the type of job you're looking for. Read job descriptions to find out what skills are required, and what the salary and benefits are. Employment opportunities (shown in Figure 8.14) may include cruise line staff, au-pair services, sales people, and camp counselors, to name a few. Employer contact information is also provided.

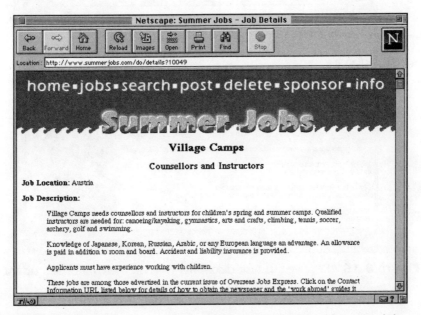

Figure 8.14 One of many employment opportunities at Summer Jobs.

Student Travel

Many college students head overseas to experience a new culture, learn a new language, experience a new lifestyle—and earn credit towards graduation in the process. Loaded with sites about international study, from non-profit travel organizations to student identification cards, the Web is a great resource for researching study-abroad programs.

International Student Travel Confederation
www.istc.org

An International Student Identification Card, shown in Figure 8.15, is proof that you're eligible for student discounts. It's used at museums, art galleries, and restaurants world wide. Find out what discounts you're eligible for by visiting this Web site. You'll read about card benefits and receive detailed information on currency, transportation, festivals, budget accommodations, and "off the beaten track" excursions at many destinations.

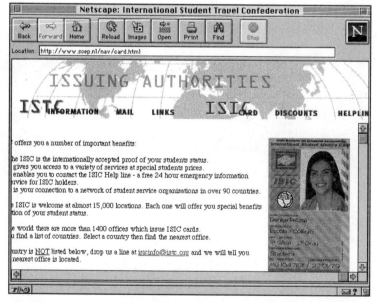

Figure 8.15 Receive student discounts with an International Student Identification Card.

Council on International Educational Exchange
www.ciee.org

Students craving travel should stop by this site, shown in Figure 8.16, to read about study-abroad programs, including locations and firsthand accounts from students who've done it. You'll also find information on volunteer service opportunities abroad, and on finding temporary employment in a foreign city. See where the CIEE offices are located world wide, and take a look at special deals and offered packages.

American Institute for Foreign Study
www.aifs.org

Read about numerous study opportunities in Asia, Australia, Europe, Latin America, and Mexico, and find information on semester programs, summer programs, scholarships, and enrollment. Want to earn some cash? Apply to be an au pair in London, Madrid, or Paris right from the Web site. If you'd like to give someone overseas an opportunity to visit the United States, you'll find information here about hosting a foreign exchange student in your home.

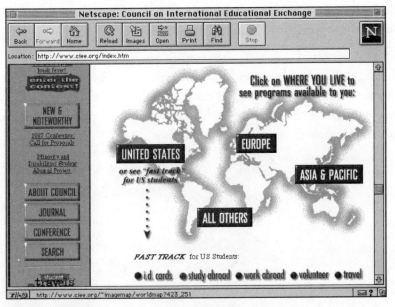

Figure 8.16 The CIEE offers aid for student travelers.

STA Travel

www.sta-travel.com

STA arranges budget travel for students on the move. Use the airfare guide to find discounted rates, and book your flight right from the Web site. There's information here on rail passes and insurance, and you can check out the featured destination and chat with other students in the "Make Tracks Online" department. Click on the interactive map to locate an STA office near you.

Travel Cuts

www.travelcuts.com

Canadian students will find this site useful for planning treks abroad. Owned by the Canadian Federation of Students, Travel Cuts offers tips of the week, special offers, and useful information about your chosen location, as well as articles from *The Student Traveler* magazine.

More Bargains To Come

Look ahead for information on one of the cheapest places to spend your vacation time—at the campground. Web sites on camping, for individuals as well as the whole family, can be found in Chapter 12.

Other chapters of this book cover more great ways to use the Web to save on your vacation. For more on how you can save by booking last-minute airline flights, in addition to saving on car rentals, look to Chapter 5. For discounted hotel rates, from last-minute deals to travel clubs, look to Chapter 6. For deals on cruises, look ahead to Chapter 11.

Trotting The Globe: Travel To Foreign Lands

CHAPTER 9 TOPICS

- CULTURAL EVENTS, CURRENCY EXCHANGE, AND REGIONAL CUISINE ON THE WEB

- FINDING INFORMATION ON EMBASSIES, PASSPORTS, AND VISAS

- ONLINE LANGUAGE LESSONS

Traveling to a foreign country is an exciting challenge. Communicating with others when you don't speak the language, converting currency you haven't quite mastered, and finding your way along ancient, winding roads can make your visit not just a vacation, but a major accomplishment.

Feeling completely overwhelmed in a new country is no picnic. The more you know upon arrival, the less confused you'll feel—and the less confusion, the better. Just as you may have prepared for a previous trip by reading a travel guidebook, the Web can help you get acquainted with unfamiliar destinations through its many sites on culture, language, and foreign travel.

Don't worry about spoiling your trip by learning "too much" about a culture ahead of time. No book or Web site can possibly describe a country, its people, and its food enough to diminish the excitement and exhilaration of experiencing it for yourself. Laying a little groundwork to smooth your arrival can be a great help.

This chapter will show you how to learn about your destination's customs, language, and current issues. You'll also be guided to Web sites that can help you get by in a foreign land, including the home pages of embassies, and Web sites about passport information, traveler's checks, credit cards, and more.

Travel Byte

When using taxis, insist that drivers use the meter. If there's no meter, or if bargaining is common, agree on a price before you get in.

Travel Tools

To get started, a smart first stop is the online travel publications provided by the United States Bureau of Consular Affairs (**travel.state.gov/travel_pubs.html**). The "Tips for Travelers" publications offer information about health, currency, and crime on a country-by-country basis—issues that travelers should know about before they leave the U.S. Other travel publications, including, "A Safe Trip Abroad" and "Foreign Entry Requirements" also provide advice and facts for anyone heading overseas.

Tips For Travelers To South Asia

The following excerpt is an example of the "tips for travelers" provided by the U.S. Department of State for world travelers. This particular information is for those planning a trip to South Asia, and can be found on the Web at **www.state.gov/ tips_sasia.html**.

Afghanistan, Bangladesh, Bhutan, India, Maldives, Nepal, Pakistan, and Sri Lanka.

Foreword

The information in this pamphlet has been gathered for you by consular officers—both here and in South Asia—to assist you with your trip. We hope this brochure will be of help to you in making your trip both safe and enjoyable.

Always keep in mind, though, that wherever you are abroad, if you come into serious difficulties, contact the U.S. consul at the nearest United States embassy or consulate for information or assistance.

General Information

Your trip to South Asia can be a rich and rewarding experience. There are ancient cultures and artistic traditions to appreciate and a wealth of natural wonders to see—all co-existing with modern societies. However, the customs and local conditions can be as distant from home as the miles, and travelers should plan their trips carefully.

Weather

If you have a choice, winter is the best time to visit most areas of South Asia. South of the Himalayas, South Asian weather is warm to very hot. Hot, humid regions like Bangladesh and central, eastern, and southern India are somewhat more comfortable in December through February. Hot, dry regions like Pakistan and northern India have pleasant weather from October to March, with the winter months cool enough for light woolens. The worst weather in the dry regions, when heat and dust can make sightseeing or other outdoor activity a chore, is during the pre-monsoon period from approximately April through mid-July.

Health

In the United States, local health departments, the Centers for Disease Control and Prevention (CDC), private doctors, and travel clinics can provide information on health precautions for travelers to South Asia. Depending on your destination, immunization is recommended against cholera, diphtheria/tetanus, hepatitis, Japanese B encephalitis, meningitis, polio, and typhoid. Drug prophylaxis against malaria may also be necessary. General guidance may also be found in the booklet Health Information for International Travel, which is available for $7 from the U.S. Government Printing Office, Washington, DC 20402, or from local, or state health departments. The CDC has an international travelers hotline that can be reached at 404-332-4559.

Travelers should be careful to drink only boiled water (bottled water is not always safe) or bottled drinks, to avoid ice cubes in beverages and unpeeled fruits and vegetables, to take precautions against mosquitoes, and to guard against overexertion at high altitudes. Trekkers and mountain climbers, in particular, should take precautions to avoid frostbite, hypothermia, and altitude sickness. The latter two can be fatal if not detected in time. Modern health facilities are not always available, particularly in rural areas. Prospective travelers should review their health insurance policies to see if they provide coverage while overseas, including medical evacuation service.

Visas and Other Entry Requirements

A U.S. passport is required for travel to all countries in the region. Most South Asian countries also require entry visas. Travel to certain areas of many South Asian countries is restricted and special permits may be required for these areas in addition to the entry visa. Prospective travelers should contact the embassy or consulate of the country they plan to visit for specific information (see list of foreign embassies at end of document).

All South Asian countries require travelers who have been in yellow-fever infected areas within the last six days to show valid yellow-fever immunization certificates. Yellow fever is found in some African and some Latin American countries. If you plan to travel from Africa or Latin America directly to South Asia, check with the embassy of the South Asian country where you are going to see if a yellow-fever certificate is required. If the certificate is required and you do not have it, you will be refused entry unless you are inoculated and kept in quarantine for up to six days.

Currency and Customs Regulations

Most South Asian countries require that foreign currency and valuables be declared upon entry as a means of enforcing restrictions on the importation of items such as gold, electronic equipment, firearms, and prescription drugs. Failure to make an accurate declaration or other violations of these restrictions can lead to high fines and/or imprisonment.

Just The Facts

To get the basic stats on your destination of choice, visit The World FactBook (**www.odci.gov/cia/publications/95fact/index.html**). It can give you the lowdown on where you're going to be. View maps and get the particulars on numerous countries around the world at this Web site. Geography, population, government, economy, transportation, and communication are detailed, and you'll find data on climate, life expectancy, national holidays, currency, electricity, and more on a country-by-country basis.

Destination 'Zines

Use a search engine to see what the Web offers in the way of online magazines about your destination. Location-specific magazines abound on the Web, offering suggestions on restaurants, excursions, and activities specific to your destination. You'll also find feature articles on the culture, history, and beliefs of the people who live there. Check for these magazines at sites such as the E-Zine List (**meer.net/~johnl/e-zine-list/keywords/travel.html**) and the Monster Magazine List (**www.enews.com/monster/travel**), which provide links to hundreds of other online publications and e-zines.

The following sites are examples of what the Web offers in destination-specific online magazines.

Britannia
www.britannia.com/tours/tor.html

Stop by this site, not only for its interesting travel articles and virtual tours, but also to brush up on your British history (as shown in Figure 9.1). There are write-ups on the country's monarchs and Prime Ministers, relics, castles, cathedrals, monuments, and more. Interviews with famous Brits are provided, as are articles on British food (recipes included). You'll also find maps and timelines, and connections to Web sites about London.

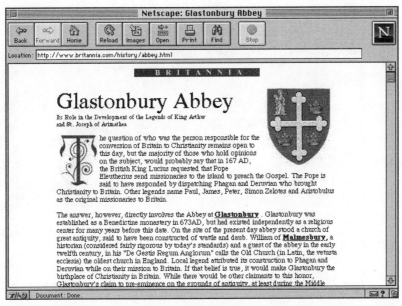

Figure 9.1   An article about Britain's history and legends on Britannia's Web site.

The Down Under Traveller
www.south-pacific.com/travel-zine/

Read this 'zine's articles to learn about cultural aspects of the South Pacific and for useful travel information. The "Moomba!" section suggests things to see and do, and reviews and impressions from readers offer a few more ideas. The Q & A department provides answers to travel questions and the "South Pacific Dictionary" gives you tips on common words and phrases used "down under."

Dolce Vita
www.dolcevita.com

This magazine is "on the net...Italian style." Check out the Travel section for features about exploring the country, and click on the interactive map for brief descriptions of cities and small villages to visit. Suggested itineraries for travel through the countryside are provided (see Figure 9.2), as well as a listing of recommended hotels and *trattorias* according to price. Articles on Italian fashion and cooking provide the traveler with a way to explore Italy at home.

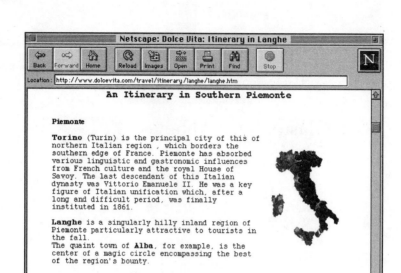

Figure 9.2   *Learn about Italy's countryside, and print out suggested itineraries, from Dolce Vita.*

Munich Found
www.MunichFound.de

Monthly issues keep you informed on German culture, history, commentary, art, and politics. Through features, columns, and departments, visitors to this site can learn about the people, festivals, language, and daily life in Germany. The Travel section contains articles on museums, historic sites, big cities, and small villages, and the calendar of events is a useful tool for travelers.

Cultural Directories

One of the reasons we travel is to learn about cultures different from our own. Whether we're exploring cathedrals in France, watching Chinese commuters peddle by on bicycles, or attending a festival in Mexico, our eyes are opened and spirits are lifted by new experiences.

Web sites about local works of art, daily life, and folk and religious traditions can help to introduce you to a national culture. Web explorers can learn about the background and history of a country or region, and begin to understand why its people live as they do. Before you travel, discover the French cathedrals: When were they built, and what's special about their architecture (**www.globalnet.net/elore/elore4a2.html**)? Learn about bicycles in China: Why are people so attached to their two-wheelers (**www.channela.com/food/yancancook/culture.html#LifeInChina**)? Or investigate Mexican heritage: What traditions are associated with the Day of the Dead celebrations in Mexico City (**majorca.npr.org/programs/seasonings/Muertos.HTML**)?

Cultural directories like the Web of Culture, shown in Figure 9.3, can link you to Web sites on cultures throughout the world. At other directories, you may find links to Web sites on the music, literature, media, and religion of a particular nation.

You can also use search engines to find cultural information on the country you plan to visit. Yahoo! (**www.yahoo.com/Society_and_Culture/Cultures**) has a department entitled "Society and Culture" that leads you to a list of countries and links to Web sites on food, music, religion, and other topics.

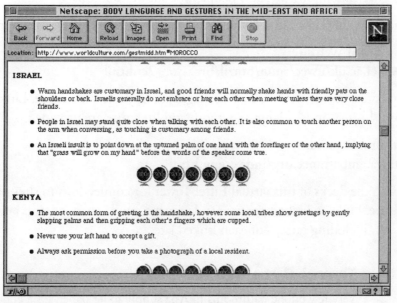

Figure 9.3 Learn the etiquette of where you plan to visit at The Web of Culture.

The Web of Culture
www.worldculture.com

This site is "the leading source for cross-cultural information on the World Wide Web." Visitors will find links to Web sites on foreign cuisine and world religions, and learn about languages, including the non-verbal body language of specific cultures. Passers-by can also stop by the chat forum for a "cross-cultural chat," and give the weekly contest a try. The Web site also lists the capital cities of countries throughout the world, as well as the street addresses of U.S. consulates and embassies overseas.

Multicultural Home Page
pasture.ecn.purdue.edu/~agenhtml/agenmc/index.html

This cultural directory was developed by Purdue University students who wanted to share information with others about their home countries. Find links to Web sites on sports and science, and maps and online magazines of nations such as Bolivia, Korea, Canada, and Israel. You can also find sites on the government, history, and people of your destination.

The following sites can tell you about the culture of a particular country.

The Brazil Web site
www.cf.ac.uk/uwcc/suon/brazil/braz-soc_2cr.html

This site connects visitors to Web pages about Brazilian culture. Links to sites about history, music, language, food, and literature are provided.

Cultural Explorer
ottawa.ambafrance.org/index_eng.html

Climb the decks of this virtual Eiffel Tower for connections to sites on French culture. Links to French poetry, art, language, food, cartoons, and news can be found, including ratings of each linked site.

Travel Byte

Very few public bathrooms in Asia supply toilet paper. It's a good idea to carry your own with you on your trip!

History of the Highland Games
sava.gulfnet.com/user_pages/kele/Games_Hi.htm

Learn the history of Scotland's caber toss, stone put, hammer throw, and other feats of strength and stamina performed at the Highland Games. Competitive Highland dancing is also featured, with historical information on the origins of the Sword Dance, the Seann Triubhas, and the Highland Fling. Read about bagpipes, kilts, and Scottish weddings as well.

The Art of Tibetan Sand Painting
www.chron.com/mandala/

View images of Tibetan Buddhist monks creating a sand painting at the Museum of Fine Arts in Houston (see Figure 9.4). Learn about the significance of sand painting, the religious ceremony that accompanies it, and the basics of the Buddhist religion, and listen to audio clips of the monks chanting.

Figure 9.4 Learn about religious and artistic traditions of the country you plan to visit.

Online Newspapers

Online newspapers make it possible for you to access news about the country you're planning to visit. They're a great way to learn about current events and the issues that affect the people living there.

Web sites, such as The Daily News—Just the Links, and Newspapers Around the World, connect you to resources on the Web that provide news updates on particular nations or regions. Through these pages, you can connect to Web sites of online news sources like the Kenya News, The Irish Times, and The Trinidad Express.

The Daily News—Just the Links
www.cs.vu.nl/%7Egerben/news/africa.html

This site offers links to daily news Web sites, including online newspapers and radio and television broadcasts. Numerous links are listed by continent. You can also subscribe to a mailing list of archived news stories.

Newspapers Around the World
www.freenet.mb.ca/community/media/newspapers/

Web links at this site connect you to newspapers spanning the globe. You'll find links to news from Canada, Africa, Central America, South America, the Pacific, and other areas, and the site informs you if a particular newspaper provides English-language content.

News Services

The following Web sites are news services in their own right, not an online version of a print newspaper. These sites deliver daily headlines and top news stories from around the world. Peruse the following news pages to read the current events of your destination.

One World Daily News Service
www.oneworld.org/news

Read headlines and news summaries on human rights issues each weekday. You can catch the top news of the week, or check into current events by theme, including free speech, democracy, human rights, health, and more. You can also choose a specific country for a briefing on its political and environmental issues. The "multimedia reports" include photos and audio clips on various topics.

The Nando Times
www.nando.net/nt/nando.cgi

Every day, The Nando Times, shown in Figure 9.5, delivers the world's top news stories. Read articles on politics, health, and entertainment from around the world. If you're a sports fan, check out the "Sports Server," which highlights sports around the globe; if you're looking for news on a particular topic, use the "Nando News Watcher" to get up-to-the-minute news by specific key words. For a lighter read, check out the linked online magazine "Third Rave."

Yahoo! News
www.yahoo.com/headlines/international

Yahoo! News posts top international headlines each weekday, as well as news summaries and features provided by Reuters wire service. Topics at this site include politics, entertainment, sports, business, technology, and health. You can use the "search news" feature to read news coverage on your destination, or review stories from the past week to catch up on current events.

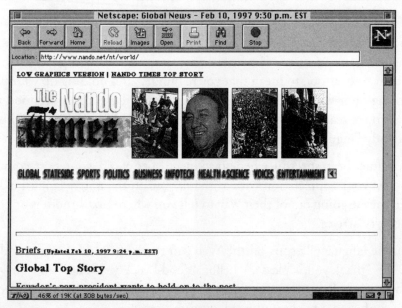

Figure 9.5 Read daily headlines from around the world at The Nando Times.

Asia Times
www.asiatimes.com

Read daily headline articles from China, India, Malaysia, Japan, and other Asian countries, or try the Editorials and Perspectives sections for personal flavor. Those sections feature comments, opinions of government officials, and "off-the-record" articles. The site also provides a daily gallery of photos, including a "picture special" and "photo-editor's choice."

Talk The Talk

Don't let language be a barrier between you and the rest of the world. Basic English, a few common phrases, and a smile can get you by almost anywhere. Luckily for us English-speaking travelers, many people around the world learn English as their second or third language at an early age.

How do you tell if a person speaks English or not? Simply ask. Using one word sentences, such as "English?" is an easy way to get your questions answered. Muddling sentences with complex words or slang may make communication more difficult. Remembering the three Ps—patience, politeness, and a positive attitude—will make communication easier for everyone involved.

While speaking louder probably won't help the situation, low-key gestures and body language may. For instance, rubbing your thumb against your index finger means "money" in almost any language. Rubbing your stomach is usually understood to mean that you're hungry, and holding up your palm and writing on it with the fingers of your other hand can be understood to mean that you're ready to pay for your meal. Web sites like Berlitz World offer tips on body language "do's and don'ts" for specific destinations.

As a rule, be respectful when speaking to people in your host country, and express your appreciation with a "thank you" in the native language. Remember, they're going out of their way to tell you where a bathroom is or how often the ferry arrives.

Online language lessons on the Web can teach you useful words and phrases such as "thank you," "please," "hello," "good-bye," "yes," "no," and "how much?" These sites often offer pronunciation keys and audio clips to help you avoid the confusion a mispronounced word can create.

Online language lessons can also teach you extended sentences, to help you carry on a real conversation with the native speakers instead of just getting by. Conversing with others ultimately brings you closer to the people of a foreign land.

Here are a few Web sites that can help you learn the native language of many different countries. Learn a thing or two, and print out vocabulary lists to memorize on your way.

Foreign Languages for Travelers
www.travelang.com/languages/

Free online lessons are offered for approximately 40 languages at this site. You'll learn numbers, times, dates, and phrases to help with shopping, dining, and getting directions overseas. A pronunciation guide accompanies the lessons: just click on designated words to hear the corresponding sound files. Online quizzes test your learning, and dictionaries can translate a specific word for you. Message boards and chat sessions are also found here.

Fodor's Living Language
www.fodors.com/language

French, German, Italian, and Spanish are the languages to learn at this site. Select a topic of interest to learn phrases that will help you communicate on your journey. Topics include "At the Airport," "Sightseeing," "Socializing," and "Finding Your Way," among others. Lessons are extensive, and accompanying audio clips help you learn proper pronunciation.

The Human Languages Page
www.june29.com/HLP/

This site is exactly what it claims to be: "a comprehensive catalog of language-related Internet resources." From here you can connect to the Web sites of translation dictionaries, language lessons, online phrase books, FAQs, foreign newspapers, and other resources. Choose from a wide variety of languages, including Czech, Nepali, Spanish, Thai, Vietnamese, and more.

Berlitz World
www.berlitz.com

Listen to and learn common travel phrases in French, Italian, German, Japanese, Chinese, Russian, Hebrew, Arabic, Portuguese (shown in Figure 9.6),

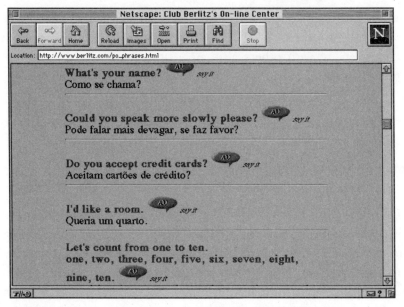

Figure 9.6 Learn useful phrases at the Berlitz World Web site.

and Spanish. This site highlights a particular country each month, providing a "tip of the week," short stories, a culture quiz, and other information on the featured country. Check out "quick tips" on the local culture, and other archived travel advice, and read about language blunders from other planet trekkers. You can also post your questions to Berlitz on the message boards, and find out about other Berlitz learners in "The Guest Room."

Hot Tips: Communication

The Europe Through the Back Door Web site (www.ricksteves.com) is the online presence for the travel guidebooks and television show of Rick Steves. At this site, the author offers travelers advice and information on visiting countries throughout Europe. The following communication tips can be found on the Web at (www.ricksteves.com/tips/commtip.htm).

If you don't speak the local language, use internationally understood words. When your car breaks down in Portugal, tell the mechanic: "Auto kaput." More international words are: self-service, restaurant, toilet, telephone, taxi, photo, sexy, chocolate, coffee, beer, O.K., no problem. Are the French rude? Or just reserved? To make Parisians suddenly 40 percent friendlier, liberally use: *bonjour* (hello), *s'il vous plait* (please), *merci* (thank you), and *pardon* (excuse me). To revel in French friendliness, use these pleasantries in the untouristy countryside. Oh, and *vive la différence.*

In Europe, gestures span the language gap. A fingertip kiss is used in France, Spain, Greece, and Germany as a form of praise. Gently bring the fingers and thumb of your right hand together, raise to your lips, kiss lightly, then toss your hand outward. This gesture can mean sexy, delicious, divine, or wonderful.

In Italy, a gesture that looks like a "cheek screw" is widely used to mean good, lovely, beautiful, and clever. Make a fist, stick out your forefinger, and screw it into your cheek (without piercing your skin!).

The "thumbs up" sign popular in the U.S.A. is used widely in France and Germany to say "O.K." The "V for victory" sign is used in most of Europe, but beware, a V with your palm toward you is the rudest of gestures in England.

Is it universal to nod "yes" and "no"? Well, yes and no. In Greece and Turkey, signal "no" by jerking your eyebrows and head upward. In Bulgaria, say "yes" by happily bouncing your head back and forth.

In southern Europe, people wave their hand palm downward to signal "come here." To Americans, this gesture looks like "go away," but it's actually an invitation.

Food

There's more to Greek food than gyros, and there's more to nibble on than cheese in Switzerland. Why not learn about the culinary delights of your destination before you go?

If you've familiarized yourself with popular local dishes, you'll have a better feel for what to order when you find yourself staring at an unfamiliar menu. Not only can you learn about common dishes the locals enjoy, but you can find out how they're made, as well as the customs and etiquette that accompany a meal in the country you'll be visiting.

For example, did you know that in countries like India, Nepal, Singapore, and parts of Malaysia, where people eat with their hands, it's only proper to eat with your right hand? The left hand is considered dirty, since it's used for self-cleaning after using the bathroom. And in China, it's very rude to stand your chopsticks straight up in your bowl of rice, as this configuration is reserved for funerals.

On a trip to Spain several years ago, I arrived in Madrid, lost, confused, and hungry. With my stomach growling, I tried to figure out why no restaurants were serving dinner at 7:00 p.m. Had I done some research before I arrived, I would have known that dinner isn't served until about 10:00 p.m. in Spain, and I would have planned accordingly.

The Web offers a wealth of information on regional cuisine, as well as regional etiquette to observe when dining. Some Web sites offer local recipes; try them out with your future travel companions while you gear up for your trip!

The Kitchen Link
www.kitchenlink.com

"Your guide to what's cooking on the Net" connects you to hundreds of food-related Web sites, newsgroups, and mailing lists. It's a good resource for locating Web sites about cooking all over the world. Just check out the "ethnic and regional cooking" department to find food facts on your destination, and stop by the cooking club message board to let others in on your secret recipes.

Cuisine en Provence
www.enprovence.com/ljones/cuisine/cuisi001.html

Learn about the many flavors of Provence at this site, shown in Figure 9.7. You'll read about staple foods from garlic to chickpeas, common dishes of the region and how they've changed over time, and the healthy aspects of Provençal cooking and regional traditions. This site will also introduce you to the many ways Provence has been represented by writers, painters, and chefs.

Travel Byte

In some countries, restaurateurs will attempt to overcharge you for your meal. To avoid getting taken, ask the waiter to write down the total cost of your meal as soon as you order. They're less likely to cheat you if they've totaled the bill before you've eaten.

Channel A Food
www.channela.com/food

Feature articles on this Web site, as shown in Figure 9.8, explore the many cuisines of Asia. You can read about traditional Asian feasts and the "dream

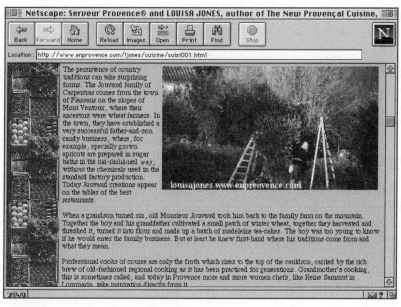

Figure 9.7   Take a virtual taste of Provence.

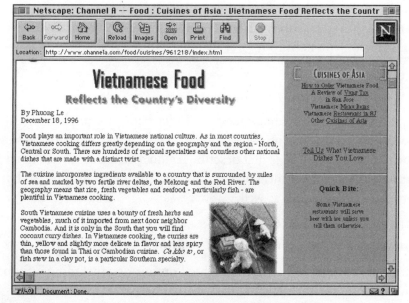

Figure 9.8   Read about the many flavors of Asian cuisine.

banquets" of noted chefs, peruse sample recipes, and read reviews of restaurants in popular destinations like Hong Kong. Also listen in on dinner conversations with famous cooks, such as Martin Yan (with a link to his Web site), and share your favorite Asian dishes with other travelers on the message boards or in the recipe exchange.

The African Cookbook
www.sas.upenn.edu/African_Studies/Cookbook/about_cb_wh.html

Learn about the traditional foods from many of Africa's countries, including Kenya, Morocco, South Africa, and Tanzania. Background is provided on formal dinners and informal meals, including the traditions that come with them. Serving customs and food presentation are described from a personal perspective, and recipes are provided so you can try making these traditional meals at home.

Tokyo Food Page
www.twics.com/~robbs/tokyofood.html

"The Culinary Explorer" features food-related attractions to visit while in Japan, from open-air markets to wine caves. In addition, articles on Japanese dishes, with ordering information and sample menus, can be found. A glossary can bring you up to date on the sushi scene, and recipes give you the information you need to try out Japanese cuisine at home.

Cuisine of India
www.incore.com/india/cuisine.html

Links to Web pages about food in India paint a complete picture of the country's cuisine. A glossary of Indian foods and an index of herbs give you the basics, and Web sites that describe regional dishes are listed, in addition to sites on the history of meal preparation and common customs. Still other sites provide Indian recipes as well.

The Italian Tradition Online
www.made-in-Italy.com/winefood/wf.htm

Regional cooking of Italy is highlighted on this site, including information on common ingredients, favored dishes, and sample recipes. Learn how climate, soil, and political history have affected the country's cuisine, and get the scoop on olive oil, pasta, parmesan, and other foods that have made Italian cooking world-renowned. Italian wines are also discussed. Articles on learning to cook Italian style are included also.

Know Your Embassy

While it's nice to know everything you can about the country you're visiting, don't forget the practical considerations that go with travel to foreign lands. My friend Jay had his neck wallet stolen after he left it outside a shower stall in a Shanghai youth hostel. (Keep your neck wallet with you at *all* times!) He found himself with no passport, no traveler's checks, and flat broke. But Jay did know where the U.S. consulate was located and went to them for help.

If you get in a jam on your journey, U.S. embassies and consulates can be of service to you, too. If your passport or wallet is lost or stolen, visit the U.S. embassy or consulate nearest you as soon as possible. The employees there can help you reach your family back home, as well as access money, cancel credit cards, and obtain a new passport. They can give aid to travelers who injure themselves and may recommend a local doctor. Embassies and consulates will also assist U.S. citizens abroad during natural disasters and political disturbances. (Keep in mind that U.S. embassies and consulates do not exist to give you directions to the Colosseum or to the best restaurant in town. They will only assist you in emergency situations.)

Embassies Worldwide
www.xs4all.nl/~airen/countries.html

Embassies Worldwide connects you to Web sites that maintain lists of specific countries' embassies. You'll find the locations of embassies of various countries throughout the world (see Figure 9.9). If a country does not have a Web site of its own to provide this information, Embassies Worldwide fills it in.

The Embassy Page
www.embpage.org

Find location and contact information for United States Embassies and Consulates in Canada, Europe, and various other places, by linking to their individual Web sites. You can also find connections to the Web sites of foreign embassies in the U.S. for updates on visa and entry requirements. You'll find lots of links to related resources as well.

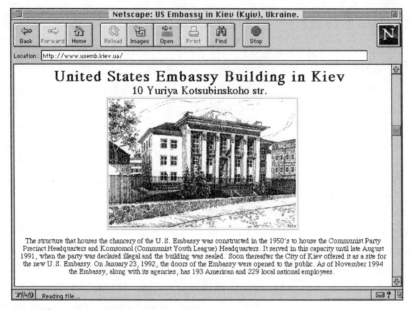

Figure 9.9 The Web site of the U.S. embassy in Kiev.

U.S. Embassies and Consulates Worldwide
travel.state.gov/links.html

The Bureau of Consular Affairs provides a list of Web links to U.S. Embassies and Consulates. Visit this site for connections to government home pages that can be useful to you overseas, from Fukuoka, Japan to Santiago, Chile.

Your Passport

Your passport is your "ticket to ride:" all travelers need this official government-issued document for international identification. You must have a valid passport to enter foreign countries, and to get back into the country you came from as well. This little booklet is the most important document you possess as you're traveling abroad—so keep it with you at all times!

If you have a passport already, you may continue to use it until the expiration date passes. (An adult's passport is valid for ten years.) You may have noticed that green passports are now being issued. If you have the older, blue version, you can continue to use it until it expires. Be sure that your passport is valid for the entire time you'll be traveling; in fact, it's a good idea to make sure it extends a few weeks beyond the time allotted in case your plans change for any reason.

If you don't have a passport already, you should start obtaining one as soon as possible. The application process can take four weeks or longer.

If you meet the requirements, you may be able to apply through the post office, state and federal courts, or one of the regional passport agencies located in 13 major U.S. cities. Passport application forms are also available via the Internet.

To apply for a passport, you will need:

- A valid driver's license, expired passport, student ID, or other proof of identity.
- A social security number.
- A birth certificate, or other proof of U.S. citizenship.
- A completed passport application form (DSP-11).
- A processing fee of $55 plus $10 for new applicants.
- Two identical 2" × 2" photographs taken within the last 6 months. (Pictures taken at vending machines in the mall are not acceptable.)

If you're taking your vacation sooner then planned, or simply did not allow enough time to get a passport, you can expedite your application by visiting passport service sites on the Web. These sites cater to those who need a passport in less than 5 days, but be sure to check on the costs of these services before you use them.

In addition to listing contact information and addresses of application locations, the following Web sites also provide downloadable application forms.

Passport Services
travel.state.gov/passport_services.html

Check out "passports the easy way" to get details on applying for a passport, as seen in Figure 9.10. After downloading them, you can print out passport applications and listings of passport agencies; you'll also find an order form to get your birth certificate, and learn how to access your passport records. Read the passport FAQ to find answers to questions such as "How do I renew my passport?" and "How do I get more pages added?"

Figure 9.10 Print out a passport application from the Passport Services site.

Travel Byte

When overseas, carry a photocopy of your passport in your luggage, separate from your real passport. If the original is lost or stolen, the photocopy will help you obtain a new one. It's also wise to leave a photocopy of your passport with a friend or relative back in the States, in case your copy is lost as well.

American Passport Express
www.americanpassport.com

DSP-82 and DSP-11 application forms are provided for passport renewals and for first-time applicants. You'll find lists of where to apply for passports by state and by passport agencies, if you choose not to use the American Passport Express service, which works in conjunction with the Boston Passport Agency. You can also find out where to obtain your birth certificate, and access visa and passport requirements for foreign countries. You can also find answers to your questions in the site's FAQ.

The Passport Express
www.tiac.net/users/passport/cafore.html

An extensive list of entry requirements for numerous foreign countries is provided at this site. Expedite your passport using express (less than 5 working days) or regular service (5 or more days). Online forms for new passport applicants, as well as renewal forms, are provided. Check the prices before you use this service to expedite your passport.

Travisa
www.travisa.com

Travisa offers expediting services for second passports and lost passports, in addition to visa processing. The site provides email links to its nationwide offices. Check out the past and current issues of the Travisa newsletter, which updates you on entry requirements to destinations abroad.

Travel Byte

If your passport is lost or stolen, contact the nearest U.S. consulate or embassy right away, as well as the local police. Carry identification with you, such as a student ID or driver's license, in case this occurs on your trip.

Visas

Visas permit you to leave and enter foreign countries. Some countries require that visitors have them, others don't. Use the Web to find out if the country you plan to visit requires one: check the embassy Web site of your destination, as shown in Figure 9.11, to read up on the country's entry requirements. Be sure to look into multiple-entry visas if you plan to travel to other countries and then return to the first one for your flight home. Do this research in advance, as processing times can range from a few days to a many weeks.

You can also visit the following site to check on visa conditions of foreign countries.

Figure 9.11   Check visa requirements at the Embassy of Switzerland online.

Visa Services
travel.state.gov/visa_services.html

Visit the "foreign entry requirements" section to access your destination's entry information from the United States Department of State and the Bureau of Consular Affairs. The site lists countries, specifying whether a visa is needed to visit, how long it is valid, and whether visas are being issued at all. Other pertinent facts are included, such as whether a letter of purpose is needed, whether photos are required, and what immunizations travelers must have to enter the country. You'll also find contact information for each country's U.S. embassy at this site.

Travel Byte

If you plan to travel between countries, many visa offices, such as those in Asia, require a photo. It's cheaper and more convenient to have these pictures taken ahead of time and bring them with you on your trip.

Exchanging Currency

When you arrive in a foreign country, one of the first things to do is exchange your U.S. dollars or traveler's checks for the local currency. Banks and currency exchanges openly display their buying and selling rates, so you can shop around easily for the lowest exchange rates and fees. Avoid exchanging currency at airports or hotels where rates are high.

Because exchanging currency can be costly, you should try to do it as seldom as possible. Estimate how much you think you will need to get you through your stay in the country, and try to get it all at once.

You can exchange your currency before entering each new country. For example, you can change your Spanish *pesetas* into Italian *lire* before you head from Barcelona to Rome.

Travel Byte

Since black market currency exchanges often involve illegal money laundering, it's never a good idea to exchange money with a person on the street.

The Money Abroad FAQ
www.inria.fr/robotvis/personnel/laveay/money-faq

This site gives travelers the scoop on world money matters (see Figure 9.12). Country-by-country, details on currency, currency exchange, banks, and traveler's checks are provided. You'll find information on commonly used credit cards, where traveler's checks may be cashed, and if ATMs can be easily located in countries like Sri Lanka, New Zealand, Tanzania, and Turkey.

The following Web sites enable you to look up current exchange rates before you leave on your trip.

Currency Converter
www.olsen.ch/cgi-bin/exmenu/pathfinder

This site allows you to view current exchange rates, as well as the rates on any day since January 1990. Submit the amount you'd like to exchange, choose the currencies you want exchanged, and the currency converter rings up the results for you, as shown in Figure 9.13. The exchange rates can easily be reversed, as well.

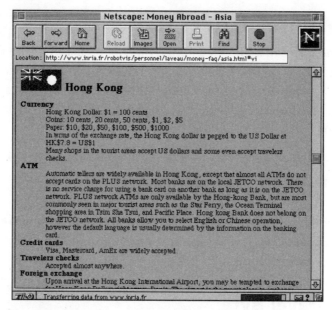

Figure 9.12 Learn about money matters in your destination.

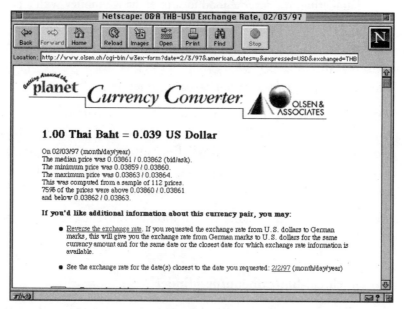

Figure 9.13 Check current exchange rates before you leave on your trip.

Exchange Rates
www.dna.lth.se/cgi-bin/kurt/rates

Choose the country whose currency you want to convert, and then select a second currency to compare to your first choice. From the Italian *lira* to the Irish pound, the Swiss *franc*, the Venezuelan *bolivar*, or the Greek *drachma*, this site offers approximately 40 currencies to choose from. The rates at this site are provided by the Federal Reserve Bank of New York, and are updated daily.

Yahoo Quotes
quote.yahoo.com/forex?update

The "Foreign Currency Exchange Table" provides current exchange rates for U.S., Australian, and Canadian dollars, British pounds, German *deutsche marks*, French and Swiss *francs*, and Japanese *yen*. This site gives the time of update, and visitors to the site may create their own personal portfolios of currencies they're interested in.

CNN Financial Network
cnnfn.com/markets/currencies.html

This site lists approximately 45 currencies for Europe, Asia, Africa, the Middle East, Canada, and Bermuda, and gives their values in U.S. dollars.

The Universal Currency Converter
www.xe.net/currency

Convert one denomination into another. Choose from numerous currencies, and sign up to have free daily currency updates emailed to you. This site encourages you to post electronic postcards from your travels, and you can read other travelers' posts as well.

Travel Byte

By the end of your trip, you may find your pockets heavy with a wide variety of foreign coins. A great way to get rid of those excess coins is to donate them to charity: attendants on many international airline flights will collect your spare change and give it to a worthy cause. American Airlines, for example, donates collected currency to UNICEF.

Traveler's Checks

Buy your traveler's checks in U.S. dollars before you leave on your trip. To be on the safe side, it's a good idea to get checks for about 20 percent more money than you expect to spend. (For more information on how to plan your budget, refer to Chapter 8.) If you have extra traveler's checks left when you return to the States, it's no problem to change them back into U.S. dollars.

Traveler's checks are a good way to carry money for a few reasons. Most importantly, traveler's checks can be replaced if they are lost or stolen. Record the number of each traveler's check you get, and keep the receipts. Carry the receipts and the list of numbers with you in your luggage, separately from your checks (which should be tucked safely away in your neck wallet). Keep a list of your check numbers, and mark them off as you use each one.

Besides their ease of replacement, traveler's checks are a good choice because banks usually give you a better exchange rate for traveler's checks than they do for cash; in addition, they can often be used in places where no ATMs can be found.

Shop around on the Web for the best services to fit your travel style, and check on fees while you're at it.

Barclays
www.barclays.co.uk

Barclays provides information on "paying for your holiday" with currency and, of course, their traveler's checks. Learn about buying your checks in U.S. dollars, British sterling, or other foreign currencies; and find out about refund locations and what to do if your checks are stolen. Instructions on how to order traveler's checks from Barclays are also found at the site.

Citibank
www.citibank.com

Find information on Citibank traveler's checks, as well as street addresses and contact numbers of Citibank branches all over the planet. You can also create a printable, customized guide to Citibank's services in the country you plan to visit, including emergency numbers, exchange information, and toll-free money management numbers.

Thomas Cook
www.thomascook.com

There are over 1,800 Thomas Cook locations worldwide—find out exactly where they are by visiting this site. There's a currency converter, and information about moneygrams in case of emergencies abroad; you'll also find advice on taking traveler's checks with you to your foreign destination. The Web site also offers travel information specific to Hong Kong and the United Kingdom.

Wells Fargo
wellsfargo.com

Wells Fargo offers customers with an online checking or savings account the convenience of ordering traveler's checks over the Internet. Travelers can order up to $2,000 worth of American Express Traveler's checks right from the Web site (shown in Figure 9.14), and they may also order up to $2,000 in foreign currency before leaving on their trip. These services are available 24 hours a day, and the travelers checks and currencies are express-delivered within two days.

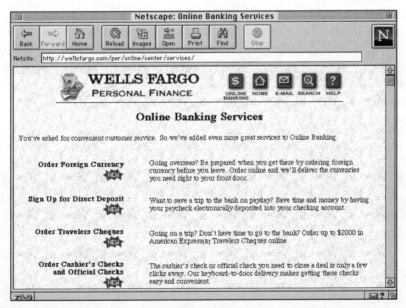

Figure 9.14 Wells Fargo allows customers to purchase traveler's checks online.

ATMs

Automatic Teller Machine (ATM) cards give you access to local currency by withdrawing funds from your home bank account. You may find the service fees charged for withdrawing money from an ATM are less than those for traveler's checks or a cash advance on your credit card. This is because ATMs use inter-bank rates, which are the rates banks use to exchange money between themselves.

In large, highly-touristed cities, ATMs can be found fairly easily. In other more rural locations, though, they may be quite hard to find.

Most ATMs feature instructions in English as well as the local language, and most ATMs overseas support four-digit personal identification numbers (the standard in most countries). But remember, some ATMs overseas are only accessible during business hours, not 24 hours a day.

The following Web sites offer specific locations of ATMs in large cities overseas, as well as in the United States:

Bank of America
www.bankamerica.com

Among Bank of America's online banking information, you'll find the "Access Guide," a directory for ATM locations around the world. Travelers can find lists of bank branches and the number of ATMs in various countries, as well as travel tips and safety advice to heed while using ATMs.

Cirrus/MasterCard
www.mastercard.com/atm

This page of MasterCard's Web site will help you locate ATMs in the international MasterCard/Cirrus network. Over 300,000 of these ATMs are found around the world. Click on the area you're heading to, and the site will inform you of how many machines are found in that country. You'll also find lists of banks where the ATMs are found, including their addresses and hours of service.

Plus/Visa
www.visa.com

The Plus/Visa network also has hundreds of thousands ATMs scattered across the globe. You can choose from a list of destinations—select a country to get information on how many Visa, Plus, and Visa/Plus ATMs are located there.

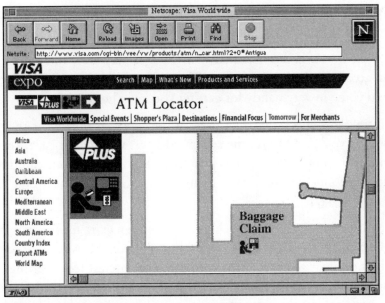

Figure 9.15 Locate ATMs in international airports.

Find out about ATMs located in baggage claim areas and terminals via airport floor plans (see Figure 9.15), or click on the interactive map of the U.S. to find ATMs at home.

Credit Cards

Credit cards like MasterCard and Visa are commonly used and accepted overseas, so world travelers can use them just as they do at home. I've used a MasterCard in restaurants, shops, and hotels in various countries, with few problems. Credit cards are recognized throughout the world, but it's still a good idea to check first before pulling out your card. Some budget accommodations, such as youth hostels, don't take them.

Still, credit cards do offer back-up security for travelers. Let's say you just arrived in Munich. It's dark, it's cold, and you didn't have time to convert your Austrian shillings to German marks. It's after hours and all the banks are closed, so you won't be able to exchange your currency or traveler's checks until tomorrow. After searching for several blocks you locate an ATM machine, but of course it's temporarily out of service! Don't panic: If you have a credit card, you're probably still safe. It shouldn't be too difficult to find a hotel that accepts an internationally recognized card. Even if the hotel costs more than you'd planned, isn't it better than being homeless for the night?

Or what if you hadn't planned your budget very well and simply ran your bank account into the ground? You'd have to end your trip ASAP. A credit card would come in very handy for getting you back home.

Like traveler's checks, credit cards can be replaced quickly if they're lost or stolen. If you should become separated from your credit card, contact your credit card company as soon as possible. They'll cancel your card for you and issue a new one; the major companies can usually get you a new credit card within two days.

Of course, there's a down side: You may incur an extra fee by charging to your credit card in some countries. In addition, credit cards are a good choice of payment only if you avoid raking in the high interest fees. Getting back from your vacation in time to pay the bill will take care of that, or you can pay it ahead of time by advancing the money to the credit card company before you leave on your trip.

Check out these Web sites to see what different services the major credit cards offer, such as cash advances. All three of the credit card Web sites offer a great deal of information for travelers, and are excellent resources to check into when planning your vacation.

Travel Byte

In an emergency, you may need to have money wired to you overseas. Visit the U.S. State Department's online publication titled "Sending Money to Overseas Citizens Services" (**travel.state.gov/money.html**) to learn how your friends or family can get money to you through the Department of State and the appropriate U.S. embassy or consulate.

MasterCard
www.mastercard.com

Find out about the services MasterCard offers its cardholders at the home page shown in Figure 9.16. The site offers information specific to travelers, such as last-minute bargains and vacation packages tailored to your preferences. There's also information on the MasterCard/Cirrus ATM network, so you can locate

Figure 9.16 MasterCard's homepage.

ATMs in locations around the world, including each bank's name, address, and hours of operation.

Visa
www.visa.com

Learn about credit cards, debit cards, and electronic banking at this site, as well as traveler's checks offered by Visa. The "ATM locator" will find automated teller machines throughout the world, including those at international airports. You can find out how many ATMs there are in the country you plan to visit, and the banks at which they're located. Take a look at the "credit card owner's manual;" emergency assistance information, such as what to do if your lose your card, is also provided. This site has lots of great travel information as well.

American Express
www.americanexpress.com

This site describes the credit card services of American Express, including cards tailored to student travelers. There are addresses of American Express offices worldwide where you can exchange currency and purchase traveler's checks, as well as information on banks around the world that have ATMs. Like Visa's site, you'll find lots of travel information here.

Travel Byte

Visit the Web sites of your credit card companies to locate emergency phone numbers. Print out the numbers and carry them with you in case your credit cards are lost or stolen.

Customs

Everything you purchase overseas must be declared upon re-entering the U.S. If you bought items costing less than a total of $400, you won't have to pay duty on them. If you went hog-wild, though, and bought over $400 worth of souvenirs, you'll be charged a duty of 10 percent.

Often Web sites of tourism boards can inform you of customs restrictions specific to the country you're visiting. Fruits and vegetables are generally not allowed to leave the boundaries of any country. In addition, no meat, fruit, vegetables, or flowers are allowed back into the U.S. The Web site of the U.S. Customs Service offers more detailed information.

Know Before You Go
www.customs.ustreas.gov/travel/pubs/kbygo.htm

Details on making a declaration, including how to pay any required duty, are highlighted on this Web page from the U.S. Customs Service. Travelers can find information on $400, $600, and $1,200 exemptions, and the countries from which these exemptions apply. Also find information on gifts; prohibited and restricted items; cigar, cigarette, and liquor limitations; and penalties.

Travel Byte

When leaving the U.S., it's a good idea to bring along the receipt for any foreign-made products you already own, such as cameras. This way you won't have to pay duty on those products upon re-entering the U.S.

Watch It

To find out what time it is at your destination, the following sites on the Web offer the current time, whatever the time zone. These sites can come in handy for family members at home: If anyone needs to get in touch with you, they can find out the time of day wherever you are. You can also use these sites to set your watch by.

American Express
www.americanexpress.com/travel/docs/resources/time/index.html

Quickly find out the time, in the U.S. or around the world, through a query. Enter the time, date, and city where you currently are, then enter the city to which you're traveling. The Web site will calculate the current time at your destination, as shown in Figure 9.17.

Local Times Around the World
www.hilink.com.au/times

Click on one of the listed continents, countries, and cities to find out the local date and time. This site lists numerous locations, so you have a good chance of

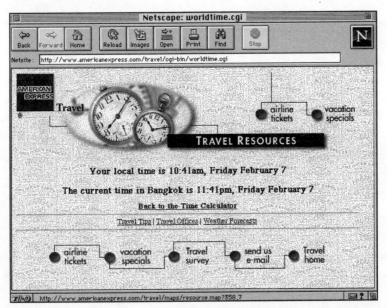

Figure 9.17 Find the time in Bangkok, or wherever you're heading to.

finding the time no matter where you're spending your vacation. And while you're at it, why not check out the information on time zones?

Moving On

If it's adventure you're looking for, Chapter 10 will guide you to Web sites on kayaking, canoeing, white water rafting, and eco-tourism. You'll also learn how sites about California's wine country and the world's greatest golf courses can help you plan the theme vacation of a lifetime!

Exploring The Wild Life: Adventure Trips

CHAPTER 10 TOPICS

- DISCOVER THE ADVENTURE OF A LIFETIME

- GET NATURE-FRIENDLY WITH A "GREEN" ADVENTURE

- ON THE SLOPES AND ON THE LINKS

- LIVING THE HIGH LIFE: WINE-TASTING TOURS AND CASINOS

Need a pick-me-up? Something to give you a little get-up-and-go? A personal adventure can test your limits and revitalize your spirit. There's an adventurer lurking in each of us, begging us to let loose, to take a break from the daily grind and get that adrenaline pumping again.

Use your vacation time to do something you've always wanted to do: Go white-water rafting down the Colorado River; bicycle through California's wine country; or get up-close and-personal with elephants, chimps, and zebra on a safari in Kenya. Make your vacation a trip *extraordinaire*.

Of course, a personal adventure doesn't necessarily mean hiking the Himalayas. Adventures come in all shapes and sizes, depending on your interests. The adventure of choice of an outdoor aficionado may be very different from that of a golfer, or of someone who loves to play the odds on the slot machines.

The Web can help you arrange the adventure of a lifetime. Online magazines, personal travelogues, and interest-specific Web sites can give you ideas on where to go, how to get there, what to do, and why. In addition, articles and features on the Web can point you to quality outfitters that operate kayaking, rafting, and mountaineering trips.

Outside Exposure

If you long to explore the wilderness, hundreds of informative Web sites with sound, video, 3D photos, and stimulating graphics await you. If you think you might like to test your limits in the wilds of nature, but aren't sure exactly what to try, consider what aspects of nature you'd like to explore, and then visit the following sites to get ideas for your journey.

GORP
www.gorp.com

At this site you can select an activity you're interested in, then read about recommended places to pursue it. You'll find articles on biking, caving, birding, hiking, rafting, climbing, and eco-tourism opportunities, among others (Figure 10.1). The site provides details on national forests, scenic rivers, and national trails—click on an interactive map and learn what each region of the world has to offer the outdoor enthusiast. Chat forums let you communicate with others.

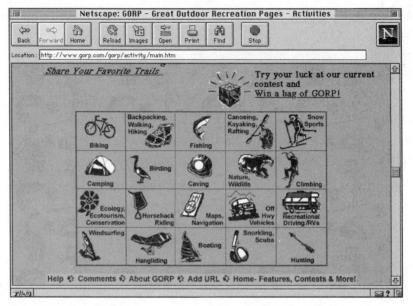

Figure 10.1 Find travel information according to the activity you're interested in.

Mungo Park
www.mungopark.com

Explore the far regions of the world at this online adventure magazine. Every month you'll find new travel articles and personal accounts, with lots of photos, graphics, animation, and sound and video clips. Rap with other adventure seekers in the "@ the park" department and stop by for scheduled chats with experts in the field.

Adventure Sports Online
www.adventuresports.com

Get acquainted with paddle sports, climbing, cycling, skiing, and other outdoor activities through the informative articles at this site. You'll find information on outdoor etiquette and cooking on the road, as well as safety advice, packing checklists, and how-tos and event calendars specific to your interests. Links are provided to the sites of outfitters, tours, schools, and clinics, as well as to other adventure-related Web sites.

The Adventure Channel
www.180.com

Read about the adventures of those who travel on the edge, doing things like kayaking the Nile River and cycling the Ho Chi Minh Trail. Some of the stories include daily updates, journal entries, photos, and interviews with the adventurers, and you can also follow links to related Web sites.

Outside Online
outside.starwave.com

Read daily features in the travel department and other articles from *Outside* magazine on cycling, paddling, mountaineering, hiking, and other adventure activities (see Figure 10.2). The "Active Traveler Directory" provides information and Web links to numerous tours and expeditions, according to where you plan to travel, and the "Adventure Advisor" can answer any travel questions you may have.

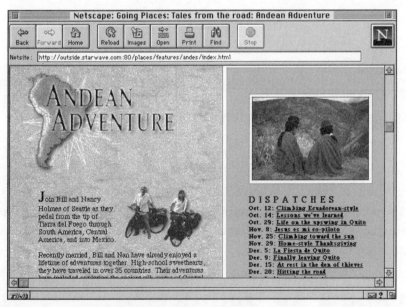

Figure 10.2 Read features about adventurous journeys at Outside Online.

Go West
www.GoWest.com

Read informative articles on biking, rafting, climbing, and camping in America's western states. Simply click on a state on the interactive map to learn about great trails and opportunities for adventure in the area. You'll find useful advice, slide shows, how-tos, and guides to activity-specific terminology, and you can communicate with others in the chat rooms and on the bulletin boards.

Adventure West
www.adventurewest.com

This site features travelogues and photos of birding expeditions, climbing in Utah's canyon country, and ski getaways, as well as treks through South America. Would-be adventure travelers can check out articles and information about regional activities, organized by state, and the "Western States Calendar of Events" provides updates on festivals, celebrations, races, parades, rodeos, and other events.

 Travel Byte

The Sportsite Sports Talk Web site (**www.sportsite.com/chat**) offers chat forums on cross-country skiing, cycling, golf, mountain biking, rock climbing, downhill skiing, snow boarding, hiking, and water sports like kayaking and scuba diving.

To find more adventure sites check out the World Wide Wilderness Directory (**www.wbm.ca/wilderness**), OutdoorLink (**www.outdoorlink.com**), Adventure Travel 2000 (**www.travel2000.com/fun/adventure.html**), and Outdoor Resources Online (**www.azstarnet.com/~goclimb**) to find links to lots of Web sites on outdoor activities. Some provide calendars that can help you plan your trip around an event.

Choosing An Outfitter

Many outdoor adventures can be enjoyed on your own. If you want to take a scenic cycling trip, you can easily pack a road map, fly to Hawaii or some other picturesque region, rent some bikes, and create your own adventure. One of my undauntable travel friends cycled across Germany and France with only a map to guide her.

On the other hand, some outdoor sports are too dangerous for novices to explore on their own. To learn about activities like white-water rafting and mountaineering, you should have a guide to lead you and teach you the ropes as you go.

Adventure tour companies and outfitters don't just supply the boats, the climbing equipment, and the food. They also provide guidance and look out for your safety as well. Traveling with outfitters that employ educated and experienced guides can bring even the most challenging adventures within reach of novice explorers.

Many adventure tour companies provide basic information on their Web sites, along with great graphics, photos, and video clips. But don't book your trip with an outfitter simply because they have a cool Web site! It's the detailed information, the real fine print, that's most important when choosing an expedition package. While these details are not often posted on Web sites, most companies provide an electronic form or email address where you can request further reading materials. So use the Web to get a basic feel for what an outfitter offers, and then request further literature to get the fine print on their tours.

Travel Byte

Purchase your adventure package with a major credit card for financial security. If the operation goes under, you won't get stuck with the bill.

When booking your trip, always (and I mean *always*) find out what's included in the quoted price. Be sure to inquire about additional fees, and about what you'll be required to pay for on your own. Also find out about the company's refund policy, in case you have to cancel.

It's also a good idea to ask outfitters about their instructors' qualifications, the size of the group, and the lodging arrangements, daily activities, and any additional equipment you should bring with you.

Choose a company that's been in business for a number of years. Ask for references from other travelers who've participated in programs with the outfitter or adventure tour company you're considering. Comparison shop by looking at various itineraries and prices.

To learn more, visit How to Choose an Outfitter or Guide at **www.viewit.com: 80/wtr/tn/t/outfitter.html.**

Travel Byte

Book ahead, especially during peak travel seasons. Some outfitters and adventure tours fill more than a year in advance.

To find Web sites of outfitters, visit sites related to your interests, such as cycling or rock climbing. You can use the sites listed in this chapter, or find others by using Web search engines. Wild Dog (**www.wild-dog.com**), an online adventure travel directory, is also a useful resource.

Outward Bound
www.outwardbound.org

Outward Bound is a non-profit organization that leads expeditions designed to challenge participants. You can search for a course that appeals to you by the location you'd like to visit, or by the activity you'd like to participate in. Read about mountaineering, canoeing, mountain biking, rock climbing, white-water rafting, and sea kayaking trips, and check out video clips and accounts from adventurers who've traveled with the organization.

Backroads
www.backroads.com

Backroads, shown in Figure 10.3, offers cycling, hiking, cross-country skiing, and multi-sport excursions. Choose your activity of choice and select from a list of destinations around the world, including Thailand, Chile, Turkey, Portugal, and such areas of the United States as the Rocky Mountains and California's wine country. The site provides information on leisurely trips as well as more arduous expeditions, from luxury lodging and cuisine to camping under the stars. You can ask specific questions in the Back Talk department.

Outdoor Adventure River Specialists (O.A.R.S.)
www.oars.com

You'll find details and itineraries here for numerous river expeditions in the Western United States, including trips through the Grand Canyon. This site has information about the O.A.R.S. staff, expedition safety, the boats you'll

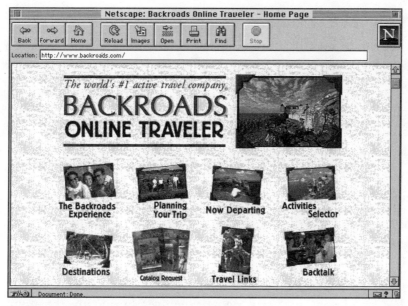

Figure 10.3 The Backroads home page.

travel in, riverside camping, and the food that's cooked up at the end of a day on the water (including recipes). Watch video clips of rafting and kayaking trips, and check out the "Hot Deals" section to find out about special offers.

Mountain Travel Sobek
www.mtsobek.com

Read about hiking treks, mountain climbing expeditions, river rafting excursions, sea kayaking trips, and safaris. The interactive map at this site will put you in touch with adventure trips offered in your destination of choice, and the "Multimedia Gallery" offers audio and video clips to give you a taste of the adventures. You can also read stories from other Mountain Sobek travelers, exchange questions and answers on the bulletin board, and look over a collection of photos from past trips.

Travel Byte

If you'd like to spend a little time on an outdoor sport like mountain biking or cross-country skiing, but don't want to make it the focus of your vacation, you can always rent the necessary equipment when you get there and just be adventuresome for a day or two.

River Rafting

River rafting is one of the most popular adventure sports for travelers. Rollicking trips along rivers like the Snake on rubber boats can be enjoyed by most anyone.

If you'd like to take your trip at a slower pace, rowing expeditions may be more your style. On these trips, you paddle your way downstream in a kayak or canoe, taking in the scenic views and the sounds of wildlife with a more relaxed approach.

The length of river trips vary. You can go for just a long weekend, or for a more in-depth experience, take a week to ten days or even longer.

Be sure to travel with a respected outfitter and knowledgeable guides, so that running the rapids is as safe as it is thrilling.

Transportation

Most expeditions don't start right at the river. Frequently, the group you'll be traveling with will meet at a pre-arranged location, often a hotel, to get started. The outfitter should give you detailed information on this meeting place in advance. From there, transportation will be provided to the staring point of your river journey. (And of course, after you've taken on the rapids, the outfitter should return you to the initial meeting spot.)

It's up to you to arrange your transportation to and from the prearranged meeting point. Be sure to get detailed information on the meeting place for your trip before you arrange your transportation, so you can fly into the closest airport possible. Use the Web sites listed in Chapter 5 to arrange initial transportation.

Travel Byte

Before you leave on your river expedition, stop by the Outdoor Action Guide to Planning a Safe River Trip at **www.princeton.edu/ ~oa/rivplan.html**.

Sites like the Grand Canyon River Running Web site (**river.ihs.gov**) offer stroke-by-stroke information about specific rivers. Grand Canyon River Running fills you in on the caverns, grottos, rapids, and gorges encountered along a trip down the Colorado. At this site, you'll find photos and descriptions, as well as an FAQ with answers to common questions on rafting trips such as "Where do I sleep?" and details on river fees. Links to Web sites of numerous river outfitters are also provided.

Online travelogues are also great ways to learn about river expeditions from a more personal perspective. Down the River (**www.discovery.com/DCO/doc/ 1012/world/specials/colorado/river1.html**), a site brought to you by the Discovery Channel, delivers the day-by-day details of Jim Malusa's trip along the rapids of the Colorado (see Figure 10.4). Read about his adventures and see photos and video clips, all collected from the trip via laptop computer and digital camera. Jim's notes include information about the geology and wildlife along the river.

Check out sites with connections to other Web sites. Paddlesports Links! (**pubweb.ucdavis.edu/Documents/oa/watersites.html**) helps you get connected to Web sites on rafting. Canada's Canoe Source (**canoe.info-pages.com**) provides links to Canadian canoeing Web sites. Use a search engine to find links to organizations like the World Kayak Federation (**www.worldkayak.com**) and American Whitewater Affiliation (**www.awa.org**) in addition to online magazines like Canoe & Kayak (**www.canoekayak.com**).

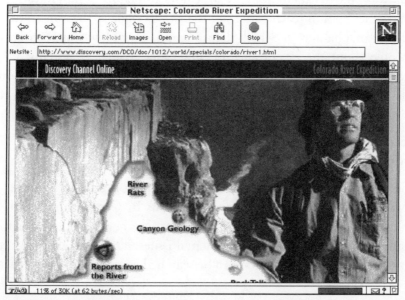

Figure 10.4 Join Jim Malusa on a trip down the Colorado River.

Gear To Go The Distance

An adventure vacation requires special items in your backpack that you might not take on other trips (see the "Pack It Up" section in Chapter 4). Here are a few extras you may want to take along on your next adventure:

- Wide-brimmed hat
- Gloves
- Flashlight
- Binoculars
- Bandanna
- Field guide
- Water bottle
- Compass
- Pocket knife
- Compact energy food, like granola bars

Eco-Travel

Every year, more and more travelers plan nature-based journeys. Eco-tours allow people to experience the exotic flora and fauna of rain forests, coral reefs, and other hard-to-reach corners of the world, while at the same time respecting the natural habitats in which they're found. These low-impact tours can teach people about the importance of preserving ecological systems; in addition, eco-tourism can support conservation by infusing currency into economically depressed countries and providing government officials and local communities with a motivation to preserve their natural resources.

Eco Travels in Latin America
www2.planeta.com/mader

Stop by this site to access extensive information on "green travel" through Mexico, The Amazon, and other locations in Central and South America. You'll find personal travel accounts and articles about places to visit, as well as information on current environmental issues. There are also links to numerous related Web sites, which can be searched according to your destination.

Eco Travel
ecotravel.com

Eco Travel is a good starting point for the environmentally-conscious traveler. Links to Web sites about outdoor education excursions, adventure camps, photographic tours, and ecological research trips can be found here. In addition, there are links to Web sites for cycling, skiing, hiking, climbing, and wildlife watching, among many other activities.

Trips With Nature Organizations

Many non-profit nature organizations like the Sierra Club (**www.sierraclub.org**) and The Nature Conservancy (**www.tnc.org**) offer environmentally friendly excursions to their members. You can often join a local chapter of one of these organizations right from their Web site, and a membership doesn't cost much. (Besides, it's for a good cause!) Check out the excursions offered by the following organizations.

The Nature Conservancy
www.tnc.org

Take a look at the list of "Field Trips" to learn about expeditions for Nature Conservancy members in the United States and other countries. You can find out about trips to waterfalls in Bolivia, sanctuaries in Belize, rain forests in Panama, and journeys to the Amazon River and the Galapagos Islands (Figure 10.5). Access a calendar of upcoming trips, read descriptions of what you'll see and do on these trips, and join The Nature Conservancy from the Web site.

National Audubon Society
www.audubon.org

Look in the "Audubon Marketplace" to find a list of upcoming Nature Odysseys, the National Audubon Society's international wildlife watching excursions. Trips include bird-watching cruises through the Caribbean, Alaska, Costa Rica, Sweden, and other places, and are led by senior staff members of the society. Fill out the questionnaire to provide the organization with your travel interests and preferences. You must be a member to participate in these outings; you can join online.

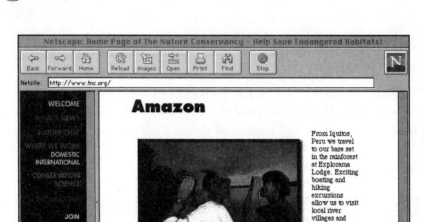

Figure 10.5 Read about offered eco-excursions at The Nature Conservancy Web site.

National Wildlife Federation
www.nwf.org

Read about Conservation Summits, week-long "environmental discovery programs" for individuals and families, hosted by the National Wildlife Federation. Trips include classes, lectures, hikes, and cruises, during which participants observe and learn about wildlife. The Web site includes photos from last year's excursions, as well as conservation news, action alerts, and articles from current National Wildlife magazines.

Travel Byte

Don't take natural souvenirs home with you. Keep rocks, flowers, shells, driftwood, plants, and seeds in the environments where they belong.

Going On Safari

Picture yourself making game runs at dawn, snapping photos of lions in the brush from your guide's Land Rover. Or sitting beside an evening campfire with monkeys swinging overhead and hippos wading and grunting in the nearby Rufiji River.

I grew up listening to engaging stories of my parents' safaris through Kenya, Tanzania, and Uganda: elephants slurping at watering holes, and up-close views of giraffes, baboons, zebra, warthogs, and impalas. It's no wonder that taking a safari is right there at the top of my vacation to-do list!

Safaris conjure up romantic images for any traveler, and from what I hear from people who've had the experience, those images are a reality. Along with the sites listed here, many safari tour operators have Web sites. Use the word "safaris" with your search engine to find extensive lists of companies that operate throughout Africa.

AfricaNet
www.africanet.com

AfricaNet is an informative Web site that can help you decide which areas of Africa you'd like to explore in person. The Country by Country Guide in-cludes such regional details as geography, language, and safety information, and you can read about featured destinations or chat with other adventurers in the Travel Forum.

On Safari
www2.onsafari.com/default.htm

This site lets you click on interactive maps to get in-depth information on game reserves, camps, and lodges throughout Africa (Figure 10.6). You'll find information on ballooning and bird watching, and walking, elephant, rail, and four-wheel safaris. There's also helpful information on regional climates, what to pack, visa requirements, and the food you'll probably eat on safari, as well as suggested itineraries, contact information for safari consultants, and online auctions. And the "Cyber Safari" lets you follow virtual wildebeasts on their migration across the Serengeti Plain.

Travel Byte

Be sure to take a telephoto lens (250mm or longer) for your camera when you go on safari. It will allow you to take close-up photos without disturbing the animals, and will also keep you out of harm's way!

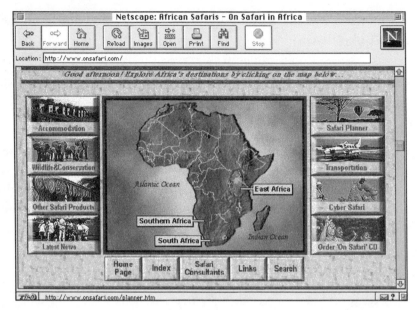

Figure 10.6 Gather information for your trip to Africa at the On Safari Web site.

Ski Trips

If your definition of adventure includes taking on the slopes, the Web can be a great resource for you. Numerous Web sites offer travel articles, information on the world's ski slopes and resorts, and the latest snow reports.

Begin planning your trip by reading articles by people who've traveled and skied all over the planet. These articles, found on SkiNet (**www.skinet.com**), SnowLink (**www.snowlink.com**), and other sites, can give you unbiased opinions of what specific resorts have to offer—from the exceptional to the inadequate. Read them to get a feel for places where you might like to test your skills.

You can also find information on ski resorts you already have in mind, like Sugarloaf (**www.sugarloaf.com**), Steamboat (**www.Steamboat-Ski.com**), and Stowe (**www.stowe.com/smr**). Using search engines like Yahoo!, you can get connected to Web sites about locations that interest you. From a search using the words "skiing" and "Lake Tahoe," I discovered a great site called SnoWeb (**www.snoweb.com**), which details the slopes and resorts in the Lake Tahoe Region.

There are sites about larger ski regions, too. The Ski Colorado Web site (**www.aescon.com/ski/index.htm**) provides information on the slopes, elevation, lifts, rates, and schedules of ski resorts throughout the state of Colorado. Skiers can look up the Colorado locations they have in mind, and follow links to other Web pages with snow reports, ski maps, and info on skiing lessons. Stop by the "Ski Instructor's Message Board" to get your questions answered; you'll also find articles on waxing skis, high-altitude health tips, and the latest ski news.

A number of ski sites offer information on regions and resorts all over the world. The following Web sites provide information that can help you plan the ski trip of your dreams.

The Virtually Complete Skier
easyweb.easynet.co.uk/~michaell

This online companion to the print book, *The Complete Skier*, offers information on skiing and resorts in various countries, and the best seasons to take your vacation. You'll also find advice on equipment, tips for skiing with children, and descriptions of the basic skills you'll need. Submit a ski-related question to the authors, and they'll provide and post the answer.

Skigate
www.skigate.com

Listen to RealAudio ski reports at this site, and check out live ski camera shots from all over the country. The "Swap Shop" is a great place to find bargains on skis, boots, and snow boards, and you'll also find numerous links to other ski pages and the Web sites of ski resorts and lodgings, ski products, and ski tours.

SkiNet
www.skinet.com

Brought to you by *Skiing* and *Ski* magazines, SkiNet delivers the daily news to people who love to hit the slopes. A travel chat forum, articles on ski trips, and a guide to great resorts can be found here (Figure 10.7), as well as daily webcam images and snow reports from across the United States and Canada. Pages geared specifically to women, teens, and families are provided, as are gear guides, classifieds, picture galleries, tip-offs on "cool deals," and ski trivia.

Figure 10.7   Check out recommended resorts at SkiNet.

SnowLink
www.snowlink.com

"Snow sport news" and information on new products and ski trends can be found at this site. Travel features offer advice on where to spend your ski vacation, and snow reports for slopes in the U.S., Canada, and Europe are available. SnowLink even features online skiing and snow boarding lessons. You can also find links here to the Web sites of ski clubs, organizations, festivals, and special events.

Ski Travel Online
www.skito.com

Click on the interactive map to learn about ski resorts in the region of your choice. You'll find facts on the slopes, information on lodgings, and details on the local area so you'll have something to do when you're not heading downhill. You can shop for choice ski packages and find answers to your questions on the message boards, and articles on skiing all over the world can be found in the "BootLoose" department.

Ski The World
www.wu-wien.ac.at/usr/h94/h9450102/skiing.html

In its own words, this site is a "comprehensive guide to the finest skiing, the warmest welcomes, and the wildest scenery." Read brief reviews about the ski regions of the U.S., France, Switzerland, Austria, Italy, Canada, South America, Australia, and Japan, and find information on terrain, snow conditions, the surrounding countryside, popular resorts, and area history.

WinterNet
www.iion.com/WinterNet

The "Resort Guide" provides contact information for ski resorts throughout the United States and Canada. Find information here on how to get to the slopes by air, rail, road, and bus—even book your transportation and accommodations from the site. You can also check out virtual slopes, snow reports, and weather forecasts.

SnowCountry
www.snowcountry.com

SnowCountry's articles about ski excursions and lodgings offer lots of advice about where to travel, including their top-pick list of ski resorts in North America. Skiers can read updates on new products, field tests, and the latest gear at the Equipment Hotline. Also available here are snow reports, screen saver images, and information about upcoming events for ski bums.

Travel Byte

When participating in outdoor activities, acting like you know more than you do can result in accidents. Don't pretend to be a professional if you aren't one!

Adventure On The Links

For golf enthusiasts, a vacation devoted to hitting the links can be the ultimate adventure. Testing your skills on superior courses like Pinehurst in North Carolina or, for the more adventuresome golfer, the links of Scotland where the sport originated, can be a thrill of a lifetime. I've visited the old course of

St. Andrews in the Kingdom of Fife, Scotland, with its rough and untrimmed greens, and trust me, it would be an adventure for even a master golfer.

Check out the old course for yourself at the St. Andrews (**www.standrews.co.uk**) Web site, shown in Figure 10.8. On its pages, golfers can read hole-by-hole descriptions of courses and find information on fees, tee-off times, and how to make reservations. The site also offers a historical overview on St. Andrews, and information on places of interest in the area, such as castles and parks, eating and drinking establishments, and accommodations.

There are numerous Web sites that provide information on the world's courses, from well known links to smaller, off-the-beaten-path courses. You'll read descriptions of the links and resorts, and you can also find contact information for making your reservations. Some sites not only provide course information, but offer links (no pun intended!) to Web sites of other courses.

At the following sites, you'll find abundant information on hundreds of golf courses, not only in the U.S., but in Europe, Asia, and South America as well.

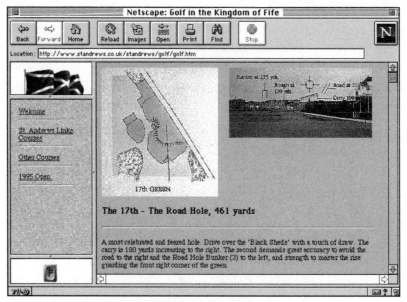

Figure 10.8 Survey the links of St. Andrews on the Web.

GolfWeb
www.golfweb.com

The "On Course" database provides you with information on public and private courses worldwide, including those in Argentina, Japan, and Australia. GolfWeb also offers rankings of the top 100 courses in the world and the U.S., monthly columns, golf news, and weekly polls, as well as numerous links to the Web sites of golf courses, resorts, contests, tours, and online magazines. An added feature is the list of discussion groups on topics such as "Women in Golf," "Tiger Talk," "Golf Action," "Juniors," and "Architecture/Golf Courses."

Golfcourse.com
www.golfcourse.com

The "Course Locator" at this site helps you access information on thousands of courses in the United States and abroad, including maps to help you get there. The travel section includes information on golfing the world's links, including those in Canada, the French Riviera, Italy, Scotland, Ireland, and England. Articles about golf course architecture and featured resorts are also available here, as are contests and message boards on golfing the world over.

Golf Travel Online
www.gto.com

This site includes details on more than 300 golf resorts. Search for a specific resort, search for resorts by region, or submit your preferences to find a resort that fits you "to a tee." For each resort, you'll find particulars on amenities and prices, how to get there, and the golf course itself. Check out information on what to do in the area when you're not hitting the links, read resort reviews, and browse travel packages here as well.

World Golf
www.worldgolf.com

At this site you can discover courses located all over the planet. Read articles on golfing adventures in the Rocky Mountains, Africa, India, and other far away lands, and find details on greens, bunkers, and sand traps. A golf glossary, advice to improve your skills, and current deals on golf getaway packages can all be found here as well.

Golf Universe
www.golf universe.com

Find a golf course that's right for you by searching the 24,000 listed at this site, including the one shown in Figure 10.9. You can use the interactive maps, or search by keyword to find just what you're looking for. You'll read specifics on all the courses, including seasons, fees, and location information, and you can also register to win golf getaways.

Travel Byte

Golf resorts are not just for golfing anymore. Many resorts offer fitness centers, swimming pools, horseback riding, cycling, and other golf-unrelated activities.

Virtual Vineyards

Take your palate on an adventure by visiting the world's great wine regions. Imagine driving through the rolling hills of Tuscany's Chianti region, or taking

Figure 10.9 Access useful information on numerous golf courses at the Golf Universe site.

in the picturesque views and grand estates of California's Sonoma Valley as you cycle along its winding roads.

A trip to the wineries of California, Italy, France, Germany, New Zealand, or any other corner of the globe, can be a learning experience for wine enthusiasts as well as for travelers with novice noses.

Guided tours may take you deep into caverns and cellars among rows of vintage-filled caskets. You'll learn the details of wine-crafting particular to each winery, and maybe catch a history lesson along the way, and of course, tasting the various vintages of a winery is the grand finale of any visit. Some wineries, like some in the Napa Valley, charge about $3.00 a person to taste, but in many other areas tasting is free of charge.

You can also visit wineries right from your home. If you have a particular vineyard in mind, use a Web search engine like Excite to see if the winery has a Web page.

At the Chateau Haut-Brion Web site (**haut-brion.com/chb/wine/index.html**), there's information on the winery's wines, vines, and history. The site also offers a virtual tour of the grounds, including a visit to the chateau, the laboratory, the vat room, and the cooperage. Virtual travelers may also read news on the latest harvests, or chat with other wine enthusiasts in the "Haut-Brion Forum."

Travel Byte

An appointment may be required to visit a winery. Get contact information at the Web sites listed in this chapter and make your reservation ahead of time.

You can also use a search engine to locate Web sites about vineyards in the country you plan to visit. The Wines and Food from France Web site (**www.frenchwinesfood.com/index.html**) offers descriptions of the land and wine of some of France's wine regions, shown in Figure 10.10. Wine Country (**www.winecountry.com**) provides information on taking a wine-tasting trip through California, and NapaNet (**www.napanet.com**) has links to Web sites of wineries located in the Napa Valley.

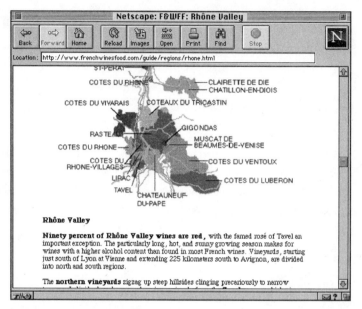

Figure 10.10 Learn about French wine regions at the Wines and Food from France Web site.

For links to other wine pages, visit the Wine Guide (**www.wineguide.com/wgpg2.htm**), or the Wine, Wineries, and Wine Products list (**www.geocities.com/NapaValley/1824**). The following Web sites also offer links to other pages, as well as information on visiting wineries.

Wine Lovers Page
www.xs4all.nl/~wincoop/Winepage/Winepage.htm

Check out the "Wine Travel Tips" for suggested vineyards to visit and advice on wine tasting in particular regions. This site lists contact information for numerous vineyards, and you'll find a listing of the favorite wines of other Web surfers. A collection of photos and text from several French vineyards take you on cyber-wine-tasting trip at "The Virtual Chateau."

The Grapevine
www.valuenet.com

You can find visitor information for various wineries, such as tasting and tour schedules, in addition to contact information and email links. Also get the scoop on upcoming auctions, festivals, and places to stay. Access maps of wine regions in the U.S., like Sonoma and Napa Valley, and look over the wine glossary and advice on sampling wines before you leave on your trip.

Smart Wine
smartwine.com

The "Wine Calendar" offers contact information for vineyards throughout the U.S., tasting room schedules included. Read travel articles, check out the Wine of the Day, and get updates on news in the industry. The chat forum allows you to communicate with wine experts about their vineyards, or you can take a look at the "Photo Album" to view images of wine country.

Wines on the Internet
www.wines.com/wines.html

At this site you'll find descriptions and history of numerous wineries and their wines, mostly in California, as shown in Figure 10.11. There's visitor information, contact information, and driving directions and maps. The "Virtual Wine Tasting Room" lets you browse the labels of new releases, or you can check out the "best wine of the week," wine reviews, the Q & A, and an online database to learn the ins and outs of wine tasting.

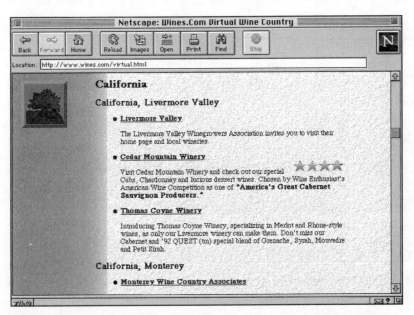

Figure 10.11 Access information about wineries to plan your trip.

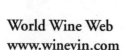

World Wine Web
www.winevin.com

This site's "World Wine Encyclopedia" provides maps of various wine regions throughout the world. Choose from a list of destinations for information about wines produced in the area, the grapes used, and the price range of the wines.

Travel Byte

Consider visiting up-and-coming wine regions, where wines cost less than those from California, France, and Italy. Spain and Chile, for example, boast flourishing vineyards you may want to explore.

Adventure Indoors: Hitting The Casinos

If you're seduced by flashing lights, the sounds of raking in chips, and the promise of winning it big, your ultimate adventure probably involves a visit to Las Vegas. To plan a trip to the "adult Disneyland," you'll want to check out the place where you'll be spending most of your time—the casino.

Luckily for you, the World Wide Web is home to numerous hotel casino sites. Look up the most popular casinos on and off the infamous strip: Caesar's Palace (**www.caesarspalace.com**), Treasure Island (**www.treasureislandlasvegas.com**), Luxor (**www.luxor.com**), MGM Grand (**www.mgmgrand.com**), and The Mirage (**www.themirage.com**). You can also find out about accommodations, restaurants, upcoming shows, shown in Figure 10.12, and theme-park-type attractions at these Web sites.

For more on making a visit to the city where Elvis still reigns supreme, look up the Las Vegas Online Entertainment Guide (**www.lvol.com/lvoleg/index.html**), Las Vegas (**www.intermind.net/im/lasvegas.html**), and Vegas.com (**www.vegas.com**).

Still Feeling Adventurous?

If you're interested in more outdoor adventures, read Chapter 12 to find out about camping and hiking in national parks. If a voyage on the high seas is

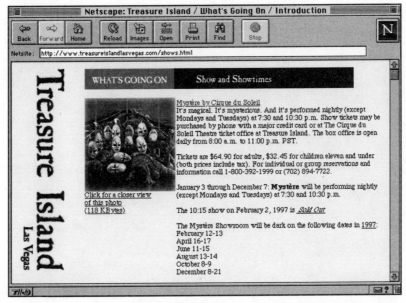

Figure 10.12 Find out about show times and ticket prices of Las Vegas shows, like Cirque du Soleil.

what you're looking for, keep reading. Chapter 11 offers advice on booking a cruise, and leads you to Web sites of cruise lines, resorts, and other resources to help you plan a tropical getaway.

Paradise Found: Cruises And Tropical Getaways

CHAPTER 11 TOPICS

- CHOOSING AND PURCHASING A CRUISE

- EXPLORING PORTS OF CALL

- RESORTS ONLINE

Cruises appeal to a variety of travelers. From singles to honeymooners, kids to seniors, everyone can find something on the sea that appeals to their tastes. Numerous cruise lines, with equally numerous ships and itineraries, give travelers many options to choose from.

Some cruise lines cater to those who want to be waited on—people who long to sit back in their deck chairs, soak up the sun, and relax as the ship's crew cooks the meals, plans the entertainment, and serves the strawberry daiquiris. Others appeal to more active types by providing a variety of activities on board: shuffleboard competitions, dance lessons, wildlife lectures, wine tastings, murder mysteries, jazz concerts, discos, casinos—non-stop entertainment all day and all night long!

These resorts-at-sea deliver vacationers to not-so-far-away locations like Mexico and the Caribbean, as well as to exotic islands like Tahiti and Bora Bora. Even travelers interested in exploring less tropical climates, like Alaska, can travel by cruise ship. Many lines sail to major world ports; these cruise excursions to the cities of Europe or Asia allow you to visit many destinations in a short amount of time and provide you with a quick impression of communities around the globe. Visiting the world's great cities on a cruise is an easy way to visit celebrated relics, browse renowned art galleries, and explore bustling city centers. Just think—each night you wine, dine, and get a good night's sleep, while your ship sails on to your next port of call.

Cruise in ultra-luxury, dining on gourmet cuisine and taking in classical concertos, or go casual, meeting your favorite football stars on sports theme cruises, as shown in Figure 11.1. There's so much to choose from, it would be hard not to find a cruise that suits your interests.

Cruise The Web

Use the Web to see what cruises have to offer. The Web pages of cruise lines will fill you in on the ships in their fleets, their various destinations, and the ports-of-call they visit. You can get a feel for the general atmosphere onboard, as well as the size of the ships, ranging from small vessels to megaliners, and many sites offer detailed cruise itineraries for your review.

In addition, check up on the details that are important to you, like wheelchair accessibility, onboard activities, low-fat menus, and extras for couples celebrating

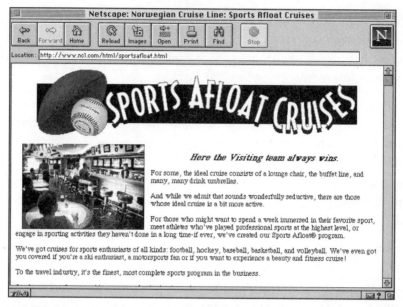

Figure 11.1   Find out about theme cruises on cruise line Web sites.

an anniversary. Some Web sites even recommend cruises based on your travel preferences. Also be sure to take an online look at the cabins, and find out how much more a suite or a cabin with an ocean view or balcony costs.

The following Web sites contain information on the cruises offered by the most popular cruise lines. To find more cruise line Web sites, visit Coolwater.com (**www.coolwater.com**) or the List of Official Cruise Web Sites (**members.aol.com/tomraynor/cruises/index.html**). The Yahoo! search engine also provides an extensive list of cruise Web sites when you search using the key words "cruise lines."

Carnival Cruise Lines
www.carnival.com

Choose from listed cruise packages to see detailed itineraries and cruise maps, or select from lists of activities, such as casinos, salons, shore excursions, and the "captain's gala dinner" to learn more about what you can do onboard. You can also read articles about the cruises from "the traveling reporter."

Celebrity Cruises
www.celebrity-cruises.com

This site provides itineraries of cruises to Alaska, the Caribbean, Bermuda, and Europe, including maps of stops along the way. You'll find details about each Celebrity ship, including accommodations and cabin amenities, facilities for disabled travelers, and notes on the ship's crew. Check out the cruise line's special features, like spa programs, the onboard art collection, the casinos, and find out from the sample dinner menu what the onboard cuisine is like.

Clipper Cruise Line
ecotravel.com/clipper

Visit this site to read about Clipper Cruise Line's vessels, the Yorktown Clipper and the Nantucket Clipper. You can look at cruise photos and get information about onboard atmosphere and amenities, cuisine, and dress code, as well as about environmentally conscious travel. You'll also find deck plans, itineraries (including price information), and information about rail/cruise excursions.

Cunard
www.cunardline.com

To find a cruise that's just right for you, go to the "Ask the Cruise Consultant" section of this site. Select your desired ports, ship, theme, cruise length, and when you would like to travel, and the "Cruise Consultant" will make suggestions—mine are shown in Figure 11.2. For each suggested cruise, you can view the itinerary and read about each port of call. In addition, this site has information about theme cruises focused on food and wine, fall foliage, guest chefs, musical theater, and jazz. You'll also find details about the ships in the fleet, and learn about discounts for those who book early. Just for fun, look up the "famous travelers of the month."

Holland America Lines
www.hollandamerica.com

Use the "Cruise Line Selector" to discover a Holland America cruise tailored to your preferences. You can read about their many destinations, including European capitols, the Panama Canal, and the Far East, and you'll find extensive information about their ships, including photos of staterooms, as shown in Figure 11.3. The site also offers information on activities for kids, teens,

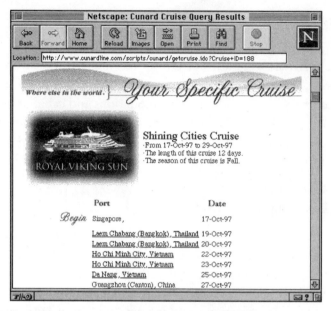

Figure 11.2 Get cruise recommendations according to your travel preferences at the Cunard Web site.

Figure 11.3 View photos of cabins before choosing your cruise.

and "tweens" in the kids' club section, and you can request further info on individual cruises using an online request form.

Norwegian Cruise Line
www.ncl.com

You can read about Norwegian Cruise Line's ships and the destinations they sail to, with detailed itineraries and maps. Find out about theme cruises on sports and music, and check out the special discounts offered at the Web site. Frequent cruisers should check out the Latitudes passenger club.

Premier Cruise Lines (The Big Red Boat)
www.bigredboat.com

Take a "Guided Tour" to learn about cruise activities for families, couples, and kids, as well as shore excursions. You'll find information about "last minute, unadvertised super bargains," and about cruise packages that include admission to the Magic Kingdom. There's a sample menu to give you an idea of the food served onboard, and you can access tropical drink recipes, download their television commercial, and even enter the photo contest when you return home.

Renaissance Cruises
www.rencruises.com

At this site you can read descriptions of ports of call, and learn about the shore excursions offered on various cruises. Take a virtual cruise, play online contests, and read comments from others who've sailed with Renaissance Cruises. You'll also find out about discounted prices, and you can sign up to receive updates on future last-minute discounts. You can even book your trip from the Web site.

Royal Caribbean
www.royalcaribbean.com

This site has details on Royal Caribbean's many destinations, and the site's "Cybercruise" takes you along for the ride. You'll find extensive information on excursions, with maps and schedules included, and you can read about the many activities available onboard, including gambling, fitness classes, swimming, and deck games, as well as nightly entertainment (see Figure 11.4). In addition, you can look at photos, read remarks from the crew and past passengers, check out the staterooms, and stop by the chat room and bulletin board.

Figure 11.4 Learn about onboard activities, from nightly shows to the casinos.

Windstar Cruises
www.windstarcruises.com

Visit this Web site to get a general feel for what you'll experience on a Windstar cruise. You can find out what a typical day at sea is like, as well as details about the fleet. The site provides cruise itineraries for the South Pacific, the Caribbean, the Mediterranean, and Costa Rica, and you can request additional literature according to your interests.

What To Do If You Feel Seasick

While most ships have stabilizers and are big enough to keep passengers from getting queasy, some travelers still get a bit nauseated on a cruise. Here are some tips to help steady your stomach if you feel sick on your trip.

- Eat light, low-fat foods like fruits, which are easy to digest.
- Avoid alcohol. Being tipsy or having a hangover while on rough water can cause disorientation and make you even more nauseated.
- Ginger can often ease an upset stomach. Drinking ginger ale or taking ginger capsules may help.

- Be as active as possible. Lying down aboard a moving ship can make your stomach feel even worse.

- Motion-sickness medicines like Bonine can help, but don't take so much that you can't function.

- Don't go below deck until you have to; instead, remain on the top deck in the fresh air.

Purchasing Your Cruise

When you book a cruise, you're booking an entire vacation package. Your meals (including the infamous midnight buffet), accommodations, and activities on board are all included in the price, as is the entertainment, which includes glitzy revues, stand-up comedy acts, and magic shows.

Usually you can purchase a cruise package that includes round-trip airfare and ground transportation to and from the ship's harbor. When you purchase a package like this, it's up to the cruise line to get you to the ship on time. If your flight is late, or you get held up in traffic, the ship will wait in port for your arrival. Because of the peace of mind a package like this offers travelers, I recommend booking your trip this way if you plan to cruise.

If you'd rather purchase your flight separately, use the Web sites listed in Chapter 5 to hunt for great promotional discounts and get the cheapest fares. In addition, booking your own flight allows you to fly with the airline of your choice so you can rack up those cherished frequent-flyer miles.

Travel Byte

Be sure to let all the travel personnel know if you're on your honeymoon. Tell the travel agent when you book your cruise, alert the airline staff, and most importantly, inform the ship's crew. Extras like free champagne and candlelight dinners are customarily offered to newlyweds.

Book Early

Some cruise lines, like Renaissance Cruises, offer last-minute bargains to travelers, similar to the closing discount rates available from airlines and hotels. In addition to advertising promotional discounts at their Web site, as shown in

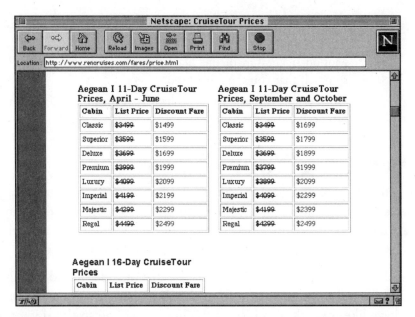

Figure 11.5 Discover discount prices by visiting cruise line Web sites.

Figure 11.5, Renaissance Cruises will also update you on last-minute low prices via email.

For the most part, though, getting the best deal on a cruise means booking early—as early as you possibly can. The cruise industry rewards travelers who reserve far in advance with great discounts—as much as 30 percent off a cruise's list price.

Cruise lines offer these discount rates to early shoppers because it benefits them to fill as many cabins as far in advance as possible. A plus for travelers today is that cruise lines are building more and more ships, and building them bigger and bigger, so you have more opportunity to get a budget price.

If you book your cruise early and then find the retail price has been lowered at a later date, you'll probably receive the cheaper price as well. Cruise lines want to encourage early booking, and guaranteeing that you'll get the lowest price advertised keeps customers happy. Be sure to check that this is the case with the cruise line you plan to travel with.

Getting A Deal

Some cruise lines list the costs of their cruises on their Web pages. Before you buy, check the Web sites for promotional deals, and get on mailing lists that inform you of advertised discounts, like the mailing list of Royal Caribbean.

Remember, only uninformed travelers pay the retail price of a cruise. Booking early, booking using a promotional discount advertised on a Web site, or booking through a travel agent informed about air/sea packages (which aren't often detailed on Web sites), can get you a lower price.

If you discover a special deal advertised on a Web site, keep in mind that the cheap price probably doesn't include airfare or ground transportation, but simply covers the cruise itself.

Travel Byte

Keep track of your additional charges, such as alcoholic and even non-alcoholic drinks, by asking the crew for a daily printout of your bill.

Most industry experts recommend that travelers book a cruise with the help of a travel agent. Most cruise lines recommend you take this route also, and will help you find an agent from their site. Booking a cruise with an agent is a good idea because they can help you arrange an air/sea package—information that is often not found on Web sites at this time. To get the best price, be sure to let your agent know about any discounts you come across on the Web before (and even after) you make your purchase.

Finding a certified travel agent with a Web site, or one located near you, is easy using the Internet. The American Society of Travel Agents (ASTA) (**www. astanet.com**) is "the largest association of travel professionals in the world," with 25,000 members located in 136 countries. The ASTA Web site enables you to conduct a search to find an ASTA agent in your neighborhood: Enter the town where you live, submit that you're looking for an agency that specializes in cruises, and select the destination you'd like to visit on your travels. You'll then receive location and contact information for any member agencies in your area.

Using the Web pages of the Cruise Line International Association (CLIA) (**www.ten-io.com/clia**), you can easily search for CLIA-affiliated agencies; find one located near you by submitting your area or ZIP code. You can also check out "Cruise News," a cruising FAQ, and profiles on CLIA member cruise lines at the Web site.

Ship Tipping

As if tipping at a hotel isn't confusing enough, tipping on a cruise can be absolutely mind-boggling, so here are some pointers on offering compensation for service. There are a lot of people to tip on a cruise. Expect to spend about $10 a day or more on tips.

- Waiters should be tipped about $3 to $4 a day per passenger at the end of your trip. Assistant waiters or busboys should get about $2 each day.
- Cabin stewards should be left approximately $3 for each day your room was tidied up, paid at the end of your cruise.
- Tip bartenders 15 percent. (If you find a 15 percent gratuity added to your bar tab, there's no need to add anything more.)
- For services at the hair salon, tip at the time of service.

Pay all of your tips in U.S. currency (in cash). If you're on an extensive voyage, offer tips once a week, or every other week. Take note of your cruise line's tipping etiquette. Some cruises have a no-tipping policy, while some (presumptuous) cruise lines provide guests with tipping guidelines.

If you would rather offer a tip at the beginning of the cruise (which may get you better service), use the cruise line's tipping guide. At the start of your voyage offer half of what the cruise line proposes, and let the crew know there is more to come.

Ports Of Call

Cruise lines often offer guided tours of ports of call to their guests. Be aware that these tours are not included in the price of your cruise, and they're often quite expensive.

To avoid a high-priced walk-through, learn about the ports of call on your ship's itinerary before you leave on your trip by using the information and Web sites listed in this section, as well as in Chapter 3.

When you learn about St. Lucia, Barbados, Aruba, or any other port-of-call on your cruise ahead of time, you'll know what to see and do upon arrival. Find out where to rent a moped, and learn about the great restaurants, clean beaches, and natural wonders on the island. And of course, don't forget to look up the best golf courses and places to shop. You can even print out maps to take along with you, as shown in Figure 11.6.

Virtual Bermuda
www.bermuda.bm

Virtual Bermuda can tip you off to the best beaches and the facilities available at them, including changing rooms, beach lounge chairs, umbrellas, snorkeling equipment, and snack bars. The site also tells you how to get around, about interesting areas to explore, places to dine, and upcoming theater performances, celebrations, and other events.

U.S. Virgin Islands
www.usvi.net

Learn about the islands of St. Croix, St. Thomas, and St. John at this site. You'll find maps, a photo gallery, current news items, and a calendar of events for the islands. Information on sightseeing and restaurants is available to help

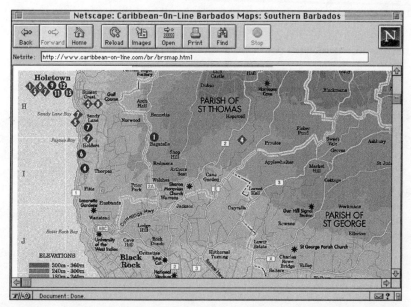

Figure 11.6 Print out maps of ports you'll be visiting, from Caribbean On-Line.

you plan your trip, and you can also investigate diving instructors, boat charters, places to shop, and golf courses.

Travel Byte

If you get off the ship to visit a port of call, be sure you can get back on! Remember to take your boarding pass with you when you leave.

Cayman Islands
www.caymans.com

Use the calendar of events to plan your trip around festivals and celebrations, take the "Culinary Crash Course" to learn about Cayman cuisine, and find out about diving, fishing, boating, sightseeing, and other leisurely pursuits. You'll also find island music and video clips at this Web site.

Caribbean On-Line
www.caribbean-on-line.com

Click on the interactive map of the islands to explore destinations throughout the Caribbean, including Jamaica, Barbados, St. Lucia, and the Dominican Republic. You'll find guides to each area, including information on currency, languages, transportation, climate, and cultural heritage. The site also features descriptions of restaurants, and information on what cruise lines sail to the area. In addition, you can look at detailed maps of your destination of choice.

Saving Your Skin

Getting sunburned can ruin a vacation. From the lingering anguish of an initial burn (blisters included) to fearing the sunlight for the rest of the trip, burning is nothing but a pain in the neck (and back, and shoulders, and arms, and forehead...). Here's how to avoid getting fried:

- Apply sunscreen everywhere. Not only noses get burned: Hands, ears, and feet are susceptible to the sun's rays too.

- Allow enough time for the sunscreen to sink in. Slather it on at least a half-hour before you go out in the sunshine.

- One SPF unit equals 20 minutes of protection. For example, SPF 4 sunscreen gives you about 1 hour and 20 minutes of protection.

- Ultraviolet rays penetrate through water and through clouds, so you can wind up red after swimming or even at the end of a gray day.

- Don't sunbathe when the sun's rays are most intense, from about 10 a.m. until 1:30 p.m.

- Apply sunscreen about every two hours, and always after swimming, even if your sunscreen says "waterproof."

Read More About It

If you want to read more cruising information, KL Smith's Cruise Letter (**www.chevychase.com/cruise**) provides updates on various cruise lines and articles on holiday cruising. You'll learn what to pack, how to save money, how not to gain weight on a cruise, and more. You'll also find tips from readers and information for disabled travelers.

Another resource is Going Places, the Web site of Al Roker's travel program on PBS (**www.pbs.org/wnet/goingplaces/caribbean.html**). The site offers information on cruises, and describes Al's trip through the Caribbean, as seen in Figure 11.7. Read about various destinations and cruise lines, look at maps and a slide show, and watch clips from the program.

Use the Destination Gateway Web site (**www.jwg.com/vacation/cruiseinfo.html**) to search for information on numerous cruise lines, or visit the Cruise Review Library (**www.pagesz.net/~jbdavis/rtc/rtc.html**) for cruise line contact info, cruising tips, and cruise reviews.

Finally, here are two more excellent resources on cruising.

Fielding Travel Guides
www.fieldingtravel.com

The Web site of the famous travel guides provides the complete edition of their *Worldwide Cruises '97* book online. Here you'll find "descriptions of 60 cruise lines and over 150 major ships." You can browse the list of cruise lines and ships, or search by the destination you'd like to visit. The site provides informative reviews on cabins, as shown in Figure 11.8, as well as itineraries and details on amenities.

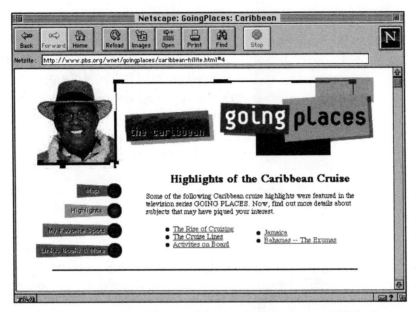

Figure 11.7 Learn more about cruising at Al Roker's travel Web site.

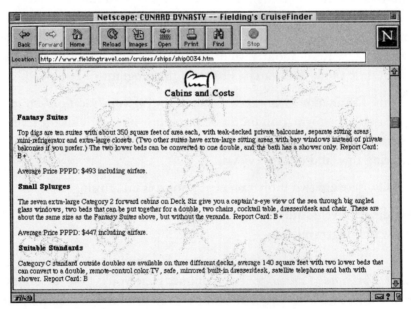

Figure 11.8 Read cruise reviews at the Fielding Travel Guides Web site.

Cruising the Americas
www.nationalgeographic.com/modules/cruise/index.html

Brought to you by *National Geographic Magazine*, Cruising the Americas recommends cruise lines to match your travel preferences. You can click on an interactive map to read about the many islands and countries that cruise lines sail to. The "Brochure Rack" provides photo collections on various cruise lines.

Resorts

If you're interested in being pampered and having fun in the sun, but you'd rather do it on solid ground, check out resort Web sites. Resorts Online (**www.resortsonline.com**) is a great resource for learning about vacation spots; with descriptions of resorts and links to each resort's Web site, you can search for a resort by name, location, or the activities you'd like to participate in.

Many hotels, like Westin, Sheraton, Hilton, and Hyatt operate resorts, too. Look up the Web sites listed in Chapter 6 to read about resorts associated with major hotel chains.

You can also use a search engine to look up a favorite resort or one you've heard about. At Web sites like that of Club Med (**www.clubmed.com**), you can find information tailored to your needs, whether you're traveling alone, as a couple, or with your family. Choose a destination by specific location (there are lots to choose from) or by your specific preferences regarding price range, comfort level, and activities. For each Club Med resort you can view a collection of photos and read about the accommodations, facilities, restaurants, and social activities.

Travel Byte

To find information on beaches all over the world, look up the Beaches Web site at **www.oneweb.com/infoctrs/beaches.html**.

Sail On

For information on cruising with the kids, keep reading. Chapter 12 offers advice and Web sites that can help you plan a trip the whole family will enjoy.

If you're interested in escaping to a tropical getaway, but would rather fly than go by boat, read up on destinations using the sites listed in Chapter 3, then go to Chapter 5 to learn about airlines online. In addition, the Web sites found in Chapter 6 can help you make room reservations for almost anywhere under the sun.

Are We There Yet?
Trips For The
Whole Family

CHAPTER 12 TOPICS

- Planning Kid-Friendly Vacations

- Online Camping, National Parks, And Dude Ranches

- Traveling With The Family Pet

Ahhh—the family vacation. Most everyone has memories from their own childhood: cramming into the back of the station wagon with brothers and sisters, waiting in anticipation to take off on that first flight out West, meeting Chip & Dale in the magical world of Disney....

And today you may find yourself packing up diapers and coloring books for your own kids, and playing travel games like *I Spy*, *Hug-Bug*, and of course, every parent's favorite, *The Silent Game*. Family vacations create memories that last a lifetime, for parents and children alike.

Each family has their own idea of where to go and what to do when it's time to take a trip. Maybe an educational excursion is up your alley, to teach the children something about U.S. history or about other cultures. On the other hand, you might want to focus on just having fun, and visit a theme park on your trip.

This chapter lists some Web sites that can help your family explore different vacation ideas, such as taking a camping trip, or letting loose at a dude ranch. If you have an idea for your family's vacation that's not covered in this chapter, use the information in the rest of this book to help with your plans. For example, if a ski trip is what you have in mind, you'll find related Web sites and information listed in Chapter 10.

Travel Byte

Check the Web to find out about discounts for kids. Children's rates are offered by certain international airlines, as well as on international flights of some domestic airlines. At some hotels, kids under 16 stay free, and kids can ride the rails at half price with Amtrak.

Planning The Trip

Most kids appreciate having a say in the family vacation plans. When your children aren't having a good time, their fidgeting and complaining will probably make it hard for you to enjoy the trip as well. Listen to them and consider their suggestions, and surf the Web together for ideas. The sites listed in Chapter 3, as well as the ones mentioned in this chapter (like the Disney Web site, which is a bit more kid-friendly than many online magazines) are great sites to visit as a family. In addition, there are Web sites that teach children about the history and cultures of other countries, such as Global Learn (**www.globalearn.org**), shown in Figure 12.1. Colgate toothpaste's Web site also offers travel information tailor-made for kids (**www.colgate.com/Kids-world/World-tour/index.html**), and Delta Airlines hosts a "Teen Travel" section on their site (**www.delta-air.com/teen/world/wld_frm.htm**), shown in Figure 12.2.

When planning your trip, consider the ages and interests of your kids. Do they show particular interest in the arts or science? Maybe a family camp would be a good vacation idea to explore. Are they interested in animals? Perhaps a trip to Sea World would be a fun and educational experience. If your kids have never left the city, a trip to a national or state park can give them a better understanding of the outdoors and natural environments.

It's also a good idea to choose a destination that offers a variety of activities, so that each member of the family can plan one day's itinerary.

Travel Byte

If you have a young child and plan to rent a car, be sure to specify to the car rental company that you'll need a safety seat.

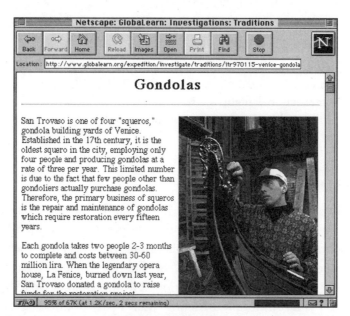

Figure 12.1   *Kids can learn about the family's vacation destination at the Global Learn Web site.*

Figure 12.2 Delta's Web pages, especially for teen travelers.

Parents who plan family trips with their kids in mind are more likely to enjoy themselves as well. Sharing in the children's happiness as they make new discoveries creates cherished memories that last a lifetime. Three great resources for parents planning a trip for the family are Parent Soup, Family.com, and Parent Time.

Parent Soup
www.parentsoup.com

Visit the Parents' Picks travel department to read reviews of various vacation spots from parents who've been there, with a focus on kid-friendliness. In the travel discussion group, parents share their views on vacationing with the kids, and you'll find travel tips and articles in the library when you search using the keyword "travel."

Family.com
family.com

At this site you'll find numerous articles on traveling with the family, as shown in Figure 12.3. Select from a list of travel topics including experiencing the outdoors, eating at restaurants, and visiting museums and theme parks, or

Figure 12.3   At Family.com you can read articles on a wide variety of vacation ideas.

find travel information according to the ages of your children. You'll find resort reviews, ways to save money, useful advice on family travel, and vacation recommendations.

ParentTime
www.pathfinder.com, then click on "ParentTime"

This site features age-appropriate information. Specify the age of your child, then click on "Activities and Adventures" to read articles about things to do with the kids on vacation, including camping, visiting zoos, and fishing. You can also stop by the chat room to exchange travel ideas with other parents.

Family Trip Tips

Keeping the kids occupied is the key to a successful family vacation. Here are a few ideas for keeping boredom at bay:

- Let your little ones carry their favorite toys with them in their own duffel bag or backpack.
- Let older kids take a cassette player and headphones, along with their pick of tapes. Make a family visit to the library

before you leave so your kids can choose new and different tapes and books to take with them.

- Pack snacks to keep away the "crankies" between meals. Foods like granola, dry cereal, pretzels, raisins, and crackers keep well and are easy to take along.

- On long car trips, make plenty of pit stops at playgrounds, mini-golf courses, and other places for kids to let out their pent-up energy. In addition, try to avoid driving more than seven hours in one day. It's worth the extra day of travel time to keep everyone smiling!

- Instead of eating in restaurants, have family picnics outside, so the kids can run around and let off steam.

- Choose family-friendly hotels, especially the ones that have pools.

- When staying at hotels, reserve adjoining rooms so you and your kids can get some privacy.

- So the kids can help preserve family memories, give them cameras to take their own pictures of the trip. Some toy companies sell durable plastic models especially for young photographers. Purchasing a disposable camera is a less-expensive option.

- Pack away a coloring book, painting kit, or hand-held video game for a bright surprise on that inevitable rainy day.

Camping

A camping trip is a favorite for travelers of all ages. It's inexpensive, and it's a great way to bring families together, around the campfire and under the stars. Parents enjoy getting back to the outdoors, and for kids there's often no bigger thrill. Helping out around the campsite, gathering wood, and setting up the tent are all enjoyable activities, and during the day a hiking excursion is a great opportunity to teach kids about plants and wildlife. (Bring along a field guide to learn a thing or two yourself!) For more on hiking, visit BaseCamp (**www.bpbasecamp.com**) or The Hiking and Walking Homepage (**www.teleport.com/~walking/hiking.html**).

For first time campers, campgrounds with showers, outhouses, game rooms, playgrounds, and other facilities may be more to your family's taste. Using the directories listed here is a good way to locate these campgrounds, or you can look up a favorite chain like Kampgrounds of America (KOA). KOA's Web

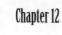
site (**www.koakampgrounds.com**) tells you where KOA campgrounds are located in the U.S., Canada, Mexico, and even Japan. You can find out about campsite facilities, fees, and location, including directions and maps. In addition, there's information about making reservations, and you can follow links to individual KOA campgrounds with their own Web sites.

CampNet America
www.kiz.com/campnet

Use this site to locate campgrounds, RV parks, and state parks in the U.S. and Canada. Read articles from other campers, look over the camping FAQ to learn more about the outdoors, and check the chat forum for recipes for cooking beneath the stars.

Camping Directory
www.rving.com/welcome.htm

Search the database to find campgrounds throughout the U.S. Specify the state you want to visit, then select the campground features you're interested in. You'll get connected to campgrounds with sites on the Web, and you can stop by the "Let's Talk" forum to hear from other campers.

Campgrounds.Net Directory
www.campgrounds.net

Find out where you can set up camp by indicating the state, and if you want, the town where you'd like to stay. Thousands of campgrounds are listed, with links to their Web sites so you can access photos and more detailed information, including fees. Chat with other campers, and find advice on maintaining your RV.

Travel Byte

Because campsites like those found in the U.S. are few and far between in foreign countries, outdoor enthusiasts often must set up camp on private property. Be sure to ask the property owner for permission before you settle in.

National Parks

For me, there's no better place to go on a family camping trip than a state or national park. Wandering among towering pines, spotting a moose, or hearing the hoot of an owl can be inspiring to both kids and adults. To avoid the usual summer flood of tourists, make your visit during the off-season, or better yet, make a trip to one of the less popular parks; there are plenty of them in the United States and Canada. There's no doubt that the Grand Canyon is awe-inspiring and Yellowstone's geysers are fascinating and exciting, but abundant natural wonders can be found in other places, too.

To find out about the many national and state parks, use the following directories. They provide photos and useful information to help you plan your trip, no matter which reserve you choose to visit. The park directories listed in this chapter provide information on entrance fees, camping regulations, and the activities available in each area.

National Park Service
www.nps.gov

"Park Net" is where you'll find information for a family trip to the national parks, from the most popular to the least explored. Find the park you'd like to visit by state, or by natural features such as "geysers." You'll find descriptions of each park, with plenty of details on entrance fees, location, facilities, and operating hours. Stop by the "Preparing For Your Visit" section for more information.

L.L. Bean
www.llbean.com

Visit the "Explore the Outdoors" section on the L.L. Bean Web site, shown in Figure 12.4, to look at photos and read about national and state parks; over 1,500 outdoor areas are listed in all. You'll find details on biking paths, hiking trails, and campgrounds, including park addresses and entrance fees. Search for a park by name, region, state, or activities and services available.

GORP
www.gorp.com/gorp/resource/US_National_Park/main.htm

You'll find detailed descriptions of the wildlife, scenery, and natural wonders of the national parks, as well as information on campgrounds, trails, and parking. In addition, you can find articles by other travelers about hiking, biking, canoeing, and camping in various national parks. There are also details about parks in other countries, such as Zimbabwe, Australia, Nepal, Canada, and others.

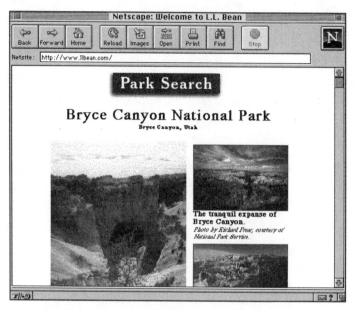

Figure 12.4 Learn about national parks online to plan a trip to the great outdoors.

Outside Online
www.outside.strarwave.com:80/npf/index.htm

The Outside Online Web site offers campers lots of information on national parks. Click on an interactive map, or search for a park according to your interests. You'll read about activities, camping, and average weather conditions, and find other useful information from Outside Online and its readers. Directions to the park of your choice are also available here.

Camping Considerations

While camping trips can be easygoing, they do require careful preparation, and family members must be aware of certain rules and regulations. Here are a few points to bear in mind before you set up camp:

- Many popular campsites and parks require reservations if you'll be visiting during the peak camping season.

- Pack as though it will rain. Bring waterproof boots and ponchos for the whole family, just in case. To check on the weather before you leave, visit the Web sites listed in the "Weather to Go" section of Chapter 4.

- You'll probably need a permit to camp away from established campsites.

- Make sure your kids stay on established trails around your campsite, so they don't destroy the surrounding plant life.

- Perfumes attract insects, so avoid using scented deodorants and shampoos. In addition, use biodegradable soaps for bathing and for cleaning pots and pans.

- To avoid sibling squabbles about who will do what, give each child a list of daily campsite responsibilities.

- Use plastic cooking utensils that won't burn small, curious hands.

- Keep your kids comfy. Inflatable sleeping mats will protect family members from the cold, hard ground.

- Make sure your group packs up all their litter. If your family is staying at an established campsite, deposit your trash in the designated receptacles. If not, take it with you to dispose of later.

Dude Ranches

You and your kids can experience the wild west with a trip to a dude ranch. These vacation homes-on-the-range offer a variety of activities for every age: horseback riding on winding mountain trails, fly-fishing in trout streams, river-rafting, line-dancing, hayrides, and campfire sing-alongs are just a few examples.

Use the Web to learn more about dude ranches, and to find one that you and your little cowpokes would like to visit.

Dude Ranch Directory
www.duderanches.com

Find out about numerous dude ranches in the United States and Canada from this site. You'll find contact information, addresses, and links to dude-ranch home pages, as well as descriptions of the authors' favorite ranches.

America's Best Dude & Guest Ranches
www.virtualcities.com/~virtual/ons/dude.htm

Read descriptions and view photos of choice ranches in the U.S. and Canada, as shown in Figure 12.5. You'll find out about facilities and activities, such as

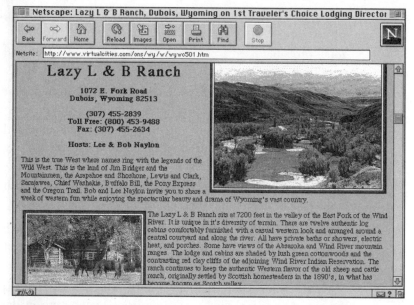

Figure 12.5 You and your kids can read about dude ranches at Web sites like America's Best.

trail rides, fishing, and nights around the campfire, as well as information on location, rates, meals, and making reservations.

The Dude Ranchers Association
www.duderanch.org

At this site you can read brief descriptions of member ranches, and find contact information for each ranch listed. The name of the closest airport is provided to help you with your travel plans, and don't miss the "Helpful Vacation Information" offered here as well.

Theme Parks

Ever wish you could be a kid again? Take the family to America's favorite theme parks. Spending some time with Mickey or Shamu is practically a guarantee of a good time!

Visit The Fun Guide at **www.funguide.com** for contact information for amusement parks located all over the world, or use a search engine to find out if your favorite theme park has a Web site. The following are a few family favorites.

Walt Disney World/ Disneyland
www.disney.com

Learn about the rides, parades, and food at the Disney theme parks, including Walt Disney World, Disneyland, Epcot, and MGM Studios. Choose from various multi-day passes, and order your selection from the Web site. You'll find details on rooms and amenities at the resorts, and you can make your reservations online. There's also information about the Disney Institute, where you can take classes in cooking, painting, gardening, and even animation. View live images, download maps, enter contests, and check out the calendar of events here as well.

Sea World and Busch Gardens
www.4adventure.com

You'll learn all about the Busch Gardens and Sea World theme parks at this site, shown in Figure 12.6. Recommendations for adventure are featured according to your age and preferences. Learn about the animals you'll see, take virtual roller-coaster rides, check out the "Shamu Cam," and find out about special events taking place throughout the year.

Figure 12.6 Your kids can gear up for a trip at the Sea World Web site.

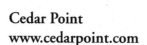
Cedar Point
www.cedarpoint.com

In addition to finding out about the latest attractions at this Ohio park, you'll find information here about roller coaster speeds, rides for little ones, the marina, and the IMAX theater. Read descriptions about hotels and campgrounds at Cedar Point, including their location, history, and associated restaurants. Entrance fee and schedule information is also available.

Universal Studios Hollywood
www.mca.com/unicity

Watch movie clips as you read up on the shows, rides, and movie lots at Universal Studios, and don't forget to take a virtual "tram tour" of the grounds. You can also participate in "online adventures" that accompany attractions. Park hours, admission fee info, and maps are available here as well.

Travel Byte

To avoid doling out cash at your children's every whim, give each child an allowance for use over the course of the vacation. Then they can decide for themselves how to spend their money, and when to save it.

Other Favorite Family Vacations

There are endless possibilities to explore for your family vacation. Here you'll find where to learn more about other household favorites on the Web. Cruises that cater to kids are growing in popularity, and family camps, which can be educational and fun, are the first choice of many families. And even a short trip to the seashore, or to renowned city zoos, can be enjoyable for both children and adults.

A Family Cruise

Cruises aren't just for grownups. Royal Caribbean (**www.royalcaribbean.com**), Premier (**www.bigredboat.com**), and Norwegian (**www.ncl.com**) are a few of the many cruise lines that offer activities for the whole family.

On these cruises, keeping children entertained is part of the package. Facilities like playrooms and arcades are available, as well as supervised activities like craft workshops, contests, games, and ice-cream socials. Some cruise ships have baby-sitters on board as well.

For more information on cruising, including specific cruise lines, ships, itineraries, and onboard activities, turn to Chapter 11.

Travel Byte
Many cruises offer discounts for children who share accommodations with their parents.

At The Beach

If you plan to hit the beach with your kids, be sure to pack essential seaside supplies. Sand molds, shovels, and buckets, as well as fins, snorkels, and face masks for underwater exploration, keep kids busy for hours on end while you relax in the sun. Don't forget the life preservers and floatation devices, which can save lives, or the sunglasses, to keep your kids from squinting and sunscreen to keep them from burning.

At The Zoo

Want to visit a zoo or two on your family vacation? Visit the Web site of the American Zoo and Aquarium Association (**www.aza.org**) to get connected to the home pages of numerous zoos and aquariums. These zoo home pages will fill you in on the animals, facilities, and entrance fees of zoos like the San Diego Zoo (**www.sandiegozoo.org/Zoo/zoo.html**) and The National Zoo in Washington D.C. (**www.si.edu/natzoo**).

Family Camps

Have you ever considered taking your kids to camp? At camps like Space Camp (**www.spacecamp.com**), shown in Figure 12.7, family programs offer parents and children the opportunity to work together to achieve a common goal while having fun. At others, like Chautauqua (**www.chautauqua-inst.org**), separate classes and workshops are offered for kids and parents to explore their personal interests according to age and ability. Week-long classes include writing, philosophy, dance, music, and language. Time to spend together as a family includes daily free time, meal times, and the evenings, which feature concerts and performances. Stop by Camp Search, at **www.campsearch.com**,

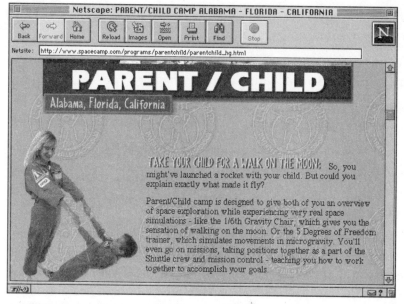

Figure 12.7 Learn more on the Web about a family trip to Space Camp.

to read descriptions of family camps located around the world and get connected to their individual home pages.

The cost of most family camps include meals and accommodations, as well as activities. Visit the parenting Web sites mentioned at the beginning of this chapter to learn more about these camps.

Travel Byte

Give your baby a bottle when ascending and descending on airline flights. Continuous swallowing helps to reduce inner-ear discomfort and pain.

Traveling With The Family Pets

For many families, their dogs are considered part of the family, and deserve a vacation just like everyone else. If you plan to take your family pets on vacation, remember to keep them leashed (or caged) to prevent harm to themselves or others. (Traveling can disorient an animal. A pet that's normally well behaved may act differently in a new place.) Be sure to take their medication and health certificates with you, and add tags to their collars specifying what hotel you're staying at in case they get lost.

Visit the TravelDog Web site (**www.traveldog.com**), shown in Figure 12.8, for information about "pet-friendly lodging and recreation," as well as advice and safety tips.

Roaming The Roadways

If you'd like to take your family on the road in a roomy RV, keep reading: Chapter 13 lists Web sites that inform you about purchasing and maintaining a recreational vehicle. In Chapter 13 you'll also find information on preparing for a road trip, from ideas on places to visit, to the scenic roads you'll take to get there.

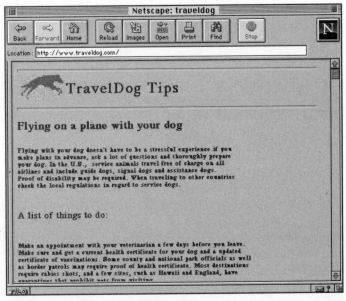

Figure 12.8 Read advice for traveling with the family pet at the TravelDog Web site.

Virtual Americana: The Road Trip

CHAPTER 13 TOPICS

- Preparing For Your Road Trip

- Get Your Kicks Online On Route 66

- America's Tackiest Attractions

- Stopping At Roadside Diners

- RVs

Since their creation, America's highways have lured city dwellers, suburbanites, and country folks out of their homes, into their cars, and onto the open road. With the construction of Eisenhower's interstate system, networked highways gave contemporary explorers easy access to all regions of the country.

Restaurants, stores, and lodging moved from town centers to the side of modern superhighways, and blinking neon signs, offbeat attractions, and whimsical oversized animal sculptures beckoned drivers off the road. Americans in their beloved cars reveled in the promising stretches of new asphalt, and a roadside culture was born as mobile America took off into the sunset.

Road trips are about as American as apple pie. Travelers enjoy the freedom of setting their own itinerary, turning off the road whenever and wherever they wish. Deteriorating relics of the past dot the roadsides along with newer motel chains, fast-food franchises, and gas stations, but the mystique of the road trip is still alive and well.

Experience America's love affair with the road for yourself. You'll see classic roadside architecture and time-honored signs, as well as alligator farms, U-Pick-Em fruit stands, and of course, spectacular views from the scenic highways that run through national parks and along coastlines.

Interstate highways, constructed to bypass towns and city centers, don't provide a close up and personal view of America. Leaving the turnpike for the back roads gives you a chance to explore the villages and people that make up this nation. Remember to stop often and explore the world around you, instead of just watching it pass you by through the car window.

In this chapter, you'll discover where roadside America still thrives today— both along the country's highways, and on the information superhighway. Web sites will tell you about silly roadside attractions, classic motels, and original diners, and online magazines, virtual guidebooks, and the home pages of other road warriors can direct you to roads and points of interest across the country. You'll also find recommendations on everything from great towns to visit, to tourist traps to avoid. The Web sites listed in this chapter offer abundant information on roadside America: the good, the bad, and the wonderfully tacky!

History

Before you pack up the car and head out on the highway, make a pit stop on the Web to brush up on your U.S. history. Learn more about America's love affair with their cars and the birth of the roadside culture, and find out how the construction of the interstate system shaped a country—the people, the culture, and the landscape.

Web sites like that of the American Public Works Association (**www.fileshop.com/apwa/roads.html**) may teach you a thing or two about an aspect of America that isn't often taught in history books. This information can give you a better understanding of the effort that went into constructing the highways, and the people who first rode them.

History by the Side of the Road
www.chevron.com/chevron_root/explore/history/hst_road/index.html

A chronicle of the American gas station, this site describes the first station, "a shed, a 30-gallon tank, and a garden hose," and follows gas station trends to the present day. Read about the rise of the service station, the flamboyant stations of the 1930s, the "freebies" of the 1950s, and the homey look of the 1960s. Photo galleries accompany the text.

Celebrating 100 Years of the Automobile in Southern Arizona
www.azstarnet.com/auto100

The automotive history of the southwestern United States is the topic of this site. Learn about the automobile's first women drivers, and how their enthusiasm for driving boosted Arizona's economy. Significant cars in American history are featured here, as well as "a century of car costs" and more current information on "Carhenge" and the new electric cars.

The Best Part Was
www.synapse.net/~sensato

Travel into the past at this site, and learn what life was like on the road in the 1920s. The diary of Doretta Beach recounts her family's trip around the United States, departing from Ontario on October 18, 1921. This personal account describes places the family visited, such as Buffalo Bill's grave, and continuous car problems like tire punctures and treacherous road conditions. Family photographs taken on the trip are included (Figure 13.1), as are topics

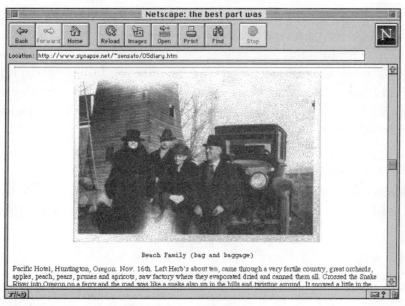

Figure 13.1 A family photo from a road trip in 1921.

in the news of the day. In addition, the site provides many links to photographs and historical information related to the text.

The Lincoln Highway
www.ugcs.caltech.edu/~jlin/lincoln

The Lincoln Highway was America's first attempt to construct a transcontinental highway. This site describes how Carl Fisher's dream came very close to reality with the backing of the president of the Packard Motor Car Company. You can also check out a comparison between the Lincoln Highway and Route 66, look at state-by-state historical routes and maps, and find out how to support the Lincoln Highway Association.

Getting Your Kicks By Car

When preparing for a road trip, give your car a thorough examination to make sure it's ready for the road. Take heed of unusual noises and puddles under your car in your garage or driveway. If you notice something out of the ordinary, you may want to have your car professionally checked. Long distances and intense heat can bring about a major breakdown as you roll merrily along, so put the odds in you and your car's favor by taking action.

Make sure your car has plenty of oil and water and that your drive belts and radiator hoses are crack-free, firm, and flexible. Check your tires for the correct air pressure, and give your spare tire a good squeeze also. Inspect your lights to make certain all are in working order, and fill 'er up with plenty of windshield-washer fluid for cleaning those friendly moths off your windshield. To learn more about your car, stop by Tom and Ray Magliozzi's Car Talk Web site at **www.cartalk.com**.

What To Pack In The Back

When traveling by car, its always a good idea to err on the side of caution: Breakdowns and accidents always happen when you least expect them. So do as the Boy Scouts do, and be prepared!

Here's a quick-pick list of items to pack in your trunk:

- Flares
- First-aid kit
- Lug wrench and jack
- Two-liter plastic water bottle (full)
- Fire extinguisher
- Flashlight
- Blanket
- Jumper cables
- Phone numbers—emergency numbers and personal contacts

Travel Byte

If you're traveling in winter weather, keep your gas tank filled above the halfway point at all times. You may also want to pack extra warm clothing, an engine heater, and extra blankets.

Driving Safely

While a road trip can be a great vacation, it's not all fun and games. Driving is serious business. Your safety, and the safety of other travelers and pedestrians, should be of major concern to you. Wearing a seat belt, driving the speed limit, slowing down in residential areas, and calling it a day when you start to get drowsy behind the wheel can all help to save lives.

Travel Byte

Never pull over to the side of the road to sleep in your car. It's dangerous, and you become a prime target for theft or assault. Always check into a motel when you're nodding off at the wheel.

The Web site of the U.S. Department of Transportation (**www.dot.gov**) can connect you with the department's various administrations, including the Office of Highway Information Management (**cti1.volpe.dot.gov/ohim**), the Federal Highway Administration (**www.fhwa.dot.gov**), and the National Highway Traffic Safety Administration (**www.nhtsa.dot.gov/new**). These sites contain current information on automotive and highway safety, and topics such as air bag protection and child restraint systems are addressed. In addition, you can find particulars on traffic trends, road conditions, and current highway safety campaigns.

You may want to consider joining a motor club in case an accident or crisis occurs while you're on the road. Motor clubs like the American Automobile Association (AAA) can provide emergency assistance when and where you need it (Figure 13.2). AAA (**www.aaa.com**) provides members with free towing and emergency service anywhere in the United States. The Montgomery Ward Auto Club (**www.mward.com**) provides limited free towing services and may cover lodging costs in the event of a breakdown or accident. The Mobil Auto Club (**www.mobil.com**) also provides emergency service and limited free towing.

Travel Byte

Always keep drinking water in the car with you to prevent dehydration (and don't forget to drink it!).

Highways On The Superhighway

Before you hit the highway, check out your road's Web site. Many highways and interstates have their own Web pages with maps, photographs, and current road construction information. The following sites are examples of what you can find about America's highways on the Net.

Figure 13.2 The AAA Web site provides information on roadside services.

U.S. Route 40
users.aol.com/usroute40/route40.htm

Check out photos and historical information here on the first federally-funded interstate highway in the United States. This site includes biographies of supporters, authors, photographers, and others who shaped and recorded the road's history—including George Washington. Museums along the route are listed, and there are songs to sing while on the road. Read about the people promoting Route 40, and about those contributing to its destruction. You can stop by the classified ads to sell your maps and automotive paraphernalia, or post a notice of the items you've been hunting for, as shown in Figure 13.3.

The Alaska Highway
alaskan.com/bells/alaska_highway.html

This site is a must for travelers heading to Alaska on the highway that stretches from Delta Junction, Alaska to Dawson Creek, British Columbia. Road conditions are detailed for those heading north, with information on rough and patchy sections and road width. Suggestions are offered on when and how fast to travel, as well as tips for maintaining your vehicle and points of interest along the way. There are also emergency service phone numbers to print out and take with you.

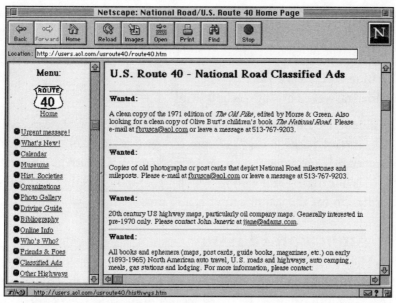

Figure 13.3 Hunt down roadside memorabilia at the U.S. Route 40 Web site.

Travel Byte

Interstate highways with even numbers run east to west, and decrease in route number the further south you drive. Interstates with odd numbers run north to south, and decrease in route number the further west you drive.

Interstate I-95
www.webpress.net/isl

Plan your trip along I-95 with information about lodgings, attractions, and cities and towns along the way. Content is offered state-by-state, and covers not only I-95, but intersecting interstates throughout Wisconsin, Michigan, Ohio, Illinois, and Tennessee. At this site you'll also find links to other Web sites with more detailed information about points of interest along the road.

Pennsylvania Turnpike
www.paturnpike.com

This Web site of "America's first superhighway" has information on expansion projects, construction schedules, and safety improvements, as well as a detailed history and "fast facts" about the turnpike. The "Turnpike Traveler" online newsletter profiles vehicles and people associated with the highway, including articles on "the oldest toll collector," and a day in the life of a safety patrol manager.

The Blue Ridge Parkway
outside.starwave.com/npf/NC/0.html

The Blue Ridge Parkway runs between the Shenandoah and Great Smoky Mountains national parks. This Web site for park visitors offers information on campgrounds and where to purchase food supplies. Find out about museums, activities like hiking and wildlife watching, and intersecting highways; contact information for the visitor center is also provided.

An American Classic

U.S. Highway 66, better known as Route 66—but also referred to as "The Mother Road" and "The Will Rogers Highway"—was constructed in the 1920s, and immortalized by the lyrics of Bobby Troup. Fanciful tourist attractions, custard stands, curio shops, and colorful motels sprung up along the celebrated highway that stretched from Chicago to Los Angeles, emerging as the epitome of American roadside culture.

While Route 66 is no longer one continuous highway, sections of roadway, intertwined with modern interstates, are still drivable.

Preservation organizations are striving to keep the legend alive and save what's left of the highway from extinction. Web sites like that of The Route 66 Museum and Visitor's Center, in Rancho Cucamonga, California, (**www.citivu.com/rc/rte66/rte66.html**) offer historical information and current news about "America's Main Street." You can also get your kicks at the Web sites of travelers who've navigated their way West on Route 66, such as Graeme Ware's Mother Road Web site (**ourworld.compuserve.com/homepages/GWare/route66.htm**). These sites can direct you to great roadside stops, and provide maps to help you stay on track.

Historic Route 66
route66.netvision.be

Be sure to stop by this site before hitting old Route 66. Read state-by-state road descriptions, get detailed route directions, and find maps for every stretch of the road. This site tells you what towns you'll pass through, provides mileage information, and points out interesting relics along the way. There's also contact information for classic motels, as well as quick facts about the highway, video clips, and tips for getting through tricky areas.

Virtual Voyage 66
www.chron.com/content/interactive/voyager/66

Follow two journalists from the Houston Chronicle Interactive on their trip along The Mother Road. You'll find descriptions of recent treks by the writers, roadside adventures, and pit stops. Sit in on the slide show for images of classic Americana, or check out the "back seat cam collage" for an alternative view of the road. A chat forum, trivia quiz, and video clips complete this "virtual voyage" along Route 66.

Route 66 Photo Lounge
www.bekkoame.or.jp/~toisa

Check out the photo images taken by Isao Saito on his journey along America's main street. Photos of Illinois, Missouri, Kansas, Oklahoma, Texas, New Mexico, Arizona, and California are included. The photo collection, categorized by state, include views of roadside attractions, wildlife, and natural landscapes. This site also includes a gallery of neon sign images, and state-by-state maps.

Route 66: Cruising the American Dream
www.cis.yale.edu/amstud/r66/map.html

Historical information on the birth and slow death of Route 66 is recorded at this site. Learn how boom towns suffered with the construction of the inter-state system, and read comments by some of the people affected. There's information about car advertisements of the day, service stations along the road, the rise of the Howard Johnson's franchise, and other related topics. View photographs, postcards, and ads, as shown in Figure 13.4, and listen to audio clips of cruising music, including the famous rendition of "Route 66" by Nat King Cole.

Route 66 West Online Edition
www.kaiwan.com/~wem/r66_west/wtr96/01ndx.html

This quarterly online magazine takes readers on a virtual tour of various stretches of The Mother Road, pointing out renovated hotels, historic sites, and distinctive buildings. You can read features about neighborly towns, landmarks

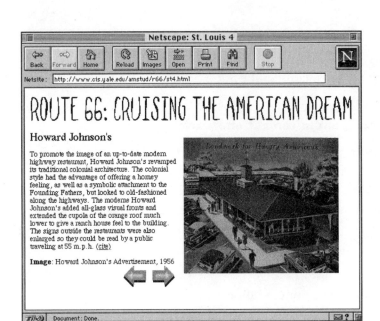

Figure 13.4 Read about the roadside franchises built along Route 66.

popular in days gone by, and the people who helped make Route 66 a legend. Directories provide information on museums, motels, RV parks, campgrounds, and restaurants along the way.

The Route 66 Virtual Voyage Trivia Quiz

The Route 66 Virtual Voyage Web site (**www.chron.com/66**), brought to you by the Houston Chronicle Interactive, presents images and information about America's Main Street in an entertaining format. The following quiz is excerpted from the Route 66 Virtual Voyage Web site and can be found at **www.chron.com/66/quiz/trivia.html**. (Copyright 1996, Houston Chronicle Interactive. Used by permission.)

1. Who wrote the song "(Get Your Kicks on) Route 66?"
2. Route 66 starts in this city.
3. The Illinois Route 66 Hall of Fame can be found at the ?
4. What famous outlaw supposedly hid out at Meramec Caverns in Missouri?
5. Baseball great Mickey Mantle's hometown is ?

6. Stanley Marsh's Cadillac Ranch is located in ?

7. Albuquerque, N.M. is home to ?

8. In "Take It Easy," The Eagles sing about a street corner in the city ?

9. This city is the endpoint for old Route 66 in California.

10. In the TV show *Route 66*, the two main characters drove a ?

11. In the 1920s, C.C. Pyle's International Trans-Continental Foot Race promoted Route 66. It was better known as ?

Answers

1. Bobby Troup

2. Chicago

3. Dixie Truckers Home in McLean

4. Jesse James

5. Commerce, Okla.

6. Amarillo, Texas

7. The National Atomic Museum

8. Winslow, Arizona

9. Santa Monica

10. Corvette

11. The Great Bunion Derby

Scoring:

11 correct = King of the road

7-10 correct = Big-time gear jammer

4-6 correct = Back-seat driver

2-3 correct = Learner's permit

0-1 correct = License revoked

Taking The Scenic Route

Not all highways are created equal. While some of America's highways can be mind-numbing, others wind their way through mountain peaks, thick forests, quaint villages, and rolling meadows. Many run through the lush landscapes of our national and state parks.

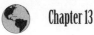

Many travelers take note of the roads that offered them such unbelievable views and scenery, and suggest them to others. You can find many of these recommendations on Web sites about America's great drives. Think about highlighting some of these routes on your map and making a point of traveling them. They could turn out to be the highlight of your trip!

The Roads of America
rossby.uoknor.edu/~sgaddy/roads.html

Look up one of the U.S. states listed at this site to discover scenic roads across the country, including recommendations from the author, state residents, and other road warriors. Read about selected highways and landscape descriptions, and find out about common weather conditions to watch out for and small towns to stop at. You can also email other motorists to get more details.

Road Trip USA
www.moon.com/road_trip

This online "cross country compendium" includes all the text of its sister guidebook now in print. Covering 11 highways across the United States (Figure 13.5), the site details routes with names like "The Great River Road,"

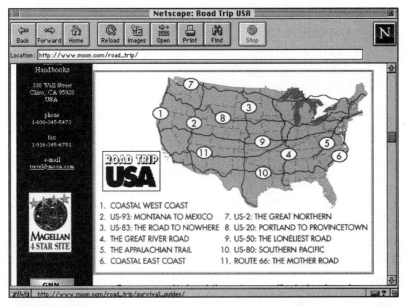

Figure 13.5 Check out road trips recommended by the online travel book Road Trip USA.

"The Great Northern," and "U.S. 93: Montana to Mexico." The site suggests itineraries, and provides historical facts about towns on each highway; descriptions of bakeries, cafes, and village greens not to be missed are also included.

Roadway Express Online
www.roadway.com/rexwrli.htm

Each month a new profile of one of America's roadways is presented on this "library of links," brought to you by Roadway Express Online. Highways profiled include "U.S. 1, The Boston Post Road" and "Texas State Route 21, El Camino Real." You'll find photos and maps, as well as history and current descriptions of these North American classics. Also check out the monthly stories of America's timeless diners.

The World Wide Web Scenic Roads Registry
www.motorists.com/states/roads.htm

This Web site of the National Motorists Association suggests scenic roads throughout the United States. You can read about routes, campgrounds, and hazards to watch for on your trip, and learn how the NMA can be of assistance to you and how to join. Find information here on speed limits, fighting traffic tickets, state seat belt laws, and fuel economy and emissions, and take a look at goofy road signs submitted by other travelers!

Great Drives
users.why.net/ajax/gdrives.htm

You can find out about numerous scenic thoroughfares at this Web site. Read about the choice highways that run through California, Wisconsin, Wyoming, coastal Oregon, and other areas in the U.S. There are details on the amount of traffic (or lack of it), advice on clothing, and descriptions of towns that might be worth a stop, as well as suggestions for motorcycle trips.

Road Tripping 'Zines

Editorials and features written by professional travel writers can inform you about interesting places to stop along the byways. Online magazines may also include accounts from recreational motorists, providing assorted viewpoints about both popular and unfrequented attractions.

Out West On-Line
www.outwestnewspaper.com

This "quarterly on-the-road newspaper" is produced by Chuck Woodbury from his "24-foot motorhome-newsroom." Articles about America's western roadways cover such topics as people, ghost towns, and attractions like fiberglass dinosaur parks. Find out about eclectic diners with good eats from other travelers, and read about recommended routes such as U.S. 50, which follows the path of the Pony Express. You can subscribe to the print magazine, or ask to receive the free "Out West Update Newsletter."

Sierra Highways
www.sierrahighways.com

This online magazine features virtual tours of Lake Tahoe, Grass Valley, Auburn, and other areas of California and the United States. Maps, activities, and recommended cafes and museums are included. Read articles from previous issues on topics such as travel to state parks and specific roadways, such as "Discovering Highway 88." Join the free travel club to receive travel updates by email and exclusive discounts.

Figure 13.6 The home page of Sierra Highways' online magazine.

Monk
www.neo.com/Monk

This 'zine for roadies is produced by "two grown men who quit their jobs, sold everything they owned, and hit the roads with their cats." The site includes features on the eccentric people they've met and the places they've explored in their eight years of traveling. City guides describe neighborhoods, natural sanctuaries, restaurants, bars, coffee houses, and more. You'll also find guides to regional slang and clickable, animated "Monk Maps," that pinpoint recommended attractions in a given area.

Vagabond Monthly
www2.globaldialog.com/~tpatmaho

Feature articles are written by travelers with a love for American kitsch. Read about museums dedicated to Liberace, cheesy theme parks, and diners with waitresses who've served their clientele for over 50 years. You'll find recommendations for eating on the cheap in Las Vegas, bad urban camping, hitching a ride, and more. Check out the "Vagabond's Strangest Journeys" section to read classic travel accounts.

Travel Byte

Buckle up. Wearing a seat belt is the law in most U.S. states, and in most areas of Canada. Even if wearing a seatbelt isn't required by law in the area you're visiting, it's still a good idea to wear one.

A Road Trip With A Mission

While some road-trippers are content to wander the country aimlessly, following off-ramps on a whim and taking detours to unknown places without hesitation, others feel the need to follow some sort of general plan. To give their trip a sense of purpose, they decide to explore and investigate a specific aspect of the good ol' USA.

You may want to jump-start your road trip by devising a quest of your own. Think about what piques your interest: Are you particularly interested in visiting national parks? Maybe you'd like to investigate the nation's tackiest tourist traps. Or perhaps capturing images of small-town America through photography appeals to you.

No matter what you choose to explore, focusing on a theme or topic can make your trip more coherent and meaningful, and can leave you with a sense of accomplishment upon your return home.

The following is a list of ideas you may want to investigate as you travel the country:

- Antebellum plantations
- Beaches
- Capitol buildings
- Civil War battlegrounds
- Colonial landmarks
- Crime sites
- Fire stations
- Ghost towns
- Harbors
- Historical landmarks
- Major or minor league ball parks
- Microbreweries
- National parks
- Native American battlegrounds
- Paranormal phenomena
- Pioneer wagon trails
- Presidential libraries and boyhood homes
- Revolutionary War battlegrounds
- Speedways
- Theme parks
- Tourist traps
- Universities

Numerous resources on the information superhighway can help you decide where to stop. For example, Primarily Petroliana (**home.stlnet.com/~jimpotts/ index.html**), a Web site for petroliana paraphernalia collectors, provides a list of automotive museums and restored gas stations to visit across the

American landscape. Or check out the Ghost Town of the Month Web site (**www.goodnet.com/wm03094/ghost.html**) for information on abandoned mining towns you can visit (if you're brave enough!).

Use the Web resources of this chapter (and other chapters in this book) to discover the best places to explore the subjects that interest you. For example, if the nation's theme parks is a topic you want to tackle, you can use the resources listed in Chapter 12 to find out where they're located.

Travel Byte

As you travel from one point to the next on your map, don't forget to stop and smell the wildflowers by the side of the road. Making a plan for your road trip doesn't mean giving up on dropping in on small towns, eating leisurely lunches at diners, or stopping to chat with locals along the way. Take the time to enjoy and interact with the scenery around you.

America's Tackiest

For many interstate excursionists, kitschy Americana is the topic of choice. Hunting down, or stumbling across, oversized Paul Bunyans, Elvis museums, miniature golf courses, and the world's largest soup kettle can be the highlight of a trip. My personal favorite is a gas station along Highway 45, near Clintonville, Wisconsin, which is easily spotted by the immense free-standing badger and colossal chipmunk-on-a-log store that sit beside it. You don't need to look far to find fiberglass relics of the past, but some are truly tackier than others. The following Web sites can help you find the most creative attractions around.

Roadside America
www.roadsideamerica.com

Pet cemeteries, prison museums, gator farms, beer can houses, and giant twine balls: This site's got it all. If you're into oddities, stop by to get your fill of attractions to include in your travel plans, as seen in Figure 13.7. "Hyper tours" take you on the road with the creators of the Web site, chronicling stops along the road with routes and itineraries included. This site has a great sense of humor, and even includes video clips of attractions like miniature golf courses in funeral homes!

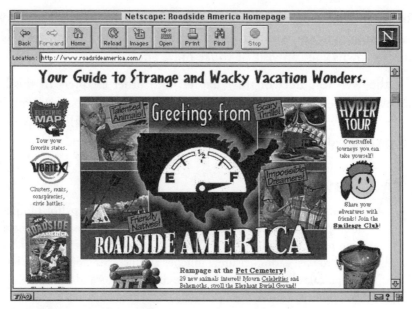

Figure 13.7 Virtual roadside oddities await you on the Web pages of Roadside America.

The White Trash Tour
marigold.colorado.edu/~arbetter/whitetrash.html

For the ultimate in cheesy attractions, check out this site. The author lists the roadside attractions he visited in his '85 Cherokee. Popular as well as seldom frequented attractions are included, such as Wall Drug, various meteor craters, and the Jack Daniels Distillery. This site may give you a few ideas for your next road trip.

Roadside Art Online
www.mcs.com/~billsw/ii/western.html

Crumbling road signs and motels are considered works of art at this site. Photographs, complete with commentary, offer a sampling of roadside architecture. You'll visit homes and cemeteries bedecked with colorful concrete sculpture, and check out blues clubs, donut shops, hamburger joints, and an over-sized hot dog. Photo galleries include "View Vistas Large and Small," "See the Signs," and "Visit Environments."

ROADSIDE ATTRACTION HOME PAGES

Some of the tackiest roadside attractions have their very own home pages. The content may be provided by the people who maintain the attraction, or by those who visited and got a kick out it. Some Web sites, such as that of Fred Smith's Wisconsin Concrete Park (**outsider.art.org/fred/fred.htm**), let you know what you can do to help preserve their associated attractions.

From Windmills to Whirligigs (North Carolina)
www.sci.mus.mn.us/sln/vollis

Meet Vollis Simpson and his wind-powered whirligig farm in North Carolina. Browse through the online scrapbook to get a good glimpse of these imaginative creations through photos and video clips. You can get a peek inside the shop where his whirligigs are created, and you'll also find a map of the grounds at this Web site, as well as activities inspired by a visit to the farm.

The Coral Castle (Florida)
www.netrunner.net/~coralroc/Coralintro.html

The Coral Castle, which first opened to the public in 1923, was carved from over 1,100 tons of coral rock, all for unrequited love. Read about Ed Leedskalnin, the man who created the castle and then moved it without the known aid of humans or machinery. Find out why his feat has baffled scientists and been featured in newspapers and on television shows like "That's Incredible." Included is a map to the structure's location in Florida.

The Orange Show (Texas)
vellocet.insync.net/~orange

Read an extensive history of one man's quest to build "the ninth wonder of the world." Creator Jeff McKissack spent over 25 years building "The Orange Show," a handmade colorful piece of "architecture." Although the dream was not realized within his lifetime, over 18,000 tourists visit annually today. The site also provides information about the attraction's location and daily hours, as well as about special events hosted by The Orange Show Foundation.

The Big Duck (New York)
www.newsday.com/az/bigduck.htm

"Hatched in 1931," the Big Duck is 20 feet tall and weighs approximately 16,500 pounds. Made of wire, wood, stucco—and Model-T Ford taillights as eyes—

this duck is relished as a classic. The history of the Big Duck, including its three moves in 1936, 1988, and again in 1993, is detailed at this Web site. You can also find out about Christie Brinkley's audio recording detailing the duck's history, and text from two *Newsday* articles is provided to fill you in on current restoration efforts.

Travel Byte

If you've spotted some less-than-classic roadside architecture, signs, or attractions, stop by the Web site of The Tackiest Place in America Contest (**www.thepoint.net/~usul/text/tacky.html**). Write a description of what you saw, take a picture, and submit your entry. It could be posted on the pages of this ongoing online contest.

At The Drive-In

Another popular topic to explore is the bygone days of the drive-in. Scattered about the landscape, you can spot some drive-ins that have been abandoned, and some that are still going strong. Catch a flick on your next road trip: Pull in and sample this classic example of how daily life and the automobile merged in the early years of this century.

Drive-In Theaters
www.driveintheater.com

Learn about Richard Hollingshead, the man who invented and patented the drive-in movie. You'll find out about "drive-through oddities" like "fly-ins" for planes, a theater with 260 screens, and drive-ins with playgrounds, restaurants, and space for over 2,500 cars. Check out the rise and fall of the drive-in in America from 1948 to 1987.

Evil Sam's Drive-In Theatre Guide
www.driveintheatre.com

The site lists theaters that are still in operation—even outside the United States, in Australia, Canada, and Europe. There's information here about efforts to save this taste of Americana, including theaters in need of aid and the attempts by big businesses to destroy them. You can also connect to the home pages of individual drive-ins across the country.

Dining Out

How does taste-testing your way across the country sound? Stopping to eat at roadside and small-town diners not only offers you as-close-as-it-comes to home-cooked meals, but a taste of America's past and present as well. Recently, sleek new (and franchised) retro-diners have been popping up in city centers and shopping malls. While these burger joints can be fun places to get a bite to eat, they don't hold a candle to the originals, many of which are still in operation today.

The first diners of the 1930s were freestanding, prefabricated structures offering drivers their initial sample of fast(er) food. Lunch counters served up American staples like meatloaf and mashed potatoes. Not only did they offer travelers a respite from the desolate highways, they provided a place for neighborhood folks to relax and chat with friends—to meet for breakfast, lunch, or a late-night cup of joe.

Today, diners along America's main streets still offer down-home meals at cheap prices. All that was true about the originals is still true for many road-side diners today. While you're traveling, why not make a detour from the same old fast-food chains: Take a turn off the interstate and enjoy a meal at a diner. Take in the atmosphere, chat with waitresses, and meet the firemen, farmers, and other locals who stop by to socialize with friends. Meals at diners are a must for any classic road trip.

Like so many other businesses, diners have turned to the Web for alternative advertising and customer service. Check out the Web pages of the following hometown diners on the Web.

Maine Diner
www.mainediner.com

This restored diner uses fresh vegetables from the back garden, planted during its first days of operation approximately 30 years ago. At their Web site you can check out the specials on the menu, such as "Meatloaf Madness," "New England Boiled Dinner," and "Yankee Pot Roast;" get to know the staff, and look over customer comments. The online newsletter lets you know what's new and what the local weather conditions are, and provides recipes to fix at home.

Rosie's Diner (Michigan)
www.rosiesdiner.com

This site introduces you to the three diners, including Rosie's Diner, that form Dinerland U.S.A in Rockford, Michigan. Rosie's was built by the Paramount company in 1946, and was moved from Little Ferry, New Jersey in 1990. Rosie's sits next to a converted diner, formerly Uncle Bob's of Flint, Michigan, which is now an art gallery. The third diner, the Garden of Eatin' from Fulton, New Jersey, is now called The Delux Diner and is still serving customers.

Jiggers Diner (Rhode Island)
www.saturn.net/~bozone/Jiggers.html

Established in 1917, this diner still offers "Blue Plate Specials," and the food is still homemade, including the ice cream. Read the about the diner's history—when it was built, and how it thrived, fell into ruins, and was revived by Carol Shriner in 1992 (Figure 13.8). Drawings from local children are featured at the site, as are T-shirts, postcards, mugs, and menus for sale. You can also learn a thing or two about Rhode Island Johnny Cakes!

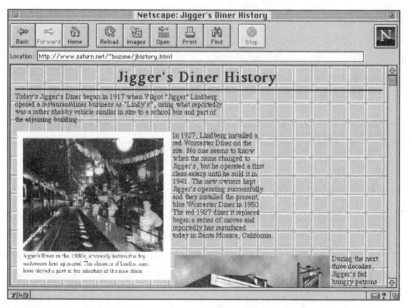

Figure 13.8 Read the history of a roadside diner still in operation today.

DINER REVIEWS

The following Web sites are brought to you by diner aficionados, who have rated the best and worst of 'em. Check out the reviews for where you'll be traveling, jot down the addresses, and stop by on your travels. You can even write your own reviews as you dine your way across roadside America.

Roadside on the Web
www1.usa1.com/~roadside/index.html

This 'zine features diners found along the American landscape. Take virtual tours of distinctive diners, or find out about the ones in a particular town. Reviews and accounts of recent visits are available as well, as shown in Figure 13.9. "Napkin Notes" provide news on renovations, reopenings, and closings, and "Diner Alerts" inform you about soon-to-be-extinct diners. Read interviews, help identify "The Mystery Diner," look at photos, and try out recipes to "bring the diner home."

EatHere.com
www.eathere.com

Dedicated to the "traveler who wants to make each driving trip a great eating experience," this site reviews drive-ins, carhops, truck stops, buffets, and barbecue

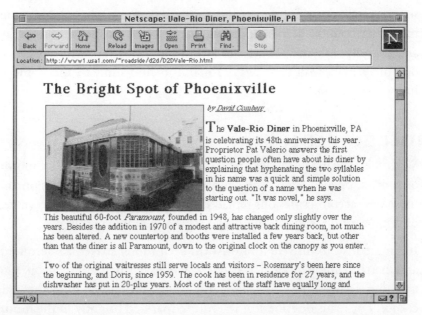

Figure 13.9 A Web review of the Vale-Rio Diner in Phoenixville, Pennsylvania.

joints along America's highways. Travelers share favorite road trip memories, from licking frosty freezes to reading the Burma Shave signs, and post stories of interesting encounters and edibles. Restaurant ratings, hours of operation, price ranges, and specialty dishes, such as beef barbecue hash, are also provided by road ramblers.

Chrone's Virtual Diner
www.neb.com/noren/diner/Chrones.html

Chrone's Virtual Diner includes a personal list of the best and worst in American diners. Diners are reviewed by taking atmosphere, food quality, architecture, and entertaining waitstaff into account. Categories include: Best Diner, Worst Diner, and "Most Hideous Remodeling of a Classic Diner." The author also recommends desserts of choice, like coconut cream or peanut butter pie. Contact information for diner manufacturers is included, and a state-by-state directory is in the works.

The Diner Page
www.astro.princeton.edu/~goldberg/diner.html

The "Diner Directory" reviews numerous lunch counters across America. Menu items such as grilled cheese, omelets, onion rings, corn muffins, coleslaw, and of course coffee, are put to the test. Atmosphere is also considered, including counter stool condition, background music, classic architecture, and friendly wait staff. "Places to Avoid" are listed too, with reviews that will definitely make you stay away! You'll also find links to the home pages of individual diners.

Vintage Motels

With the advent of America's new super-highways in the 1950s, motor hotels, or motels, opened across the country. Geared towards families on the move, these new accommodations replaced the home-style hotels in town centers by offering easy-on, easy-off highway access and ample parking.

In an attempt to lure the motorist in, each motel strived to become brighter and better equipped than the next. Motels with flashing neon signs, eye-catching architecture, and standardized conditions became the lodging of choice. For roadside America, the future sparkled brightly in the headlights of Chevys, Fords, and Pontiac station wagons.

Today, many of these classic motels still survive and are open for business, and you can revisit the automotive era by checking in and calling it a night. While their heyday has come and gone, many still offer clean rooms and comfortable beds at very affordable prices.

Many travelers, writers, and photographers have looked into the past by visiting these fading examples of roadside culture. Web sites like Motel Americana offer reviews, personal accounts, and directions to classic motels.

Motel Americana
oak.cats.ohiou.edu/~aw148888/motel.html

Discover the unique and intriguing motels that scatter the American landscape, such as the one shown Figure 13.10. You'll find descriptions of architecture, decor, and sometimes tacky atmosphere from a couple who have devoted themselves to this "poignant part of Americana." There are also stories from others with a passion for the road, including descriptions of motels, conversations with proprietors, and strange occurrences, and postcards from motels with names like "Edge-O-Town," "Star," and "Thunder Bird."

Figure 13.10   Explore America's roadside motels at the Motel Americana Web site.

Excellent Motels
stefan.www.media.mit.edu/people/stefan/photos/motels.html

Read about a traveler's favorite motels from a trip across the United States. "El Rancho," "Big Sky," and "Allen's Rocket Motel" can be found here. Motels with scenic views and hand-painted murals of Elvis are preferred.

Travel Byte

It's a good idea to ask to see your motel room before agreeing to spend the night. Remember, you're under no obligation to stay if the room doesn't meet your standards.

Motels Of Today

While glittery motels of an earlier era may be passé, the budget motels of today thrive just off the interstates and highways. With set standards of decor and cleanliness, you can be pretty sure what to expect when you stop for the night. Many budget hotels offer swimming pools, cable TV, and in-room coffee makers—amenities also found in more expensive city hotels. For information about today's motel chains, such as Econolodge and Days Inn, look to Chapter 6. Numerous Internet addresses are listed so you can read up on roadside rooms, facilities, and nightly rates.

Written On The Road

As you already know, other travelers can offer useful advice for your vacation. This includes those road warriors who have set out to "discover America" in their cars, mini-vans, and RVs. Some of these motorists have created Web sites about their adventures to let you know what life on the road is really like. While many post the details about their trip on the Web after returning home, many others do it while they're still going strong. Some of these road warriors have been rambling across the country for years!

Gather ideas about where to go, what to visit, and what to avoid on your next road trip by reviewing the Web sites of those who took the time to explore the back roads. The following home pages may give you some insights about road travel, and maybe you'll get a few ideas for creating a road trip Web site of your own.

Travels with Samantha
www-swiss.ai.mit.edu/samantha

This travelogue is about a photographer's journey across North America with his camera and laptop computer named Samantha. The detailed account of his journey from Boston to Alaska and back describes a "summer spent seeing North America, meeting North Americans, and trying to figure out how people live." Download all 215 pages excerpted from his print book, and browse through approximately 250 accompanying photos.

Road Trip America
www.RoadTripAmerica.com

Follow Mark, Meagan, and Marvin the road dog as they roam the United States (Figure 13.11). The family, who took to the road after losing their home and business in a California wildfire, share their experiences through articles, memorable signs, slide shows, and goofy quizzes. Check out recommended diners, read about the special people they've met, and find out about the interesting sights they've seen, from hot springs to Las Vegas wedding chapels. You can also send a virtual postcard from the site.

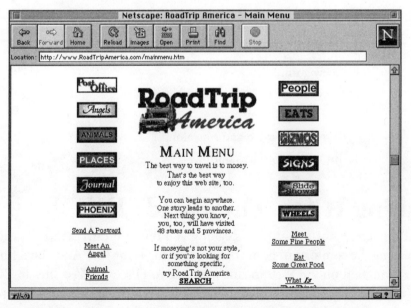

Figure 13.11 Head out on the highway with Road Trip America.

The Road Warrior's America
www.bergen.com:80/roadtrip

Travel with "the road warrior" and photographer Rich Gigli on "a journey from sea to shining sea on and off Route 80." The travelogue records visits to America's small towns, such as What Cheer, Iowa, and recounts conversations with people who live in them. Look over photos of the countryside, farms, sunsets, and roadside attractions like John Wayne's birthplace. You'll also find quick facts on the interstate highways. (Did you know there are no interstates in Alaska?)

Paul and Carol's Great Adventure
mindlink.bc.ca/pklym

A Canadian couple decides to leave it all behind to explore British Columbia and the U.S. in an RV named "Chief." The travelogue is separated into regions: the Southwest, Midwest, and "Alaska & The Yukon" are covered. Numerous photos with captions take you along on the ride: camping in Utah, trout fishing in Yellowstone Park, and meeting "modern-day gold miners" along the Yukon River.

 Travel Byte

Top five ways to avoid highway hypnosis:

1. Chew gum.
2. Drink coffee or cola with caffeine.
3. Open the window.
4. Turn up the radio and sing along.
5. Turn off the cruise control.

Taking It On The Road: RVs

If the lure of the open road is calling you but you can't stand the thought of leaving the comforts of home behind, RV-ing is for you. And you'll find lots of information on the Web to suit your needs. Discover Web sites for RV parks, dealers, rentals, suppliers, manufacturers, and directories, as well as online publications catering to and focusing on the lives of avid RV travelers.

RV America
www.rvamerica.com

For the RVer in you, check out this site. You'll find a beginner's guide to living the RV lifestyle, as well as RV news, contests, and links to RV e-zines. Visit chat rooms and post messages, replies, and retorts on electronic bulletin boards. RV enthusiasts—beginners and veterans alike—will find everything they need on the RV America Web site (Figure 13.12).

Roads to Adventure
roads.tl.com

This is a great resource for RV enthusiasts. Hear from others through readers' tips and chat forums about campgrounds, technical tips, and life on the open highway. Purchase vehicles and other amenities through classified ads, and check out the schedules of upcoming RV shows, special events, and fairs. The search engine and interactive map will help you find the specific information you're looking for.

Figure 13.12 Communicate with other RV enthusiasts on RV America's message board.

RV News
www.rvamerica.com/rvnews

Keep on top of things with monthly columns, vehicle evaluations, and new-product reviews, and catch up on general industry news and check the calendar of events for RV shows and events.

Trailer Life
www.trailerlife.com

Check out this Web site, which is a companion to the popular trade publication of the same name. Read *Trailer Life's* latest round of vehicle tests and reviews of products and services, and learn how to fix up your rig on your own through "do-it-yourself" articles and feature Q&As. For the many Americans who pull a trailer on vacation, *Trailer Life's* Web site provides a wealth of info (Figure 13.13).

Traveling USA
www.travelingusa.com

To locate parks and campgrounds, take a look at the RV park index at this site. Interactive maps enable you to search by city and state, and you can view historical auto advertisements and have some fun in the kids' section as well.

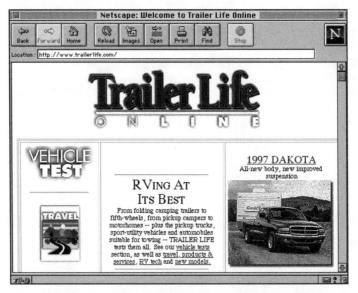

Figure 13.13   Read the latest RV news from Trailer Life.

RV Ventures
www.rvamerica.com/rv_ventures

This site is for newcomers to the "RV Lifestyle." Features include when to travel, where to travel, and how to stay safe during your travels. There's other useful information as well, on topics such as driver licenses, driving through customs, and what to look for when purchasing a vehicle.

Rental Resources

If you're looking for information on renting a car, turn to Chapter 5, where you'll find Internet addresses of rental-car companies and details on how to save when renting your wheels.

Index

Cyber cafes, 51, 125–128, 254, 255
  locations, 254
Cyber Rentals Web site, 197
Cyber tour, 19
Cyber Travel Agent, 137
CyberCafes in Europe, The
  Complete List of, 127
Cybermalls, 102
Cyberprograms, 65–67
CyberSaver fares, 144
CyberShop, 104
Cyberspace World Railroad, 152
Cyberstores, 102
CyberTraveler auction, 139
CyberTraveler email updates, 142
Cycling, 326, 327, 328.
  See also Biking.
Czech
  language resources, 299
  Republic, 261

D

Daily News–Just the Links,
  The, 296
Damage waivers, 158
Danube River, 60
Days Inn, 185, 414
Deals, 136. *See also* Bargains
  and Promotions.
  airfares, 137
  for cyber-surfing customers, 139
Delta Airlines, 143, 258, 372
  ticketless travel, 133
Denmark, 264
  driver's guide, 162
  hotels, 195
  shopping, 247
Denver International Airport, 148
Department of Transportation.
  See Transportation.
Destination Gateway Web site, 365
Destination Maine, 83
Destinations, using the Web to choose,
  53–90

Diarrhea, 122
Diets, special, 74
Digital travel books, 62–65
Diners, 409–412
Dining, 242–247
  cars, 152, 156
  diners, 409–412
  family-oriented, 373
  frequent-flyer programs, 146
  tips, 276–277
Diphtheria, 125
Directories hotels, 178–181
Disabilities
  cruises for travelers with, 365
  email source for travelers with, 40
  theater access, 240
  travel sites for, 98–100
Discman, 109
Discounts, 7–10, 61, 62, 99, 206–208,
  210, 211, 262, 275, 284
  accommodations, 100
  airfare, 40
  airlines, 262
  British Rail, 155
  car rentals, 144
  cruises, 357, 361
  cruises with children, 383
  for children, 371
  hotels, 144, 179
  safaris, 144
  travel agencies, 140–141
Discover Spain, 89
Discovery Channel, 333
Disney
  Big Red Boat, 357
  Disney Institute, 381
  Disney World, 224, 381
  Disneyland, 381
  Web site, 20
Distance calculator, 165
Diversion Magazine, 209
Diving, 85
Doctors, locating, 305
Dolce Vita, 291
Dollar Rent A Car, 160

U

V